23 Myths About the History of American Schools

What the Truth Can Tell Us, and Why It Matters

EDITED BY
Sherman Dorn
David A. Gamson

TEACHERS COLLEGE PRESS
TEACHERS COLLEGE | COLUMBIA UNIVERSITY
NEW YORK AND LONDON

Published by Teachers College Press,® 1234 Amsterdam Avenue, New York, NY 10027

Copyright © 2024 by Teachers College, Columbia University

Front cover photo: Public School 3 in Paterson, NJ by the National Park Service via Flickr creative commons.

All rights reserved. No part of this publication may be reproduced or transmitted in any form or by any means, electronic or mechanical, including photocopy, or any information storage and retrieval system, without permission from the publisher. For reprint permission and other subsidiary rights requests, please contact Teachers College Press, Rights Dept.: tcpressrights@tc.columbia.edu

Library of Congress Cataloging-in-Publication

Names: Dorn, Sherman, editor. | Gamson, David, editor.
Title: 23 myths about the history of American schools : what the truth can tell us, and why it matters / Edited by Sherman Dorn and David A. Gamson.
Other titles: Twenty-three myths about the history of American schools
Description: New York, NY : Teachers College Press, [2024] | Includes bibliographical references and index.
Identifiers: LCCN 2023056346 (print) | LCCN 2023056347 (ebook) | ISBN 9780807769270 (hardcover) | ISBN 9780807769263 (paperback) | ISBN 9780807782170 (epub)
Subjects: LCSH: Education—United States—History. | Schools—United States—History. | School districts—United States—History. | Teachers—United States—History.
Classification: LCC LA205 .A15 2024 (print) | LCC LA205 (ebook) | DDC 370.973—dc23/eng/20231214
LC record available at https://lccn.loc.gov/2023056346
LC ebook record available at https://lccn.loc.gov/2023056347

ISBN 978-0-8077-6926-3 (paper)
ISBN 978-0-8077-6927-0 (hardcover)
ISBN 978-0-8077-8217-0 (ebook)

Printed on acid-free paper
Manufactured in the United States of America

Contents

Acknowledgments	v
Introduction: Of Education Myths and History	1
David A. Gamson and Sherman Dorn	

PART I: ORIGIN MYTHS

1.	The Myth of the Little Red Schoolhouse	11
	Jonathan Zimmerman	
2.	The Myth of a Purely Religious Motive for Harvard's Establishment	20
	A. J. Angulo	
3.	The Myth of Summer Vacation and the Agrarian Calendar	30
	Kenneth Gold	
4.	The Myth of Local Control	42
	Campbell F. Scribner	
5.	The Myth of Industrial-Era Classrooms	50
	Sherman Dorn	

PART II: MYTHS OF PROGRESS AND DECLINE

6.	The Myth of Declining Student Behavior	61
	Judith Kafka	
7.	The Myth of Faulty City Schools	73
	John L. Rury	
8.	The Myth of American School Decline	81
	David A. Gamson	
9.	The Myth That U.S. Schools Were Desegregated in 1954	90
	Hope C. Rias	
10.	Reframing the Myth of School Reform Failure: Clocking School Change	98
	Larry Cuban	

PART III: MYTHS ABOUT TEACHERS

11. The Myth That Good Teachers Are Born, Not Made   109
    Kate Rousmaniere
12. The Myth of Heroic Teachers in Special Education   118
    Neil Dhingra, Joel Miller, and Kristen Chmielewski
13. The Myth That Elementary Writing Instruction Is Recent   127
    Joan M. Taylor
14. The Myth That Schoolteachers Take the Summer Off   140
    Christine A. Ogren
15. The Myth of Harmful Teacher Tenure   149
    Diana D'Amico Pawlewicz

PART IV: MYTHS ABOUT INEVITABILITY

16. The Du Bois–Washington Myth of Black Male Educational Thinkers   161
    Dellyssa Edinboro
17. The Myth of Gender Dominance in Higher Education   169
    Linda Eisenmann
18. The Myth of the Asian American Model Minority, American Individualism, and Meritocracy   178
    Sharon S. Lee and Yoon K. Pak

PART V: MYTH-ING VOICES AND QUESTIONS

19. The Myth of De Facto Segregation   191
    Ansley T. Erickson and Andrew R. Highsmith
20. The Myth That Technology Will Modernize Teaching   204
    Victoria Cain
21. The Myth That School Spending Doesn't Affect Student Outcomes   213
    Matthew Gardner Kelly
22. The Myth That Preschool Education Is a Panacea   223
    Barbara Beatty
23. The Myth of Patriotic Education as a Unifying Force   232
    Cody Dodge Ewert

About the Editors and the Contributors   239

Index   243

Acknowledgments

As historians, we often conduct our research and writing in solitude, so we rely on our colleagues in the history of education to help us gain broader perspectives on our field. The intent of this book is to harness and share that collective understanding so that as a reader, you emerge from the book a little more armed against mistaken claims about education. We are enormously grateful to the authors who contributed chapters to this book; some agreed to our early requests to write for this volume, while others submitted successful proposals in late 2021 and early 2022. We have learned so much from our colleagues who wrote for this book, and we are confident that you will, too.

Our students are our most regular touchstones for checking how persuasive we are in explaining the importance of education history and in being conscientious about its use. The sources of the myths addressed in this book are not generally students; rather, in these chapters, we and our fellow historians frequently highlight the role played by politicians, pundits, and on occasion fellow educators in spreading false notions about American schooling. That pattern does not mean that students do not come into our classes with misunderstandings. They do, as do all of us when we enter a new field. But of the thousands of students we have taught over the years, many of them have come with a sense that their goal is to learn, which often includes the hard work of unlearning what they thought was verified history. They have all helped us hone our sense of where it is most important to address misunderstandings about history.

At Teachers College Press, editorial director Brian Ellerbeck was very encouraging early in the development of this project. We are immensely grateful to him, to senior acquisitions editor Allison Scott, and to the anonymous reviewers who provided early feedback to our proposal.

The idea for this book started in a discussion of the Policy and Reform Affinity Group at the 2019 annual meeting of the History of Education Society. HES has been a crucial academic home for each of us over the decades, and all royalties from this book go to support the Society.

Introduction
Of Education Myths and History

David A. Gamson and Sherman Dorn

Schools are not as rigorous as they used to be, and children are misbehaving more than they did 50 years ago. Colleges like Harvard were founded on religious principles and have since veered away to focus on prestige and serving the elite. Educational myths abound. Virtually every educator—whether a classroom teacher or university researcher—is familiar with loudly voiced misconceptions about the problems of American schooling. The most common focus on the present: Schools waste money, we are told, or they are badly managed by unresponsive district offices, or they make excuses for the poor performance of students. In recent years, the critiques have stretched beyond such standard fare to include accusations from politicians that the schools are teaching divisive lessons and indoctrinating students. Complaints about education are a longstanding feature of public life and reflect strong beliefs about the role of schools. Even (or maybe especially) when these beliefs are flawed and misguided, they gain enough traction to capture public attention and contribute to a general public sense of discontent with education. Even before conflicts about masking during the pandemic or disagreements about the nature of academic standards, public confidence in education had waned since the 1970s (Gallup, 2023).

As historians who study and care about education, we worry about the whole range of myths in public discussion. Still, we have a special professional interest in fact-checking politicians and other public critics of education who abuse history to justify a range of arguments about education. As teachers, scholars, and citizens, we have often found ourselves saying, "Well, that's not entirely true; let me explain." Often that happens in the context of a class, or an interview with a reporter, or a conversation with fellow customers waiting in line with us at coffee shops, bookstores, or hardware stores. This book evolved out of a casual remark at an academic conference several years ago about the need for a resource to address common myths. This book is the result. In it, we aim to drive a wedge between myths and realities about schools by exploring common misconceptions about American education history. And we want you to benefit from our division of truth from misunderstandings and occasional outright falsehoods.

HOW MYTHS CAN BE HARMFUL

Myths are not innocuous. In some cases, historical myths matter when they become the justification for ill-informed decisions; erroneous historical narratives about schooling then have policy consequences. As Campbell Scribner points out in his chapter, the U.S. Supreme Court relied on flawed and nostalgic views of local control in *San Antonio Independent School District v. Rodriguez* (1973) and *Milliken v. Bradley* (1974), rulings that dramatically curtailed the obligation of states and local school districts to ensure equal treatment in education (see also Scribner, 2016; Superfine, 2013). We do not think that justices need to be experts in history, but they should be conscientious when they use it within their analysis.

Myths can also warp common understandings of the role education serves in society—they can suggest both limits and capacities that never truly existed. Myths that claim there was a golden age of student behavior or academic rigor suggest that schools just need to return to past practices to recover both quality and prestige. Persistent myths about the magical value of new technology or people who were "born" to be teachers suggest that schools can improve by paying for the right educational technology or hiring virtuous teachers, rather than the hard work of understanding how schools might use (or abuse) technology or providing teachers with the skills and support needed for success.

The pursuit of school reform solutions based on myths can lead to bad policy. The case of a $575 million Intensive Partnerships for Effective Teaching (IP) project, designed and funded in part by the Bill & Melinda Gates Foundation between 2009 and 2016, is just one illustration of what can go wrong when leaders operate on misconceptions about education. "Over the past four decades," said Gates in explaining the initiative, "the per-student cost of running our K-12 schools has more than doubled, while our student achievement has remained virtually flat. Now we need to raise performance without spending a lot more," he insisted (Gates, 2011). The IP initiative was a multiyear effort, intended to dramatically improve student outcomes, especially for low-income minority (LIM) students, by developing more robust measures of teacher effectiveness.

The Gates initiative, however, was built on a foundation of flawed assumptions. First, Gates is wrong about student achievement: Before the pandemic, student scores on national assessments had *risen* since the 1970s (National Center for Education Statistics, 2022). Second, his statements on funding are misleading. Much of the increase in school funding can be attributed to the rising costs of special education, not education in general (Berliner & Glass, 2014). Third, and perhaps more importantly, Gates overlooks the vast disparities in income and school funding across the country. Research has shown that students living in poor communities, attending underfunded schools, do less well on achievement testing (Reardon, 2013).

The problem for those schools is not too much money. And finally, the measures of teacher effectiveness used by the project relied heavily on student scores on standardized tests, against the advice of assessment scholars, who have warned for decades about the dangers of using a single test score to evaluate teachers (Koretz, 2017).

Given the flaws in thinking, what happened with the Gates's IP initiative? It failed. "*Overall,*" concluded the evaluators of the project, "*the initiative did not achieve its stated goals for students, particularly LIM students. By the end of 2014–2015, student outcomes were not dramatically better than outcomes in similar sites that did not participate in the IP initiative*" (Stecher et al., 2018, p. 488). Moreover, not only did the initiative *not* achieve its goals, but the outcome led the foundation to throw up its hands and step back from funding large-scale "swing for the fences" education projects altogether (Gates & Gates, 2020). Such is the fate of uninformed school reform efforts.

No society is without stories about its past, and that is as true for institutions such as schools and colleges as it is for other historical myths. When historical myths about education persist, that survival reveals more about ourselves than about the history of education: what we try to explain, what concerns drive us to talk about the past, and what we think needs to change. In some ways, historical myths are akin to urban legends, stories retold because of their social value and ability to convey normative values and often warnings (Brunvand, 1981). But there is an important difference between urban legends and historical myths: While urban legends have a quasi-personal flavor with the supposed "friend-of-a-friend" origins of many of them, the historical myth has the patina of objective truth, and it is couched in a rhetorical style consistent with other historical narratives, often with dates, names, and explanations that at first impression seem plausible. A "just the facts" style helps bolster the lessons conveyed by the storyteller: It is supposedly just a fact that summer vacation is the obsolete legacy of the agrarian calendar, that students used to be more obedient in school, that the history of immigration is one of meritocracy and hard work in schools, and that the development of tenure ruined teaching and harmed students. But as the chapters in this book show, those alleged lessons of history are often built on sand.

ORGANIZATION OF THE BOOK

We have grouped the chapters by the type of myth they represent, emphasizing the trope or underlying type of argument that is at the core of a myth. The typology we use is a mix of labels that identify common errors across all such historical stories and myths and patterns specific to historical myths about education in the United States. The first section collects several *origin myths* about education, often an explanation of how something came to be, or something about the origins of schooling (or a type of schooling) that captures something important about education, for good or ill. In his chapter, Jonathan Zimmerman explores the story of the little red schoolhouse, describing the condition of one-room schools, which varied far from the myth, and also what Zimmerman believes the myth's persistence tells us about how we view education. A. J. Angulo focuses on an origin myth of higher education, the supposedly religious focus of Harvard College; the truth is more complicated and tells us a great deal about the social structure and related ambitions of colonial New England. Kenneth Gold tackles the myth of summer vacation and how its history began in urban and not rural schooling. Campbell Scribner compares the rhetoric of "local control" with the real-life historical tug-of-war over school governance. Sherman Dorn uses the modern myth of a classroom designed in the industrial era to explore the more complex reasons why some features of classrooms are stable.

Sometimes these are origin myths about the "first" schools in some way, and sometimes authors focus on what we might call late-origin myths, such as the myth of industrial-era school design. Sometimes the myth serves nostalgic aims, suggesting some "true" (singular) purpose of education, while sometimes an origin myth is an object lesson in what is wrong about schooling. Sometimes there is an explanation—the agrarian calendar myth and summer vacations. But the common pattern in these origin myths is a story of stability before or after some key transition moment in time: One-room schoolhouses fit a "little red schoolhouse" stereotype until they disappeared, or local governance reigned supreme until after World War II.

A different set of myths focuses on change, and specifically myths of uniform *progress or decline.* Historians know this pair of myths well: A story of declension from some golden age in the past is the mirror image of a story of continuous progress. Judith Kafka's chapter focuses on a common myth that K–12 student misbehavior is a greater problem today than in the past; as she observes, there was no golden age of well-behaved students. John Rury addresses the myth of city high school decline, which is tied into the history of urban high schools as important institutions in the early 20th century. Both of these are myths of decline, as is the general story of failing schools that David Gamson addresses. Hope Rias presents a reverse account of false progress: the common assumption she encounters among her college students (and students of many historians) that after the 1954 *Brown v. Board of Education* decision, segregation ended quickly and smoothly. In her chapter, the failure to desegregate schools in the 1950s meant that local activists had to push hard for any meaningful measure of school desegregation in the 1960s and 1970s.

Along with origin myths, stories of progress and decline are common fallacies in informal and thumbnail histories, whether about the history of education or larger politics (e.g., Kruse & Zelizer, 2022; Loewen, 1996). But some myths about education history are specific to the context of schools, such as various myths about *teaching*. There are a broad array of fallacies about teachers, teaching, and what goes on in American classrooms. Kate Rousmaniere explores the myth that "teachers are born, not made," the notion that good teaching requires an innate quality that some people have and others don't. The myth of the born teacher is harmful to education, she argues, because it presents teachers' work as a simplistic act of personal charisma that does not require professional or academic knowledge. Neil Dhingra, Joel Miller, and Kristen Chmielewski tackle the myth of the heroic teacher, focusing especially on the misconception that disabled children require a profoundly different type of education—taught by an almost superhuman educator—than their nondisabled peers do. Disability, they point out, is conspicuously absent from many popular narratives of teachers and students; when it does appear in cinema and literature, good teachers commonly experience a "magical breakthrough" in connecting with students; but in reality, they assert, successful teachers foster a classroom community, one focused on the common good, in which all students can participate.

Some myths have to do with the daily business of what teachers do with their time. Joan Taylor examines the long-recurring complaint about the absence of elementary writing instruction. Each new generation of teachers laments what they believe to be a tragic flaw in the generation preceding their own: that students had failed to receive proper instruction in composing written text. Utilizing robust evidence from textbooks, student journals, and memoirs, Taylor tells us a far different story. In her chapter, Christine Ogren explains that even though schoolteachers do not have regular classroom responsibilities or receive paychecks during summer, the belief that they take the summer entirely "off" from their professional roles is a misconception that discredits the many ways in which teachers contribute to the education system through their summer activities. The persistence of the "summers off" myth, she argues, keeps taxpayers and policymakers from recognizing the crucial role of summer activities in shaping a professional teaching force and from rewarding teachers appropriately.

A number of myths swirl around the concept of teacher tenure, as Diana D'Amico Pawlewicz explains, including the flawed belief that teacher tenure somehow harms students and makes schools inefficient. Tenure privileges have never granted teachers a job for life, she reminds us, nor have they guaranteed teachers academic freedom. Instead, tenure simply offers teachers due process and ensures that supervisors must document cause for dismissal.

In addition to myths about the history of teaching, some historical myths specific to schooling treat key features of schooling as unavoidable in some way. Sometimes this is an argument about the impossibility of changing some feature of schooling. Ansley Erickson and Andrew Highsmith explore one such claim in their chapter about the concept of "de facto" segregation, a legal term that divides allegedly explicit segregation policies ("de jure" school segregation) from segregation that exists outside the influence of policy. They point out that for well over a century, a broad web of social policies has unambiguously shaped where Americans live, and thus where children attend school. Some myths are not about the impossibility of change but its inevitability. Victoria Cain explores such a myth, the persistent belief that the latest technology will revolutionize schooling. Matthew Kelly explores arguments about school spending, specifically claims that additional funds make little or no difference in what schools do with and for students. And Sharon Lee and Yoon Pak explore the obstinacy of a pair of myths that have long shaped the experience of Asian American students: the persistent labeling of Asian Americans as eternal outsiders and as meritocratic strivers. As they observe, the combination is irrational and toxic.

Finally, some myths go to the heart of the educational enterprise, a set of myth-directions about whose voices count in educational debates, who has been the beneficiary of education, what schools can truly accomplish, and how we think about change. This section begins with a myth about voices most active in Black education at the turn of the 20th century. The most common emphasis is on the important contributions and differences between Booker T. Washington and W. E. B. Du Bois. Dellyssa Edinboro argues that this traditional focus reinforces a myth that the most relevant intellectual leaders in debates about Black education during this period were Black men. To broaden this narrative, Edinboro reminds us of the significance of key women who were leaders in Black education circles, and she offers the example of Dr. Anna J. Cooper, whose writings existed outside the narrow framing of a dichotomy between industrial education and elite liberal education.

Highlighting the current myth that there is a "male crisis" in American higher education, Linda Eisenmann traces the participation by women and men in higher education over time, looking for periods when gender influenced college attendance. Studying the vagaries of social and economic forces that both encouraged and discouraged women from attending college, Eisenmann finds an uphill gain for women without a concomitant loss for men. In her chapter, Barbara Beatty offers a brief history of early childhood education in the United States. She argues that big promises about the benefits of preschool have often diverted attention from the significance of program quality and from the large, systemic social problems that preschool education was said to help to solve.

In the tumultuous years surrounding World War I, groups like the Grand Army of the Republic (GAF) argued that schools had a duty to inculcate in students a sense of civic and nationalistic pride. The notion that schools can heal social and political divisions by teaching patriotism is a persistent and pervasive myth, explains Cody Ewert; in fact, it dates back to the origins of our nation (Nash et al., 1997). Over a century after World War I drew to a close, several states began considering legislation aimed at keeping "divisive concepts" out of the classroom. Ewert argues that Americans should remain deeply suspicious of leaders who seek to impose narrow definitions of what it means to be a good citizen and to bar teachers and students from asking difficult questions. Finally, Larry Cuban confronts the well-worn myth that school reforms have failed again and again. He suggests that taking a broader historical view, one that examines school innovations over a longer span of time, often produces a more complex picture of the life and death of school reform. Paying more attention to slower-paced reforms, he argues, could shift public debate to more substantial matters of classroom teaching and learning.

We have no expectation that this book will end the spinning of historical myths about education—in part because the appeal of a good myth is hard to resist, as many of us have learned in teaching our students over the years, and in part because new myths will inevitably spring from evolving debates over education. Instead, our goal here is for you and other readers to take control of the narrative away from those who tell mythical stories. You are entitled to question the thumbnail histories and look for more accurate and interesting scholarship on any issue. We also want you and other readers to see the role that historical myths about education play—why you hear or read some of them repeatedly, what explicit or hidden lessons their tellers are trying to convey with them, and the ways in which they can make common errors in historical reasoning.

REFERENCES

Berliner, D. C., & Glass, G. V (Eds.). (2014). *50 myths & lies that threaten America's public schools: The real crisis in education*. Teachers College Press.

Brunvand, J. H. (1981). *The vanishing hitchhiker: American urban legends and their meanings*. Norton.

Gallup. (2023). *Satisfaction with K-12 education in the U.S.* Retrieved from https://news.gallup.com/poll/1612/education.aspx

Gates, B. (2011, February 28). Smarter school reform. *The Washington Post*, A.15. Retrieved from https://www.proquest.com/docview/853982237/abstract/76336BC8885A405BPQ/45

Gates, B., & Gates, M. (2020). *Our 2020 annual letter: Why we swing for the fences*. Retrieved from https://www.gatesnotes.com/2020-Annual-Letter

Koretz, D. M. (2017). *The testing charade: Pretending to make schools better*. University of Chicago Press.

Kruse, K. M., & Zelizer, J. E. (Eds.). (2022). *Myth America: Historians take on the biggest legends and lies about our past*. Basic Books.

Loewen, J. W. (1996). *Lies my teacher told me: Everything your American history textbook got wrong*. Simon & Schuster.

Milliken v. Bradley, 418 U.S. 717 (1974).

Nash, G. B., Crabtree, C. A., & Dunn, R. E. (1997). *History on trial: Culture wars and the teaching of the past*. A. A. Knopf.

National Center for Education Statistics. (2022). *Digest of Education Statistics, 2022*. Table 214.10. National Center for Education Statistics. Retrieved from https://nces.ed.gov/programs/digest/d22/tables/dt22_214.10.asp

Reardon, S. F. (2013). The widening income achievement gap. *Educational Leadership, 70*(8), 10–16.

San Antonio Independent School District v. Rodriguez, 411 U.S. 1 (1973).

Scribner, C. F. (2016). *The fight for local control: Schools, suburbs, and American democracy*. Cornell University Press.

Stecher, B. M., et al. (2018). *Improving teaching effectiveness: Final report. The intensive partnerships for effective teaching through 2015–2016*. RAND Corporation. Retrieved from https://www.rand.org/pubs/research_reports/RR2242.html

Superfine, B. M. (2013). *Equality in education law and policy, 1954–2010*. Cambridge University Press.

Part I

ORIGIN MYTHS

CHAPTER 1

The Myth of the Little Red Schoolhouse

Jonathan Zimmerman

In 1872, a Boston art critic reviewed several new paintings of an age-old American institution: the one-room schoolhouse. They were the handiwork of Winslow Homer, a rising young star whose colorful depictions of rural landscapes caught the eye of a rapidly industrializing nation. Homer's new series included the soon-to-be-iconic *Snap the Whip*, which depicted nine barefoot boys playing in front of a bright red school. For the critic—and, no doubt, for many other viewers—this idyllic scene conjured happy moments of childhood. "Every person from the country knows the powerful associations lingering around the old red schoolhouse," the critic wrote. "No spot in the whole world is so full of histories and memories" (quoted in Conrads, 2001, p. 40).

Yet Homer's paintings also distorted history, even as they shaped our memory of it. Over the next century, *Snap the Whip* would become one of the most popular and recognizable images of an American school. And when people looked at it—and at countless other portrayals of the little red schoolhouse—they surely recalled that the old schoolhouse of their youth was red.

It wasn't.

Most one-room schools were coated with white paint—which was cheaper than the red kind—or simply left unpainted, reverting to a weather-beaten silver or gray. But we continue to imagine them as red, precisely because of the images from art, literature, and film that have lingered around them. We also envision them differently at different moments in time, depending on our political and social circumstances. Across our history, we have remembered the little red schoolhouse that we want—or need—to recall.

That doesn't make us dupes, or liars; it makes us human. All of us live through myths, which are the stories that tell us who we are. These stories always diverge to some degree or another from "what happened," as best historians can determine it. But they are real, nevertheless, structuring how we experience the world and choose to act within it. No spot in American education is so full of histories and memories as the little red schoolhouse.

Whatever its actual hue, it continues to color the ways we think about "school" writ large—and also about ourselves.

* * *

For the first half of American history, most Americans who went to school did so in a one-room schoolhouse. In 1830, just 9% of citizens lived in places with populations greater than 2,500. America was an overwhelmingly rural nation of small towns and villages, which could only afford to build and staff small, one-room schools. The first schoolhouses were constructed of log, like the one to which Abraham Lincoln walked (2 miles each way) in Hodgenville, Kentucky; as communities grew and stabilized, they replaced the log buildings with frame ones. But most schools still had just a single room, with a single teacher. As late as 1913, fully half of America's 212,000 schools were taught by one person. They remained ubiquitous in parts of the Midwest and Great Plains into the 1930s, when roughly three-quarters of schools in Illinois, Kansas, Iowa, Minnesota, and Wisconsin had one teacher. Only with World War II and the postwar baby boom would the one-room schoolhouse disappear, passing from history into memory. By 1960, just 1% of American students attended a one-room school (Fuller, 1994, p. 104; Gulliford, 1996, p. 35; Kaestle, 1983, p. 13; NEA, 1960, p. 9).

The little red schoolhouse wasn't red except in rare cases, but it was little. Most schools were boxlike squares or rectangles, with sides ranging from 15 to 40 feet. Each of the long sides had three or four tall windows, without shades or curtains, creating a "crosslight" effect (as it was called) that made it hard for students to see; to correct for that, schools built after 1900 typically had windows on only one side. Students entered through a single door, although later schools sometimes featured two doors—one for boys and one for girls—to prevent "improprieties between the sexes," as one educator explained (Johonnot, 1871, p. 23). Once they got inside, students sat on backless benches on three sides of the room while the teacher occupied a desk along the fourth wall. Smaller children sat on another set of benches near the center, closest to the potbellied stove, where they would often nod off to sleep; on the frigid periphery, older students donned mittens and struggled to turn the pages of their textbooks. Lacking sufficient funds to supply the inefficient stoves, which could consume a cord of firewood per week, schools burned green wood that produced more smoke than heat. Thirsty youngsters drank from a shared bucket of water, which sometimes froze in the winter because the schoolhouse was so cold (Kaestle, 1983, p. 16).

After the Civil War, most schools replaced their benches with rows of individual desks. That meant older girls would no longer have to raise their feet above their hips to exit their seats, which sparked considerable hand-wringing among 19th-century moralists. But it also made girls easy targets for mischievous boys, who would dip girls' hair braids into the inkwells on the desks behind them. Other boys climbed the roof to plug the chimney with branches—which filled the room with yet more smoke—or threw buckshot against the blackboard or into the stove, triggering loud explosions. In response, teachers often made the miscreant (almost always a boy) sit with the girls or even wear a sunbonnet. Other penalties echoed the infraction in question: A student caught chewing gum might be forced to wear it on their nose, while a liar would have a split green twig affixed to their tongue. But the most frequent penalty was corporal punishment, administered with the "board of education"—as paddles were euphemistically known—or with a ferule, a long and flat ruler that teachers kept handy for that purpose. Reformers like Horace Mann inveighed against flogging, urging teachers to develop gentler forms of discipline. But teachers insisted that they could not perform their jobs without it. Teaching as many as 100 students, ranging in age from three to 20, they needed the threat of pain to preserve order (Clark, 1994; Ellison, 1996, pp. 9–10, 17, 13–14; Grove, 2000, pp. 66–68; Johnson, 1893, p. 51).

For the most part, "teaching" meant repetition. Students would memorize passages from their textbook—often whatever book their family possessed at home—and then recite to the teacher, who awarded a "mark" or grade in return. Most teachers had neither the time nor the training to do much more than that. Primarily single women in their teens or early twenties, they possessed barely more education than the students in their charge (Benjamin, 2001).

But the one-room school also housed community events and festivities, which surely accounts for much of its popularity in American memory. Often the only public building for miles, schools hosted dances, plays, marriages, funerals, and holiday celebrations. (In the days before electricity, when schoolhouses were lit by candles or lanterns, Christmas parties inevitably concluded with Santa Claus's beard catching on fire.) Schools were also the site for political campaigns and debates over divisive local issues, including how to fund the schools themselves and where to erect new ones. Penny-pinching communities often built schools on land that nobody else wanted, such as barren hilltops and the irregular triangles created by the intersection of several roads. That presented an obvious safety hazard for children walking to school, who were injured or killed by stagecoaches and other vehicles. Merchants pleaded with local authorities to build schools near their stores, which would enhance foot traffic around them; but farmers sought to block school construction adjacent to their fields, fearing that crowds of students would trample their crops. In several hilarious instances, citizens from one side of a town hitched horses to the schoolhouse in the middle of the night and dragged it to the other side. The next morning, students arriving at school were surprised—and delighted—to find that it was gone ("78-Year-Old Recalls Life in One-Room Schoolhouse," 1999; Fuller,

1982, pp. 60–61; Gulliford, 1996, p. 163; Henke, 1998, p. xi; Johnson, 1963, p. 102; Stilgoe, 1982, pp. 244–245; Theobald, 1995, pp. 88, 71–72).

American communities were also divided by race, of course, especially in the segregated South. School boards improved or replaced one-room schoolhouses for Whites but appropriated little or nothing for all-Black schools, which remained ramshackle and dilapidated. Walls lacked paint or plaster, windows went without panes, and roofs did not have ceilings. "Many of these houses are not fit for animals," a Black newspaper in Georgia complained in 1914. "Cows, horses, and pigs should have better shelter than are furnished the Negro children in the country" ("More Schools and Better Ones," 1914). In some districts, 75 or 80 children were crowded into schools "like a parcel of sheep," the paper added. As late as 1959, baseball trailblazer Jackie Robinson devoted one of his newspaper columns to the dismal conditions of Black schools in the rural South. Many African Americans were still relegated to "rundown, unsanitary shacks" with just a single room, Robinson wrote ("Jackie Robinson," 1959).

* * *

So why is the little red schoolhouse imprinted so powerfully in our minds, long after its departure from our landscape? And why do we imagine it as a paragon of pedagogical excellence—or as a symbol of united community—when it was neither? For the same reason that we recall it as red: As the actual schoolhouse waned, we built myths around it. That was the one-two step of the one-room school. With every move into the recesses of history, the little red schoolhouse became more enshrined in our memory.

One-room schools started their steady decline at the dawn of the Progressive Era, around the turn of the 20th century. Appalled by the graft and inefficiency of local communities, Progressives developed centralized state authorities to manage and regulate them. In rural education, that meant the replacement of one-room schools with larger, "consolidated" ones. "'The little red school house' so fondly alluded to sounds very sweet when juggled about in a great collection of sentiment," an Omaha newspaper declared in 1892, demanding school consolidation. "This city wants real progress and not red paint. It wants science and not sentiment" ("Red School House," 1892, p. 4). The *Independent*, a leading Progressive magazine, was even more direct. "The Little Red Schoolhouse Is a Fake," it proclaimed in 1913, noting inadequate heat, light, and toilet facilities at most one-room schools. As Progressives correctly sensed, Americans had already developed a nostalgic attachment to the one-room school. The only way to dislodge that was by trumpeting "the facts," a favorite Progressive mantra. If the public possessed real information, it would put aside its romantic yearnings for a lost past and join the inexorable march into modernity (Hill, 1913, p. 316).

But modern society also generated mass entertainment, which popularized precisely the myths that the Progressives were trying to subvert. The best-known example was the 1909 hit song "School Days," cowritten by the vaudeville producer and composer Gus Edwards. A German immigrant to Brooklyn, Edwards probably never saw the inside of an American one-room country school. But he knew how to tug at America's heartstrings, imagining an adult couple looking back on their rural childhood:

> School Days, School Days, dear old golden rule days
> Readin' and ritin' and 'rithmetic
> Taught to the tune of a hickory stick
> You were my queen in calico
> I was your bashful barefoot beau
> And you wrote on my slate, "I love you Joe"
> When we were a couple of kids. (Cobbs & Edwards, 1906/1907)

Forty years later, *The New York Times* ranked "School Days" as one of the 10 most popular songs of the first half of the 20th century. Edwards adopted it as a theme for several schoolhouse-themed vaudeville shows he produced, including *Nine Country Kids* and *School Boys and School Girls* (Spaeth, 1949, p. SM56). It also inspired a 1921 movie, in which a young boy leaves the farm for the city but eventually returns to the sweetheart he met at his one-room school (Foster, 1930, p. 23).

The Progressive Era pattern repeated in the interwar years, when a new generation of critics blasted the one-room school and a revived nostalgia movement burnished its memory. Under Franklin D. Roosevelt's New Deal, the Farm Security Administration hired Dorothea Lange, Walker Evans, and other leading photographers to document the poverty of rural America, including its decrepit single-room schools; meanwhile, the Works Progress Administration and Public Works Administration helped fund the construction of consolidated schools alongside the bridges and roads that would bring children to them. But these changes also brought renewed appreciation for the little red schoolhouse and—especially—for the brave young women who taught there. Novelist Laura Ingalls Wilder struck gold in the late 1930s with her enormously popular *Little House on the Prairie* children's books, which drew on her experiences teaching in a one-room school 50 years earlier. Readers thrilled to her adventures as she faced down the big boys, while sunshine streamed through cracks in her schoolhouse wall; poor but proud, the school captured a pioneer spirit that was supposedly dissolving in the faceless bureaucracies of modern America. Others looked to the last living remnants of rural simplicity, the Amish, whose own one-room schools enjoyed a media vogue during these same years. *The New York Times* published over 20 articles about efforts by Amish parents in a Pennsylvania town to preserve their "little red schoolhouses," as the *Times* pointedly called them, even though the schools were gray and white; likewise, *House and Garden* ran a full-page black-and-white photo of four Amish students "wrestling with the three R's in little red schoolhouses," as the caption noted (Their schools weren't red, either.) (Miller, 1998, pp. 3, 181–183; Provenzo, 2006, pp. 177–180; Weaver-Zercher, 2001, pp. 61, 214n35, 67, 69–70).

The end of World War II and the postwar rise in national fertility ushered in the final demise of the one-room schoolhouse, which simply could not accommodate America's skyrocketing young population. But it also triggered another round of sentimentality, fueled by the sad recognition that a beloved institution was fading away. "We oldsters know all the advantages of the larger, more impersonal, better equipped consolidated school," wrote a Detroit high school teacher, who had walked a mile each way to his childhood one-room school in rural Kentucky. "But we can't help looking backward over our shoulders at the warm, cozy memory tinted school days of yesteryear" (Logan, 1959, p. 78). Nor could his fellow Kentuckian Rebecca Caudill, who freely admitted that she had "a genuine case of nostalgia" when she wrote her popular children's book *Schoolhouse in the Woods* (1949) (Caudill, 1949). Businesses happily capitalized on the same mood, selling toys and children's clothing that displayed schoolhouse motifs ("Everybody's Happy Playing Famous Parker Games," 1953, p. SM67; "Parker Games Are Family Games," 1952, p. 75).

In the white-hot atmosphere of the Cold War, meanwhile, the one-room schoolhouse also came to symbolize America's democratic virtues in the face of a totalitarian foe ("Germans Capitulate on All Fronts," 1945, p. 1). That spirit was already apparent at the end of World War II, when American newspapers reported that German generals had surrendered to Allied forces at a "little red schoolhouse" in Reims, France. Never mind that the red brick building was actually a technical college, three stories high and half a city block in length. The enemy had to surrender in a little red schoolhouse, which "played a most important part in the growth of the democracy we cherish so fondly and fight so bravely to defend," as one reporter wrote (Vorpe, 1945). Within a year, the little red schoolhouse would be invoked to bolster America's campaign against a new tyrannical enemy: Soviet Russia. Laura Ingalls Wilder's *Little House* series witnessed another burst of popularity, this time reframed as a prophylaxis against communism: By demonstrating frontier self-sufficiency, in the one-room schoolhouse and beyond, Wilder's books would supposedly teach children to resist Soviet propaganda (Zimmerman, 2002, p. 91).

Such claims rested on an imagined national consensus that simply did not exist. As the surface-level unity of the 1950s exploded into the open conflicts of the 1960s—over civil rights, the war in Vietnam, and much more—people across the political spectrum pressed their own vision of the nation onto it schools. And every side invoked the little red schoolhouse, which became a shared icon with diametrically different meanings. To the Right, it symbolized the rigor, discipline, and patriotism that America had allegedly forsaken; on the Left, meanwhile, it embodied a communal ethos that would correct for poverty, racism, and the country's other social injustices. Both claims distorted the actual history of the one-room schoolhouse, as memory campaigns inevitably do. But they also spoke volumes about Americans' mutual commitment to education, even as they disagreed—deeply and fundamentally—about its meaning and purpose. The one-room school united "nostalgic old-timers and sophisticated radicals alike," as historian David Tyack wryly observed in 1972 (Tyack, 1972, p. 17). Whatever their politics, it seemed, everyone could find something to like in the happy, harmonious little red schoolhouse.

The actual schoolhouse wasn't harmonious, of course, any more than America was. The one-room school ranked children via spelling bees and other competitions, labeling some "dull," "slow," or even "retarded"; it almost never served mentally challenged children, who were dismissed as uneducable or warehoused in asylums; and it routinely punished children for assisting—or even for speaking with—their peers (Lewis, 1978). In her 1986 poem "Trouble with Math in a One-Room Country School," Jane Kenyon recalls asking for help with an arithmetic problem from a student sitting next to her. The teacher "sprang from her monumental desk," forcibly removed Kenyon from class, and shut her in the dark closet housing the school's furnace. Kenyon sat on a bucket and hummed to herself until the teacher retrieved her. Straining to adjust to the light, she returned to her class "blinking and changed" (Kenyon, 1999, p. 101).

Do we misrepresent—and, most of all, misremember—the little red schoolhouse? Of course we do. And we have done so for a very long time. "The historical ghost of the little red school-house stalks the land," wrote a frustrated educational official in 1939, bemoaning Americans' nostalgia for it. "It seems a ghost that just cannot be laid. It may have ninety-nine lives" (Rice, 1939, p. 18). Each of us has only one life, of course, just as the schoolhouse had only one room. But we live and remember with each other, spinning stories that bind us together. However much we distort its history, the little red schoolhouse remains the most important icon in American education. So it also provides us with a shared vocabulary for interpreting—and, we might hope, for improving—contemporary schools. Anyone who wants to make them more rigorous—or more equitable, or more inclusive, or more anything—will have to embrace this quintessential American symbol. Blinking and changed, we look back on it from our own particular perspectives. Yet we should not lose sight of the ways it can connect us, even amid the bitter divisions of our present-day moment. The little red schoolhouse is all we have, symbolically speaking, and all of us have it. It has departed, but it will still be here when we are gone.

REFERENCES

78-year-old recalls life in one-room schoolhouse. (1999, December 19). *Muskegon Chronicle*. "L" Binder, Bess Britton Michigan One-Room Schoolhouse Collection, Van Buren District Library, Decatur, Michigan.

Benjamin, K. (2001). The decision to teach: The challenges and opportunities of a one-room school teacher in turn-of-the-century Texas. *Thresholds in Education, 27*(1 and 2), 18–30.

Caudill, R. (1949, May 9). Mrs. James S. Ayars [Rebecca Caudill] to Nancy E. Valtin. Folder 1, Box 7, Rebecca Caudill Papers, Special Collections, Margaret I. King Library, University of Kentucky, Lexington, Kentucky.

Clark, C. (1994, February 14). Memories. *Fowlersville [MI] News and Views*. "Bowens Mills-Beyers" binder, Bess Britton Michigan One-Room Schoolhouse Collection, Van Buren District Library, Decatur, Michigan.

Cobbs, W., & Edwards, G. (1906/1907). *Will D. Cobb's School Days (When We Were a Couple of Kids)*. Gus Edwards Publishing Company. "Introduction: General History and Non-Michigan Schools" binder, Britton Collection.

Conrads, M. C. (2001). *Winslow Homer and the critics: Forging a national art in the 1870s*. Princeton University Press in association with the Nelson-Atkins Museum of Art.

Ellison, H. A. (1996). *The old one-room country school*. National Writers Press.

Everybody's happy playing famous Parker games. (1953, December 13). *The New York Times*.

Foster, R. A. (1930). *The school in American literature*. Warwick and York.

Fuller, W. E. (1982). *The old country school: The story of rural education in the Middle West*. University of Chicago Press.

Fuller, W. E. (1994). *One-room schools of the Middle West: An illustrated history*. University Press of Kansas.

Germans capitulate on all fronts. (1945, May 8). *The New York Times*.

Grove, M. J. (2000). *Legacy of one-room schools*. Masthof Press.

Gulliford, A. (1996). *America's country schools* (3rd ed.). University Press of Colorado.

Henke, W. A. (1998). Preface. In W. A. Henke & E. C. Albers (Eds.), *The legacy of North Dakota's country schools*. North Dakota Humanities Council.

Hill, E. M. (1913, August 7). The little red schoolhouse a "fake." *Independent*.

Johnson, C. (1893). *The country school*. D. Appleton.

Johnson, C. (1963). *Old-time schools and school books* (2nd ed.). Dover.

Johonnot, J. (1871). *School-houses*. J. W. Schermerhorn & Company.

Kaestle, C. F. (1983). *Pillars of the republic: Common schools and American society, 1780–1860*. Hill and Wang.

Kenyon, J. (1999). Trouble with math in a one-room country school (1986). In M. Anderson & D. Hassler (Eds.), *Learning by heart: Contemporary American poetry about school*. University of Iowa Press.

Lewis, A. C. (1978, September 10). Back to the one-room school. *The Washington Post*. Folder 6, Box 10, Country School Legacy Collection, University Archives, University of Colorado at Boulder Libraries.

Logan, E. (1959). Salute to the little red schoolhouse. *The Clearing House: A Journal of Educational Strategies, Issues and Ideas, 34*(2), 78–81.

Miller, J. E. (1998). *Becoming Laura Ingalls Wilder: The woman behind the legend.* University of Missouri Press.

More schools and better ones. (1914, July 23). *Atlanta Independent.* Reel 2, Frame 759, Tuskegee Institute News Clipping File, Tuskegee Institute.

NEA Research Division. (1960). *One-teacher schools today.* National Education Association.

Parker games are family games. (1952, December 7). *The New York Times.*

Provenzo, E. F. (2006). One-room and country schools depicted in Farm Security Administration photographs. In E. T. Ewing & D. Hicks (Eds.), *Education and the Great Depression: Lessons from a global history.* Peter Lang.

Red School House. (1892, November 6). *Omaha World-Herald.*

Rice, D. F. R. (1939). The ghost of the little red schoolhouse. *American School Board Journal.*

Robinson, J. (1959, November 25). *New York Post.* Fiche 003.459-1, Schomburg Center Clipping File, Schomburg Center for Research in Black Culture, New York Public Library.

Spaeth, S. (1949, March 20). The first ten since 1900. *The New York Times.*

Stilgoe, J. R. (1982). *Common landscape of America: 1580 to 1845.* Yale University Press.

Theobald, P. (1995). *Call school: Rural education in the Midwest to 1918.* Southern Illinois University Press.

Tyack, D. (1972, March). The tribe and the common school. *American Quarterly,* 24(1), 3–19.

Vorpe, W. G. (1945, May 20). As the parade passes by. *Cleveland Plain Dealer.* Folder 6, Box 11. Country School Legacy Collection.

Weaver-Zercher, D. L. (2001). *The Amish in the American imagination.* Johns Hopkins University Press.

Zimmerman, J. (2002). *Whose America? Culture wars in the public schools.* Harvard University Press.

CHAPTER 2

The Myth of a Purely Religious Motive for Harvard's Establishment

A. J. Angulo

Harvard University caused a stir in 2021 when it selected Greg Epstein as the institution's new chaplain (Paumgarten, 2021). Epstein took the lead role for a chapel that—like many other U.S. college chapels—stands at the center of campus, offers weekly services, and reminds visitors of the historical importance of religion in American higher education. The buzz centered on how the university appeared to have broken a multi-hundred-year tradition. At the time of the appointment, the new chaplain did not identify as a Christian, a Jew, a Muslim, or a member of any other world religion. Rather, Epstein, author of *Good Without God* and coauthor, with James Croft of "The Godless Congregation," began his chaplaincy as an atheist (Epstein, 2010; Epstein & Croft, 2013).

When the Epstein story broke, common assumptions about Harvard and, more broadly, the colonial college took center stage. Media headlines suggested that the atheist appointment was a first, but that wasn't quite accurate. Several decades earlier, Tom Ferrick had founded the world's first university-based Humanist chaplaincy at Harvard. Ferrick began his tenure in 1974 and continued in the role for more than 30 years. Epstein described Ferrick, his former boss and mentor, as "America's first atheist chaplain" (Epstein, 2014).

This chapter examines the related, deeper historical assumption: that Harvard College, America's oldest educational institution, was founded for a single, unifying reason—to train ministers. It's a claim that has appeared widely and frequently for decades, and it's one that reemerged with reports about Epstein. But evidence suggests there's more myth than historical fact to the claim.

Given how often the "Harvard trained ministers" claim appears, it's not surprising why many hold this assumption. *The New York Times* kicked off their Epstein story by describing Harvard's origin in terms of "Puritan colonists who settled in New England in the 1630s" and who founded the institution "to educate the ministry" (Goldberg, 2021). *The Guardian* took a similar approach, portraying the college as originating with "a mission to educate clergymen in order to minister to New England's early Puritan colonists" (Yang, 2021). The same kind of assumption can be found in popular religious works, school textbooks, and public exhibitions. Christian heritage books have argued that higher education in America began "with a tax levied in 1637 to fund the training of ministers at Harvard" (Combs, 2011, p. 32). Widely used high school textbooks have taught students that "to ensure a supply of ministers trained in the New England Way, Massachusetts founded Harvard College in 1636" (Boyer et al., 2010, p. 61). And public exhibitions by the U.S. Library of Congress have mentioned that early American colleges emerged "to train a ministry to deliver their message" (Hutson et al., n.d.). As such, whether from newspapers, popular texts, or federally funded exhibitions, the story tends to be the same—Harvard and the country's first colleges originally had a single, religious purpose.

With its exclusive focus on religion, however, the popular origin story has limited historical plausibility. In the case of Harvard, the record paints a more complex picture. Closer inspection indicates that a variety of factors—economic, social, psychological, and political—offer equally or more satisfying explanations. They shed light on why Harvard and, by extension, other colonial colleges were founded and what role they played in early America.

UNPACKING THE POPULAR ORIGIN STORY

The first bump in the road for the popular "Harvard trained ministers" origin story comes from a vote by the Great and General Court of Massachusetts in 1636. The vote ultimately led to the founding of a college that later became Harvard. But rather than having a clear vision of starting a seminary, colonial leaders were not exactly sure what they wanted. The Court's final decision was to earmark £400 to establish "a schoale or colledge" of some undetermined purpose (Harvard University Archives, n.d.; Morison, 1936, p. 5). With this act, colonial leaders expressed a strong desire to propagate learning of some kind without specifying the educational level or course of studies. Schools, for instance, focused on children and did not train ministers. By suggesting the need for a school *or* college, the Massachusetts Bay Colony signaled an openness to a variety of options. As such, the original decision to found America's oldest educational institution left off any mention of religious or ministerial education.

Some might not see a need for colonial leaders to specify the vote's religious intent. The desire for trained clergy could be read implicitly and contextually rather than explicitly and textually (Hall, 2019). After all, the best-known colonists envisioned establishing a shining "City Upon a Hill" that would serve as a beacon of hope and religious refuge to the rest of the world (Van Engen, 2020). Why else but to prepare homegrown clergy would colonial leaders establish a college a mere 16 years after landing in the North American wilderness of 1620?

But a second setback for the popular origin story comes from historical scholarship contesting conventional views about religiosity in colonial America. Church attendance, researchers argue, served a long list of spiritual *and* non-spiritual needs for parishioners (Finke & Stark, 2005; Pyle & Davidson, 2003). On the non-spiritual side of the ledger, motives included the desire for community, the vital government announcements made during services, and the casual exchange of economic information before and after meetings, among others. For these reasons, it would have been difficult to gain or maintain social status without attending church. Even so, estimates put church membership at 10 to 20% of the overall population throughout the colonial period (Stark & Finke, 1988, pp. 39–40). Of those, 75% attended irregularly or came as "pew holders" (Bonomi, 2003, p. 88). What we learn from this scholarship is that attending church was important, but not necessarily for spiritual reasons and not necessarily on a regular basis. In this light, the Massachusetts Bay Colony's decision to found "a schoale or colledge" likely reflected the spiritual *and* non-spiritual interests of the wider population. That's how some described the idea of a college before the Great and General Massachusetts Court's vote: for "learning's sake" serving both "church and common" purposes (Hoeveler, 2002, p. 23). To color the founding of Harvard as a strictly spiritual act misses the rich and complex role that religion has played in America life.

Advocates of the "Harvard trained ministers" argument might still wonder about the institution's name, campus rules, and final campus location that all signaled religious purpose. When the "colledge" finally received a proper name, it came from clergyman and benefactor John Harvard in 1639. Campus rules projected a disciplinary regimen framed to "know God" as the "foundation of all found knowledge and Learning" (New England's First Fruits, 1643, p. 26). And the selection of Newtown, later named Cambridge, for the campus location had religious meaning, as historians have noted. It was further away from the distractions and licentiousness of Boston (Geiger, 2014, p. 2).

All of these—the name, the rules, and the location—offer compelling support for the popular origin story, but they face a final challenge: what Harvard actually taught colonial American college students. According to the earliest published record of Harvard's curriculum, students received a British-styled liberal arts education, following the pattern of Cambridge and Oxford colleges, rather than direct preparation for the ministry. They learned physics, astronomy, arithmetic, geometry, politics, logic, poetry, and history. They also learned Greek, Hebrew, the Bible, and catechism, but, as with the rest of the curriculum, these studies served the overall purpose of preparing broadly educated gentlemen. Harvard's Charter of 1650 described this broad-based purpose as "the advancement of all good literature, artes, and Sciences" (Dudley, 1650). As such, for those seeking to enter the ministry the expectation was advanced study in divinity *after* attending Harvard and, when possible, a second degree (Geiger, 2014, p. 3).

From the start, Harvard's broad arts and science coursework prepared alumni who pursued a variety of life pathways. During the first five decades following the institution's founding, the majority of graduates assumed non-ministerial roles. Some took positions as physicians, teachers, and public servants. Others became merchants, planters, soldiers, and mariners. A portion died young, and the rest entered miscellaneous or unknown fields (Cremin, 1972, p. 221). Churches, meanwhile, regularly turned to alumni of British universities rather than Harvard to fill their ministerial openings. One-third or less of colonial church leaders received training in the colonies. The rest came largely from Oxford, Cambridge, and Dublin (Stout, 1974, p. 378).

ALTERNATIVES TO THE POPULAR ORIGIN STORY

If the Massachusetts Bay Colony had no explicit vision for their "schoale or colledge," valued churchgoing for spiritual and non-spiritual reasons, and ultimately produced Harvard, with its wide-ranging curriculum and alumni, then why did colonial leaders propose founding an institution in the first place?

Economic motives, or boosterism, offers one reason. The Massachusetts Bay Colony was largely a business venture of the Massachusetts Bay Company, and Harvard served an important role in economic development. The colonial charter received by the company from the English monarchy required every settler to purchase shares of the company and, as a colony, to produce goods or precious metals for England. Trade consumed a significant part of colonial daily life and mental energy (Pestana, 2020). With every colonist a shareholder, the colonial government had direct and indirect responsibilities to support the company's interests (McWilliams, 2009; Muldoon, 2018; Robbins, 1969).

With the founding of Harvard, colonial leaders conveyed a message of economic stability in an era of substantial hardship. Approximately 50% of the settlers of 1620 died within the first 6 months (Vinovskis, 1977, pp. 274–275). Challenging winters, demands on limited food supplies, pressures created by the arrival of new settlers, and a range of illnesses—including epidemics that raged between 1633 and 1641—continued to make stability elusive for decades (Grobb, 2002, p. 39). Ten to 30% of colonial infants never made it past their first year of life (Vinovskis, 1977, p. 286). And around the time of Harvard's founding, a smallpox outbreak laid waste to 40% of infected children and adults (Duffy, 1953). The southern colonies fared even worse health-wise (Dobson, 1989; Wells, 1992), and bad news making its way back to Europe influenced prospective newcomers. The viability of the Massachusetts Bay Company and the Massachusetts Bay Colony depended on distinguishing themselves as a favorable destination. Harvard gave the company and colony a symbol of stability, prosperity, and even comfort at a time when these elements were in short supply. The college became a point of distinction for the "City Upon a Hill," attracting those considering their options among colonies. The presence of Harvard suggested higher chances of survival and success.

The case of Harvard's first president, Nathaniel Eaton, highlights these economic motives. Eaton, a college dropout with no experience training ministers, had a brief stint in the colony that had more to do with business than spiritual values. His brother was involved with organizing the Massachusetts Bay Company, and the connection likely had something to do with Eaton's appointment as college president at age 27. Although the presidency lasted only a year, it was marred by controversies over Eaton under-provisioning the 10 students in his charge, beating them and an assistant, and absconding with college funds (Geiger, 2014, p. 2).

A few years after Eaton's failed presidency, the Massachusetts Bay Colony produced a "promotional pamphlet" about Harvard that painted a rosy portrait of the settlement's financial condition (Herbst, 1982, pp. 8–9). The document targeted future colonists and investors in the Massachusetts Bay Company. It focused on the colonists' safe passage across the North Atlantic, the housing and chapels built up after arrival, the bounty providing "necessariess for our livelihood," the civil government established, and the area's converted natives, among other things (New England's First Fruits, 1643). The document failed to mention the nearly decade-long smallpox pandemic but noted the "prosperity" the survivors sought through Harvard (First Fruits, 1643). The document was silent on alarming infant mortality rates, but it celebrated being in a stable position to "advance *Learning*" (First Fruits, 1643). Prospective settlers read of the "very faire" and "comely" and "spacious" and "large" and "convenient" buildings associated with the college (First Fruits, 1643). For those in England, colleges already symbolized luxury and comfort with "bowling greens" and "tennis courts" (Geiger, xv). In terms of boosterism, few messages could rival that of a colony so advanced as to have a college.

While serving economic motives, Harvard also satisfied social and psychological needs. The colonial order included "traditional social ranks," as some have noted, dominated by the wealthy and "well-educated" (Bailyn, 2013, pp. 370–371). In this context, Harvard helped reproduce social distinctions transplanted from Europe. As in England, those with advanced education could expect to gain certain advantages and benefits, through language, culture, connections, and prestige. Harvard became a vehicle for the distribution of such advantages, limited as they were within the colonial context (Geiger, 2014, pp. 7–8). But the college also served as a vehicle for change. Harvard represented an opportunity to prevent the reproduction of the kind of sectarian-based social discord the first settlers rejected about their European roots. If Puritans sought to leave behind religious persecution and intolerance, then Harvard offered a pathway to help realize this goal, or at least create social cohesion around a brand of Puritanism (Bangs, 2020; Bremmer, 2020; Hoeveler, 2002, pp. 28, 43).

Closely related to these social needs were the psychic ones Harvard helped to address. Early colonial life came with a healthy dose of fear, even for those with the greatest faith and optimism (Bailyn, 2013, pp. 321–364). Death, disease, starvation, poverty, crime, murder, rumor, gossip, suppression, disillusionment, loneliness, sectarianism, uncertainty, and the unknown—all of these exacted their psychological toll on colonists. Early settlers worried about the waves of newcomers deemed "rough and unruly" and "rude" and "violent" (p. 339). Fear of natives, or that colonial children would turn native, was also a fixture in the emotional lives of colonists (Bailyn, 1960). The idea of losing their cultural identity as the next generation resisted European habits, customs, and ideals produced documented anxiety. The penal code institutionalized these fears and frustrations by requiring minors to be put to death if they disobeyed their parents ("Incorrigible Children," 1646) or to be whipped if young males grew out their hair like the natives ("Punishing Disorderliness," 1675).

Harvard's mere presence had the power to counter these kinds of psychological wounds. The campus symbolized "civilized" life, an antidote to psychic maladies, and food for the mind and soul. It provided evidence of prosperity, community, and stability—real and perceived. And, at bottom, few symbols could have comforted the homesick more than a college, or at least the idea of one in their settlement (Bailyn, 1960).

In addition to satisfying economic, social, and psychological needs, Harvard offered a pathway for the colony to produce homegrown political leaders. There was little point in leaving the political troubles of Europe behind if the colony continued importing its political leadership. The Massachusetts Bay Colony received a right to self-governance from the British Crown (Muldoon, 2018). To exercise this right, the colony needed its own leaders. And to have its leaders taken seriously at home and abroad, they needed an educated class of citizens—trained by and for colonists. Harvard became a vehicle for producing the colony's first homegrown political class. At least 10% of Harvard graduates between 1642 and 1689 went into public service. They assumed roles as "Governors, councilors, judges, and deputies, (if continuing for a term of years), and permanent officials" (Cremin, 1972, p. 221). Given that this estimate does not include any who served in or ran for local office, the number of graduates who assumed political positions was likely much higher.

THE STORY'S LEGACY

Debates over and assumptions about the founding of Harvard have been with us for decades. In the early to mid-20th century, historian Samuel Eliot Morison took his lumps for suggesting that Harvard had been founded for any reasons other than to train ministers. The "Morison Myth," as one scholar called it, meant that Morison had lost his way, producing questionable "conclusions" that do "irreparable damage" and downplay the "Puritan interest in education" (Hudson, 1939, pp. 148–149). Morison argued that Harvard's earliest students received a liberal arts education, rather than a ministerial one. Despite early resistance, Morison's view has stood the test of time. Evidence from the historical record continues to align with his research on Harvard's origin.

The popular "Harvard trained ministers" origin story, however, continues to shape public understanding. It receives support from the many who see America as founded on Christian beliefs (Butler, 1992; Green, 2015). Claiming Harvard was a seminary adds credibility to this belief. It puts America's oldest educational institution on the spiritual rather than secular side of the ledger. In this light, Harvard's popular origin story supports a larger web of interconnected assumptions about American exceptionalism and the nation's religious roots—from colonial America and the Revolutionary War to the present. Questioning one element of this web brings a strong response from advocates of all the other points on the web. With the election of an atheist to Harvard's lead chaplaincy, the popular origin story becomes ever more important to its supporters.

Whether America was founded as a Christian nation is beyond the scope of this chapter. But the evidence discussed complicates the idea that Harvard was founded to train ministers. It also offers insight into the origin of other early colonial colleges. The 1693 Charter for the College of William and Mary, for instance, states that institution aimed for a broad "universal" curriculum, including "Divinity, Philosophy, Languages, and other good Arts and Sciences" (Royal Charter, 1693). Yale, likewise, first appeared as a "Collegiate School" in 1701 so that "Youth may be instructed in the Arts & Sciences" to pursue "Publik employment both in Church & Civil State" (The Yale Corporation, 1976, p. 4). Based on these charters, it's safe to say the goal was to establish colleges rather than seminaries. As such, early colonial colleges did not emerge out of a single, religious purpose.

No historian, however, would rightly doubt that religious values informed the early operations of Harvard or its colonial peers. Certainly, religion shaped the liberal education taught and the regular prayers and behaviors expected. But just as it would be a mistake to think religion had little to do with the era's campus life, it's also time to put to rest the Harvard and colonial college mythology.

REFERENCES

Bailyn, B. (1960). *Education in the forming of American society: Needs and opportunities for study.* University of North Carolina Press.

Bailyn, B. (2013). *The barbarous years: The peopling of British North America— The conflict of civilizations, 1600–1675.* Vintage.

Bangs, J. D. (2020). *New light on the old colony: Plymouth, the Dutch context of toleration, and patterns of Pilgrim commemoration.* Brill.

Bonomi, P. (2003). *Under the cope of heaven: Religion, society, and politics in colonial America.* Oxford University Press.

Boyer, P., et al. (2010). *The enduring vision: A history of the American people* (7th ed.). Cengage.

Bremmer, F. J. (2020). *One small candle: The Plymouth puritans and the beginning of English New England.* Oxford University Press.

Butler, J. (1992). *Awash in a sea of faith: Christianizing the American people.* Harvard University Press.

Combs, S. (2011). *A tribute to our Christian heritage.* Lulu.

Cremin, L. (1972). *American education: The colonial experience, 1607–1783.* HarperCollins.

Dobson, M. J. (1989). Mortality gradients and disease exchanges: Comparisons from old England and colonial America. *Social History of Medicine, 2*(1), 259–297.

Dudley, T. (1650). Charter of 1650. Harvard University Archives, Harvard University. Retrieved from http://id.lib.harvard.edu/via/olvwork368905/catalog

Duffy, J. (1953). *Epidemics in colonial America.* Louisiana State University Press.

Epstein, G. M. (2010). *Good without God: What a billion nonreligious people do believe.* William Morrow.

Epstein, G. M. (2014, March 24). In memory of Tom Ferrick: America's first atheist chaplain died. *Huffington Post.* Retrieved from https://www.huffpost.com/entry/tom-ferrick-atheist_b_4646372

Epstein, G. M., & Croft, J. (2013, October/November). The godless congregation: An idea whose time has come. *Free Inquiry, 33*(6). Retrieved from https://secularhumanism.org/2013/10/cont-the-godless-congregation-an-idea-whose-time-has-come/

Finke, R., & Stark, R. (2005). *The churching of America, 1776–2005: Winners and losers in our religious economy.* Rutgers University Press.

Geiger, R. L. (2014). *The history of American higher education: Learning and culture from the founding to World War II.* Princeton University Press.

Goldberg, E. (2021, August 26). The new chief chaplain at Harvard? An atheist. *The New York Times.* Retrieved from https://www.nytimes.com/2021/08/26/us/harvard-chaplain-greg-epstein.html

Green, S. K. (2015). *Inventing a Christian America: The myth of the religious founding.* Oxford University Press.

Grobb, G. N. (2002). *The deadly truth: A history of disease in America.* Harvard University Press.

Hall, D. D. (2019). *The Puritans: A transatlantic history.* Princeton University Press.

Harvard University Archives. (n.d.). Charters and legislative acts relating to the governance of Harvard, 1650–1814: An inventory. Harvard University Archives, Harvard University. Retrieved from https://hollisarchives.lib.harvard.edu/repositories/4/resources/4113

Herbst, J. (1982). *From crisis to crisis: American college government, 1636–1819*. Harvard University Press.

Hoeveler, J. D. (2002). *Creating the American mind: Intellect and politics in the colonial colleges*. Rowman & Littlefield.

Hudson, W. S. (1939). The Morison myth concerning the founding of Harvard College. *Church History, 8*(2), 148–159.

Hutson, J. H., et al. (n.d.). Religion and the founding of the American republic. *U.S. Library of Congress*. Retrieved from https://www.loc.gov/exhibits/religion/rel02.html

Instructions for punishing disorderliness and rudeness in Massachusetts youth. (1675). In N. B. Shurtleff (Ed.), *Records of the governor and Company of Massachusetts Bay, 1628–1685* (Vol. V, 1853–1854, pp. 60–61). William White.

Instructions for the punishment of incorrigible children in Massachusetts (1646). In N. B. Shurtleff (Ed.), *Records of the governor and Company of Massachusetts Bay, 1628–1685* (Vol. III, 1853–1854, p. 101). William White.

McWilliams, J. E. (2009). Butter, milk, and a "spare ribb": Women's work and the transatlantic economic transition in seventeenth-century Massachusetts. *The New England Quarterly, 82*(1), 5–24.

Morison, S. E. (1936). *Three centuries of Harvard*. Harvard University Press.

Muldoon, J. (2018). Colonial charters: Possessory or regulatory? *Law and History Review, 36*(2), 355–381.

New England's first fruits. (1643). R. Oulton and G. Dexter Printers.

Paumgarten, N. (2021, September 11). Harvard's atheist-chaplain controversy. *The New Yorker*. Retrieved from https://www.newyorker.com/magazine/2021/09/20/harvards-atheist-chaplain-controversy

Pestana, C. G. (2020). *The world of Plymouth plantation*. Belknap Press.

Pyle, R. E., & Davidson, J. D. (2003). The origins of religious stratification in colonial America. *Journal for the Scientific Study of Religion, 42*(1), 57–75.

Robbins, W. G. (1969). The Massachusetts Bay Company: An analysis of motives. *The Historian, 32*(1), 83–98.

Royal Charter of the College of William and Mary. (1693). Royal Charter Collection, Special Collections Research Center, Earl Gregg Swem Library, College of William and Mary. Retrieved from https://scrc-kb.libraries.wm.edu/royal-charter

Stark, R., & Finke, R. (1988). American religion in 1776: A statistical portrait. *Sociological Analysis, 49*(1), 39–51.

Stout, H. S. (1974). University men in New England 1620–1660: A demographic analysis. *The Journal of Interdisciplinary History, 4*(3), 375–400.

Van Engen, A. C. (2020). *City on a hill: A history of American exceptionalism*. Yale University Press.

Vinovskis, M. (1977). Angels' heads and weeping willows: Death in early America. *Proceedings of the American Antiquarian Society, 86*(2), 273–302.

Wells, R. V. (1992). The population of England's colonies in America: Old English or new Americans? *Population Studies, 46*(1), 85–102.

The Yale Corporation: Charter and legislation. (1976). Yale University. Retrieved from https://www.yale.edu/sites/default/files/files/University-Charter.pdf

Yang, M. (2021, August 28). Harvard University's new chief chaplain is . . . an atheist. *The Guardian*. Retrieved from https://www.theguardian.com/education/2021/aug/28/harvard-university-chief-chaplain-atheist

CHAPTER 3

The Myth of Summer Vacation and the Agrarian Calendar

Kenneth Gold

Ask someone why schools are typically closed in the summer. In response, most people, including many scholars, policymakers, and journalists, will describe a tradition dating back to this nation's agricultural past. Michael Strain (2022, n.p.) of the American Enterprise Institute recently argued that "The US does not need to continue structuring children's education based on the old agrarian calendar." So did former secretary of education Arne Duncan (University of Northern Iowa, 2009) and *Time* magazine (Von Drehle, 2010) in its "Case Against Summer Vacation." They and many others assume that farmers needed their children's labor during the summer or that rural life produced a school year without the summer.

These are plausible answers if you don't know much about 19th-century farming or schools, but they're entirely wrong. They express what I call the agrarian myth of summer vacation. The standard school calendar of today—180 days of school beginning late summer and ending late spring—was not the format produced by an agricultural society. Instead, it was the intentional creation of the earliest professional educators and a collective response to prevailing medical notions, economic conditions, cultural practices, and impulses for standardization in the mid-19th century.

I took on the agrarian myth 20 years ago with the publication of *School's In: The History of Summer Education in American Public Schools* (Gold, 2002). The first half of the book focused on the evolution of the school calendar during the 19th century and generated the most interest among the general public. For over 20 years now, reporters have interviewed me—usually between Memorial Day and Labor Day—about why the school year typically lasts 180 days and avoids the summer. Each year I give the same explanation about summer vacation being created by school reformers and popular practices rather than simply inherited from farmers. Each year I wonder what makes this myth so persistent and what the cost is of believing it.

Answers to these questions are offered here. First, I take the reader through the 19th-century transformation of the school calendar by conveying the enormous variety in academic years prior to the Civil War and tracing what happened to the school years, the mechanisms used to transform them, and the reasons the changes occurred. Second, I explore the origins of the myth—how and when it took root and the public forgot that any other form of school year had preceded what had become ingrained by 1920. Finally, I consider the resiliency of the agrarian myth and whether correcting misconceptions about it would make the summer vacation any less entrenched.

TRENDS AND VARIATIONS IN 19TH-CENTURY SCHOOL CALENDARS

As Horace Mann collected data and visited schools throughout Massachusetts during the 1830s and 1840s, he identified what to him were great deficiencies. Speaking and writing in his role as secretary to the state's board of education, Mann thought too many communities lacked a proper commitment to schooling—as evidenced by their inhospitable schoolhouses, unimpressive teachers, and haphazard student attendance. Overall, there was far too much variation across the state for the system he aspired to build, reflective of the hyperlocal districts that each ran a single school. This troubling divergence included the range in school-year lengths, with many districts running schools for what Mann and other early school leaders deemed an insufficient amount of time. (Illinois Superintendent of Public Instruction, 1868; Massachusetts Board of Education, 1842). Massachusetts districts averaged nearly 7 months of schooling in 1840, but many villages ran schools for just a few months, while Boston and other cities kept their schools open nearly year-round. For example, in 1826, districts in towns with fewer than 1,250 residents averaged 127 days of schooling, while districts in larger communities of 5,000 to 10,000 inhabitants averaged 204 days. The level of agriculture in a community and population density were strong predictors of school-year length in Massachusetts in 1860, relationships that likely persisted until the end of the century (Kaestle & Vinovskis, 1980; Rury, 1988).

School terms in the Midwest were decidedly shorter but equally as varied as their counterparts in Massachusetts. In 1841, the average length of school in each Michigan county ranged from 3 to 5½ months, and the divergence was just as stark among the townships in a single county. In Washtenaw County, west of Detroit and home of the University of Michigan, schools in Sharon ran an average of 6½ months; schools in Sylvan just over 4. Schooling was so localized that each town had multiple districts. In 1841, one district in Sharon ran its school for 3 months and another one for 10 (Michigan Department of Public Instruction, 1841). Nearly 20 years later, Indiana's state superintendent reported equally disparate school terms, ranging from 22 to 246 days and averaging only 77 (Indiana Department of Public Instruction, 1859). Making rural school terms longer and more standard fit well with the larger reform agenda of the Common School Movement.

Regardless of how many weeks a district ran school, most shared one thing in common—the schools were open in the summer for much of the 19th century. In the antebellum, many cities divided their lengthy school year into four quarters, with a week or two between each one. While urban children's presence at school was often highly irregular, summer term attendance fared well in comparison to the other three quarters (Gold, 2002; Michigan Department of Public Instruction, 1852; Philadelphia Controllers of the Public Schools, 1840). It was, of course, rural school calendars that supposedly reflected the agrarian myth. In agricultural areas with little population density, school districts typically offered two terms, one in the winter and the other in the summer; indeed, this was the actual school calendar pattern shaped by local economies steeped in farming. By opening in the hottest and coldest months, schools did not compete with the especially intensive planting in the spring and harvesting in the fall. There was plenty of farmwork to do during summer, so many older students only attended during the winter, but summer terms still attracted thousands of students. Rural summer terms were an integral component of the school year and not at all supplemental. As part of the regular operation of a school district, summer term teachers largely taught the same curriculum in the same school building (Connecticut Superintendent of Common Schools, 1846; Gold, 2002; Illinois Superintendent of Public Instruction, 1866; Massachusetts Board of Education, 1842).

Nevertheless, the summer term was not well reputed. As one county superintendent from New York noted, "it is evident that the summer terms will not compare favorably with those kept in the winter" (New York Superintendent of Common Schools, 1844, p. 324). Educators and citizens associated a number of characteristics with this perceived weakness: slighter attendance, younger attendees, and female teachers (Connecticut Superintendent of Common Schools, 1839, 1840; Indiana Department of Public Instruction, 1852, 1853; Massachusetts Board of Education, 1837, 1842; New York Superintendent of Common Schools, 1843; Ohio Office of the State Commissioner of Common Schools, 1854). Gendered assumptions about inferior summer term teachers were especially potent. Even as notions of feminine suitability for teaching expanded, superintendents' dismissiveness of female summer term teachers persisted because they were young, untrained, and transient. Collectively, the variation in these criteria by school session added up to a general consensus that the summer term was inferior. It was also inconvenient.

A number of factors increasingly discouraged schools from opening in the summer over the course of the 19th century. As school districts transformed into expanding urban school systems, construction and repair of school buildings grew more urgent and summer weather lent itself to addressing those needs (Brooklyn City Superintendent of Schools, 1856; Indiana Department of Public Instruction, 1878; New York Board of Education, 1853). Attendance patterns mattered too. Urban districts often added vacation days when school attendance was vastly diminished—for example, the day of Christmas Eve (Gold, 2002; New York Board of Education, 1856). By the late 1850s, previously robust summer attendance in urban schools had become less sure, and many cities had already carved out lengthy summer vacations for their schools (Albany Board of Public Instruction, 1870; Boston Schools Committee, 1857; Cleveland Board of Education, 1858; Philadelphia Controllers of the Public Schools, 1858; St. Louis Board of Education, 1859). Summer outbreaks of illness and heat also periodically prevented schools from opening and drove a community's wealthiest inhabitants increasingly to leave towns and cities for retreats in the mountains or by the water: Saratoga Springs and Coney Island for Brooklyn and New York; Warm Springs for Baltimore and Washington, and eventually Door County, Wisconsin, for Chicago (Burrows & Wallace, 1999; Chambers, 2002; Holland, 1917; Sterngass, 2001). Summer activities took other forms as well: Revivalists attended summer camp meetings, and businessmen and professionals hosted and traveled to conventions (Dresser & Gardella, 2020; Keating, 2004; Miller, 2014).

School leaders had reasons of their own for wanting to eliminate the summer term. Ideas about the physical and mental frailty of students and teachers raised concerns that year-round schooling enabled too much mental activity in a confined space. As Mann observed, "not infrequently is health itself destroyed by over-stimulating the mind" (Massachusetts Board of Education, 1842, pp. 26–27). Such notions were grounded in the medical thinking of the day, but even after the science moved on in the latter half of the 19th century, school leaders continued to extol the summer vacation as a prophylactic for debility (Gold, 2002). They also embraced the contemporary commodification of time. Growing out of the Puritan ethic and market capitalism, time increasingly became seen as something to be spent profitably. With more and more schools closed for 6 weeks or 2 months in July and August, reformers feared teacher idleness and viewed the summer as an ideal moment to address a key plank of their agenda: teacher professionalization. Normal schools and institutes with summer courses and conferences proliferated, and journals like the *Massachusetts Teacher* urged their readers to get out into the country, especially if there was a teacher convention to attend. Professionalization also served to justify lengthening rural school terms, as better-trained teachers also needed to be better compensated through more full-time work (Gold, 2002).

Armed with these reasons for wanting a uniform school calendar that excluded the summer, school reformers implemented a few key policies in order to prod towns and districts to reshape their school year. These included the consolidation of districts; the redefining of school terms and years; and, most significantly, the intertwining of school funding with legal minimums for the length of school (Gold, 2002). States that at mid-century may have mandated 3 to 6 months of schooling in order for districts to access state school funds required 8 or 9 months by the century's end. At the state level, the 19th-century superintendency was largely a toothless position whose incumbents spoke from the bully pulpit, but eligibility requirements for state monies proved to be effective. The agrarian school calendar of the early 19th century, which included summer but excluded the spring and fall, and the urban school calendar that also contained a summer term were eliminated. By the century's end, urban and rural school calendars were converging on a familiar norm: a 180-day school year held during the fall, winter, and spring, punctuated by a 2- to 3-month summer vacation. That this change had occurred over the 19th century as the United States was industrializing was eventually forgotten.

THE ORIGINS OF THE AGRARIAN MYTH

Uncovering the origins of the agrarian myth requires an exploration of discussions about school calendars and summer vacation. *School's In* showed how social and school reformers grew uneasy about the summer vacation in cities increasingly congested with the immigrant working poor in the late 19th century. In response, they created vacation schools to provide children viewed as idle and/or troublesome with opportunities for meaningful activity. They emphasized that the nonacademic activities would have no ill effect on health but did not claim that the current school calendar was an outdated relic. Nor did the professional school administrators, who in the early 20th century transformed vacation schools into academic summer schools still familiar today: classes that offered academic credits used mostly to avoid falling behind and sometimes to get ahead (Gold, 2002). Summer schools served the needs of school systems eager to move students through the grades in a timely fashion but did not lead to a reconsideration of the school calendar.

By the 1920s, summer vacation had become an object of study for social scientists. Educator lore had long suggested that students forgot everything they learned during a lengthy break in schooling. Henry Barnard, for example, articulated that notion in 1840: "But in many of these districts, there are long vacations between the summer and winter schools, in which time the habits of study, and in a measure, the proficiency gained in a previous term, are lost" (Connecticut Superintendent of Common Schools, 1840, p. 17). Eighty years later, psychologists, education researchers, and other scholars, equipped with early versions of standardized tests, set out to verify that assumption and measure the phenomenon. They pre- and posttested students for growth in reading and mathematics, the mastery of particular subjects, and in some cases cognitive development more generally. Some investigated whether a specific intervention might mitigate the learning loss or how long in the subsequent fall term it would take to regain the knowledge or skills (Cooper et al., 1996; Morgan, 1929; Morrison, 1924; Nelson, 1928). These researchers did not express the agrarian myth to explain their query. Neither the strictures of their discipline nor their scholarly agenda warranted broaching the origins of the summer vacation at all.[1]

Inchoate expressions of the agrarian myth started to appear in the middle of the 20th century. The 1930 White House Conference on Child Health and Protection included summer vacation as an object for study, and speakers identified it as an opportune time for curricular experimentation. The school superintendent of Providence called into question the very organization of the school calendar, a theme that was amplified in the 1933 report of the Subcommittee on Summer Vacation Activities of the School Child. Chaired by no less a Progressive educator than William Kilpatrick, the subcommittee's report opened with a supposition: "*Probably* (italics mine) summer vacation for the school child grew up, as a result of an old economy, when his help was needed and utilized in the work of the farm" (White House Conference on Child Health and Protection, 1930, p. 3). Voicing of the agrarian myth, even without asserting its veracity, had granted it some legitimacy by demonstrating an argumentative purpose. The recommendations for the summer might involve new activities or less traditional vacation, and such contentions were seemingly buttressed by the claim that summer vacation itself was an outdated relic of the farm.

The agrarian myth emerged fitfully over the next three decades. Expression of it was not very common because interest in summer education did not surface all that often and summer programs were not especially prevalent. Many districts had eliminated summer sessions during the Great Depression, and by the mid-1950s, summer term enrollments still had not returned to their peak levels in the late 1920s (Gold, 2002). When writings about reconfiguring the school calendar, reinvigorating summer sessions, or improving rural education appeared, many authors did not routinely offer the justification that summer vacation reflected the economy of a bygone era (Committee on Rural Community High Schools, 1944; Fine, 1948; Studebaker, 1948). But some did. In 1952, a *New York Times* article discussing lengthening the school year quoted a Columbia University professor asserting that "summer vacation is archaic" and cited the agrarian myth as one reason to consider his ideas ("11 School Months Urged," 1952).

By the early 1960s, the attraction of altering the traditional school year had grown, often accompanied by a still embryonic version of the agrarian myth as a justification. In 1961, a proposal for a year-round school

---

1. I located only two pieces of scholarship that did address changes in the urban school year, and both presented reasonably accurate accounts. See Snow (1927) and Nelson (1929).

understood how the farming economy shaped the rural calendar and suggested that the fallacy at play was that kids still had obligations or opportunities to work on a farm during the summer (May, 1961). A subsequent polemic for year-round education understood that farm economies had supported winter and summer terms but not why, when, and how the calendar changed (Glass, 1962). Given the poor reputation of the 19th-century summer term, there was also some truth to one university president's assertion that "we have clung tenaciously to the outworn tradition of the agrarian society, which prescribes that school is an enterprise for the winter, that teachers cannot teach and children cannot learn when the weather is warm" (Fawcett, 1962, p. 128). Among some experts, the agrarian dynamics that structured the 19th-century school calendar were understood, but the summer term was largely forgotten, and the story of the creation of the summer vacation was unknown. The nuance found in such articulations was often lost in discussions by journalists. For example, a 1961 *New York Times* report of "longer school years ahead" explained that "the nine-month school year is increasingly being described as a relic of the days when the children of an agricultural nation were needed to bring in the crops" (Hechinger, 1961, p. E10).

The agrarian myth firmly took hold in the 1970s. Interest in year-round education had coalesced into the establishment in 1969 of an annual conference on the topic. Over the next 5 years, the agrarian myth steadily gained potency during the meetings. Initially, the myth was not often cited but appeared fully articulated when it was (Mt. Sequoyah National Seminar on Year-Round Education, 1969). The conferences in 1971, 1972, and 1973, however, included fully developed expressions of the agrarian myth: "Why . . . do we continue to operate schools for only nine months? Apparently it was because at one time the labor of children was needed on the farm," a University of Florida professor asked and answered (McLain & Morgan, 1971, p. 7a). Or as the president of the National Council on Year Round Education put it 2 years later, the standard school year was "an educational strait-jacket" (Lovern, 1973, p. 32). Forty years later, policymakers and scholars still perpetuate the false notion that "history tells us the reasons that school systems used only a 10-month calendar were due to agrarian needs" (Pederson, 2012, p. 54). Over the last 50 years, proponents for change in the school calendar would usually say something similar. What's the harm in them getting it wrong?

THE PROBLEM OF THE AGRARIAN MYTH

The agrarian myth—the belief that today's school calendar is a product of the farm—has proven quite resilient. People have repeatedly expressed it to me in conversations about *School's In*, but it also regularly appears in written and oral discussions of potential policy improvements to the school year. It often serves as a preamble to an argument for a different school calendar, one with summer vacation diminished or eliminated. In that context it functions as a usable past meant to portray the status quo as outdated and irrelevant. Having emerged as American economic dominance and the post–World War II order waned, the myth is commonly grounded in the assumption that schools are fundamentally economic institutions that must form human capital for society and serve the occupational aspirations of its residents. The assertion of the agrarian myth became a standard trope used to contend that a different calendar would help schools better prepare students for industrial, and later postindustrial, work in a globalized economy (Barrett, 1990; Domenech, 1998; Harris, 2011; Shepard & Baker, 1977; Symonds et al., 2001).

The agrarian myth as a rhetorical device is problematic in at least four ways. First, it misreads what has kept the school year intact. In portraying summer vacation as illogical today, it presumes that a rational basis for change is at hand. Historical experience suggests otherwise. Over the last 100 years, schools and systems have had suitable reasons to experiment with the way the academic year is structured. For some, those motives led to vacation programs, summer schools, and/or a longer school year. For others, they dictated eliminating summer vacation by running schools all year round. More commonly, year-round schools were adopted to make more efficient use of the school plant, leaving students and teachers with long vacations at varying times during the year. Still more tackle the summer learning loss phenomenon by breaking up a single long vacation into smaller blocks of time: 60 days of school followed by 20 vacation days, for example. What all of these and other approaches have in common is that they have to date failed to ignite widespread systemic alteration of the 180-day, summers-off school year. Labeling summer vacation as a relic is a poor tactic not because it's inaccurate but because it's ineffective.

Second, the real past might prove much more usable than the agrarian myth. Knowing that the establishment of the current school year was the conscious creation of a group of reformers might prove empowering and make summer vacation less inviolate. Advocates for change can draw on past accomplishments to inspire their work in the present (as opposed to recycling tactics and strategies). Conversely, treating the school calendar as something without history and never substantially altered may only serve to reify it. Reformers would also do well to understand the ways that the 19th-century calendar evolved in response to the summertime choices made by urban and rural residents. How people are using schools today in an era marked by increasing divergence between the affluent and the economically insecure may prove to be rhetorically fertile; a mismatch between current structures and behaviors will likely prove to be more persuasive than incongruence between past and present.

Most importantly, the agrarian myth functions as an ideological decoy, diverting attention away from more significant material conditions that block change. With summer vacation from school the norm for well over 100 years, powerful economic interests, cultural practices, and bureaucratic inertia have developed a firm hold in American society. Businesses related to youth programs, camps, and outdoor recreational activities are highly dependent on income earned during the summer, as are beach and resort areas. One 2022 survey identified 81% of Americans as planning to take a summer vacation; before the COVID pandemic, the travel and tourism sector accounted for nearly 3% of the United States' total GDP (Osborne, 2022; "Summer Travel Survey," 2022). Economic activity during the summer—whether near or far—has generated a host of iconic activities embedded in American culture: days at the pool, lake, or ocean; nights at the band shell or ice cream stand; and weekends in the mountains or at the shore. Americans will not lightly relinquish the family time often afforded by summer vacation; nor will teachers and other professionals who benefit from an economic slowdown in the summer. These current factors are what keep summer vacation in place, and those who would change it should heed them since neither historical fallacies nor well-constructed educational rationales for a different calendar will topple them.

Finally, the agrarian myth distracts us from a more promising direction for policy. However ineffectively it is employed, the myth is still harnessed to argue against a long summer vacation, but there is also a tradition of educators leaning in to summer vacation. From fresh air funds to outdoor education programs, summer educational experiences need not occur in a traditional classroom setting. Children of affluence largely escape learning loss because of the educative value of many of the summer activities available to them; creating and funding a host of opportunities for youth with less means will help stem their summer slide without jettisoning the cultural significance that summer now holds for Americans of all social strata. Summer learning is important, but it need not feel at all like school.

REFERENCES

11 school months urged. (1952, April 9). *The New York Times*, 25.
Albany Board of Public Instruction. (1870). *Fourth annual report of the board of instruction*. The Argus Company.
Barrett, M. J. (1990). The case for more schools days. *Atlantic, 266*(5), 78–106.
Boston School Committee. (1857). *Annual report of the school committee*. George C. Rand & Avery.
Brooklyn City Superintendent of Schools. (1856). *Annual report of the City Superintendent of Schools of the consolidated city of Brooklyn*. L. Darbee & Son.
Burrows, E. G., & Wallace, M. (1999). *Gotham: A history of New York to 1898*. Oxford University Press.

Chambers, T. A. (2002). *Drinking the waters: Creating an American leisure class at nineteenth-century mineral springs*. Smithsonian Institution Scholarly Press.

Cleveland Board of Education. (1858). *Report of the board of education*. Fairbanks, Benedict & Co.

Committee on Rural Community High Schools. (1944). Adventures in rural education: A three year report. *Journal of Experimental Education, 12*(4), 245–248.

Connecticut Superintendent of Common Schools. (1839). *Report of the superintendent of common schools*. Press of Case, Tiffany, and Burnham.

Connecticut Superintendent of Common Schools. (1840). *Report of the superintendent of common schools*. Press of Case, Tiffany, and Burnham.

Connecticut Superintendent of Common Schools. (1846). *Report of the superintendent of common schools*. Press of Case, Tiffany, and Burnham.

Cooper, H., Nye, B., Charlton, K., Lindsay, J., & Greathouse, S. (1996). The effects of summer vacation on achievement test scores: A narrative and meta-analytic review. *Review of Educational Research, 66*(3), 227–268.

Domenech, D. A. (1998). Should students attend school year round? *Spectrum: Journal of State Government, 71*(4), 24.

Dresser, T., & Gardella, N. (2020). *The rise of tourism on Martha's Vineyard*. The History Press.

Fawcett, N. G. (1962). A new challenge to education. *Theory Into Practice, 1*(3), 125–130.

Fine, B. (1948, February 26). Educators favor all-year schools. *The New York Times*, 25.

Glass, R. E. (1962). Calendar possibilities for year-round schools. *Theory Into Practice, 1*(3), 136–140.

Gold, K. M. (2002). *School's in: The history of summer education in American public schools*. Peter Lang.

Harris, D. (2011, March 14). The amount of quality classroom time is the real issue. *Indianapolis Business Journal, 32*(2), 10C.

Hechinger, F. M. (1961, May 21). Longer school years ahead. *The New York Times*, E10.

Holland, H. R. (1917). *History of Door County, Wisconsin: The county beautiful*. S. J. Clarke.

Illinois Superintendent of Public Instruction. (1866). *Annual Report*, 6. Office of the Superintendent of Public Instruction.

Illinois Superintendent of Public Instruction. (1868). *Annual Report*, 7. Office of the Superintendent of Public Instruction.

Indiana Department of Public Instruction. (1852). *Annual report of the Department of Public Instruction of the State of Indiana*. Author.

Indiana Department of Public Instruction. (1853). *Annual report of the Department of Public Instruction of the State of Indiana*. Author.

Indiana Department of Public Instruction. (1859). *Annual report of the Department of Public Instruction of the State of Indiana*. Author.

Indiana Department of Public Instruction. (1878). *Annual report of the Department of Public Instruction of the State of Indiana*. Author.

Kaestle, C. F., & Vinovskis, M. A. (1980). *Education and social change in nineteenth-century Massachusetts*. Cambridge University Press.

Keating, A. D. (2004). Chicagoland: More than the sum of its parts. *Journal of Urban History, 30*(2), 213–230.

Lovern, M. F. (Ed.). (1973). *Proceedings of the fifth national seminar on year-round education,* 32. Retrieved from https://eric.ed.gov/?id=ED083735

Massachusetts Board of Education. (1837). *Annual report of the Board of Education,* 1. Author.

Massachusetts Board of Education. (1842). *Annual report of the Board of Education,* 6. Author.

May, F. B. (1961). Year-round school, a proposal. *Elementary School Journal, 61*(7), 388–393.

McLain, J. D., & Morgan, D. (1971, February 6–8). *Proceedings of Pennsylvania State Annual Conference on Year-Round Education,* 7a.

Michigan Department of Public Instruction. (1841). *Report of the Superintendent of Public Instruction.* State Printers.

Michigan Department of Public Instruction. (1852). *Report of the Superintendent of Public Instruction.* State Printers.

Miller, D. L. (2014). *City of the century: The epic of Chicago and the making of America.* Simon & Schuster.

Morgan, L. D. (1929). How effective is specific training in preventing loss due to the summer vacation? *Journal of Educational Psychology, 20*(6), 466–471.

Morrison, J. C. (1924). What effect has the summer vacation on children's learning and ability to learn? *Educational Research Bulletin, 3*(12), 245–249.

Mt. Sequoyah national seminar on year-round education. (1969). Retrieved from https://eric.ed.gov/?id=ED040498

Nelson, M. J. (1928). How much time is required in the fall for pupils of the elementary school to reach again the spring level of achievement? *Journal of Educational Research, 18*(4), 305–308.

Nelson, M. J. (1929). *The differences in achievement of elementary school pupils before and after the summer vacation.* Bureau of Educational Research.

New York (N.Y.) Board of Education. (1853). *Annual report of the Board of Education of the City and County of New York.* William C. Bryant & Company.

New York (N.Y.) Board of Education. (1856). *Annual report of the Board of Education of the City and County of New York.* William C. Bryant & Company.

New York (State) Superintendent of Common Schools. (1843). *Annual report of the Superintendent of Common Schools.* Author.

New York (State) Superintendent of Common Schools. (1844). *Annual report of the Superintendent of Common Schools.* Author.

Ohio Office of the State Commissioner of Common Schools. (1854). *Annual report of the State Commissioner of Common Schools.* Statesmen Steam Press.

Osborne, S. (2022). U.S. travel and tourism satellite account for 1999–2020. *Survey of Current Business, 102*(2), 1–12.

Pederson, J. (2012). The history of school and summer vacation. *Journal of Inquiry & Action in Education, 5*(1), 54–62.

Philadelphia Controllers of the Public Schools. (1840). *Annual Report,* 22. J. Crissy.

Philadelphia Controllers of the Public Schools. (1858). *Annual Report,* 40. J. Crissy.

Rury, J. L. (1988). The variable school year: Measuring differences in the length of American school terms in 1900. *Journal of Research and Development in Education, 21,* 29–36.

St. Louis Board of Education. (1859). *Annual report of the board of education*, 5. E. P. Studley & Co.
Shepard, M. A., & Baker, K. (1977). *Year-round schools*. D. C. Heath and Company.
Snow, W. B. (1927). The Boston school calendar. *Elementary School Journal, 28*(2), 134–136.
Sterngass, J. (2001). *First resorts: Pursuing pleasure at Saratoga Springs, Newport, and Coney Island*. Johns Hopkins University Press.
Strain, M. R. (2022, September 26). America's educational emergency. Retrieved from https://www.aei.org/op-eds/americas-education-emergency/
Studebaker, J. W. (1948). Why not a year-round educational program? *Journal of Educational Sociology, 21*(5), 269–275.
Summer travel survey. (2022). *The Vacationer*. Retrieved from https://thevacationer.com/summer-travel-survey-2022/
Symonds, W. C., Palmer, A. T., & Hylton, H. (2001, March 19). How to fix America's schools. *BusinessWeek, 3724*, 66–80.
University of Northern Iowa. (2009, April 24). *U.S. Secretary of Education Arne Duncan* [Press release]. Retrieved from https://president.uni.edu/us-secretary-education-arne-duncan
Von Drehle, D. (2010, August 2). The case against summer vacation. *Time, 176*(5), 36–42.
White House Conference on Child Health and Protection. (1930). *Official proceedings: White House Conference on child health and protection, November 19–22, 1930: Section three: Education and training*. American Child Health Association.

CHAPTER 4

The Myth of Local Control

Campbell F. Scribner

During her 4-year tenure as the U.S. secretary of education, Betsy DeVos never missed an opportunity to delegitimize her own office. "This drives the big-government folks nuts," she told one audience, "but it's important to reiterate: Education is best addressed at the state, local, and family levels" (Brown, 2017). Like most political rhetoric, DeVos's statement was an odd mixture of common sense, ideological signaling, and outright incoherence. Condemning federal involvement in education and downplaying the conflicts between other levels of government assumes (and implicitly endorses) the decentralization of the American educational system, an arrangement that proponents describe as "local control." At various times, Americans have invoked local control to defend the freedom of parents, charter schools, school districts, municipal boards, county governments, and state legislatures, and to resist everything from standardized testing and school closures to racial desegregation and tax redistribution. The very malleability of the phrase suggests how easy it is to mythologize the history of local school governance.

This chapter makes two arguments about the myth of local control. First, it dispels any notion that there was a "golden age" of local democracy, in which state and federal governments were uninvolved in education and local participation flourished. And second, it shows how, in the 20th century, invocations of localism have been cynically and selectively deployed to stifle equal educational opportunity. The chapter concludes with some thoughts about the appropriate role of localism in educational politics, and the ways in which one might support local democracy without relying on myths or slogans.

There has always been an entanglement between local, state, and federal governments in the United States. None of them operated independently, and educational undertakings at different levels often grew in tandem. During the nation's westward expansion in the 18th and 19th centuries, for example, when the federal government took millions of acres of land from native peoples and parceled them for White settlement, Congress imposed a linear grid on the territories of the Midwest. The Northwest Ordinances (1787) established the patchwork of rectangular fields and roads still visible from airplane windows—and set aside land in the center of every township to generate revenue for local schools. As these territories became states, they expanded provisions for public education, empowering legislatures to draw district boundaries, set minimum tax rates, and establish broad curricular standards, such as mandatory Bible reading. In the decade after the Civil War, the federal government pressured former Confederate states to draft constitutional provisions for public education as a condition of their readmission, while the Freedman's Bureau (an arm of the War Department) helped African American communities build thousands of schools across the South. In both of these cases, federal authorities took steps to imagine, incentivize, and even mandate the construction of schools that they did not actually have the resources to operate or oversee. The result was what Brian Balogh (2009) describes as a "government out of sight," in which federal agencies quietly built state capacity, while state legislatures set broad parameters for the exercise of local initiative. All three levels of government were interdependent, although local institutions were the most visible.

Decentralizing educational responsibility encouraged a culture of self-reliance and civic association throughout the 19th century. Foreign visitors marveled at the democratic energy they found in town councils and school boards, which governed with almost complete independence. Local authorities assessed school taxes based on land ownership. Board members interviewed and hired teachers directly, usually on short-term contracts, while students' families provided lodging. Local residents contributed the materials and labor to build schoolhouses, which in turn hosted community meetings and events. More than 200,000 school districts had appeared by the turn of the 20th century, most of them operating a single, one-room school building.

There were many shortcomings to these strictly local arrangements. Taxes were unpopular, and local corruption could lead to neglected buildings, underpaid teachers, shortened terms, and unrepresentative elections; poorly trained teachers were often only a step ahead of their students and had to whip them to keep order; prevailing prejudice usually excluded non-White students and those with disabilities; and many communities had low expectations for academic proficiency. Nevertheless, as Jonathan Zimmerman notes in his chapter, this volume, and his stand-alone book on the subject, the one-room schoolhouse became a powerful mythological symbol, the embodiment of a particular set of democratic ideals (Zimmerman, 2009). When Americans speak approvingly of local control today, it is often the bucolic image of country schools that they have in mind and rarely a realistic rendering of those institutions (also see Neem, 2017).

A series of changes at the turn of the 20th century called into question the viability of small, locally governed schools. Particularly concerning to White, native-born Americans was the rise of immigration, urbanization, and perceptions of political corruption. One-room schoolhouses may have sufficed for a rural, agricultural society, but cities seemed to require larger buildings and the hierarchical management of experts. Business and professional organizations insisted that voters needed a uniform civics curriculum, that poverty required public health services, and that a changing labor market demanded broader course offerings than small schools could provide. To meet these needs, they lobbied urban districts to raise school funding thresholds and strengthen standards for attendance, curriculum, and facilities. Growing budgets prompted new concerns about the makeup of local school boards, which had long been sites of embezzlement and preferential hiring. To prevent self-dealing, reformers tried to depoliticize education entirely, shifting operational decisions from elected officials to unelected principals and superintendents, and requiring that school board elections be nonpartisan and held on alternate years from other offices. As a result of these changes, local voters had significantly less oversight of the daily operation of their schools, and turnout for board elections fell by more than half (Steffes, 2012).

While the particulars of school governance had previously been left to local authorities, reformers now insisted that education was a state and perhaps even a national interest. By the 1910s, most state courts allowed municipalities and school boards to exercise only those powers granted to them by legislatures. Local governments had no inherent right to exist, they claimed: Chartered by and subordinate to the state, they were merely a convenient instrument through which to discharge social services, and legislators could regulate, redraw, or dissolve them as they saw fit. Educational policy was perhaps the most dramatic demonstration of the state's newfound power. To create a more modern, efficient school system, state governments encouraged (and sometimes forced) rural schools to consolidate into larger, regional districts, which could meet increasingly comprehensive standards for funding, curriculum, facilities, and teacher certification. Of the 200,000 one-room schools operating across the country in 1915, only 1,000 remained open in 1975. Consolidation met with resistance in rural areas, but it was not enough to reverse the trend toward professionalization, centralization, and state oversight. Indeed, if the attachment to local control had remained a purely rural phenomenon, it would be of little importance to educational policy today. But the principle of local democracy became more complicated when applied to cities and suburbs (Scribner, 2016).

Appeals to local democracy during the early 20th century also resulted from a polarized political climate, leading to the "culture wars" that continue to wreak havoc at school board meetings in the present. Despite (or perhaps because of) the fact that Americans were increasingly excluded from the day-to-day operation of their schools, the 1920s witnessed a surge of local activism that responded to national issues. Voters accused teachers and school boards of pushing controversial views on impressionable children—whether around socialism, race relations, the theory of evolution, or critical interpretations of American history—and invoked either majority rule (as "the public") or minority rights (as "parents") to browbeat teachers and administrators. These campaigns had been less common in the 19th century, when decisions remained in the hands of smaller, more homogenous communities. Their eruption in the 1920s was in some ways a demand to return power to local communities, but localism was often more of a political slogan rather than a matter of principle.

Most of these incidents were driven by national organizations that were equally willing to use state and federal power to impose their preferred vision of schooling. For instance, the American Legion and the Daughters of the American Revolution protested textbooks that they found insufficiently patriotic, while at the same time pressuring state legislatures to require the Pledge of Allegiance and to prohibit instruction in languages other than English. In some states, the Ku Klux Klan targeted Catholics by banning private education statewide, forcing parochial schools to close. These campaigns were less about the site of decision-making than the defense of prevailing cultural norms: Whereas the popular will had previously been exercised through local institutions, it now shifted to higher levels of government.

Since the 19th century, the common-law doctrine of "police power" had granted states a broad mandate to protect the general welfare, even at the expense of some minority rights—for example, by allowing states to require attendance, vaccination, and tax support for public schools over the objections of some voters—and it seemed likely that laws targeting foreign languages or religious minorities would be allowed on similar grounds (Laats, 2015). Unable to defend their interests at the local or state levels, minority groups turned to the federal courts, which during the early 20th century began to apply the Fourteenth Amendment's promise of "equal protection" and "due process" to state and local governments. Education cases imposed some of the first constitutional restrictions on state policymaking. For instance, *Meyer v. Nebraska* (1923) upheld the right to teach foreign languages; *Pierce v. Society of Sisters* (1925) reserved the right to operate private schools; and *West Virginia Board of Education v. Barnette* (1943) exempted schoolchildren from compelled speech such as the Pledge of Allegiance. These civil liberties rulings underscored the increasingly ambiguous concept of local control during the 20th century. If one conceived of localism principally in terms of association, pluralism, or voluntarism—a German neighborhood hiring a teacher in their native language, say, or a Catholic diocese offering religious education—then federal courts were protecting local democracy against overreaching state governments. On the other hand, if one conceived of localism primarily in terms of majority rule, then striking down state laws seemed like an undemocratic intrusion by federal officials in state and local affairs. It was the latter interpretation that began to merge calls for local control with those for states' rights. Whereas states and school districts had previously been in open conflict over many issues of educational authority—such as the consolidation of one-room schools and rural districts—federal oversight allowed both of them (selectively) to claim the mantle of local democracy.

By the mid-20th century, the same ambiguities would reappear around questions of funding. Legislatures helped local districts meet their educational responsibilities by increasing subsidies, drawn from statewide taxes rather than the value of local property alone. State support for schools rose from $1 trillion to almost $32 trillion nationwide between 1945 and 1975. Although federal funding stalled for decades over questions about whether money would be available for racially segregated schools or parochial schools, the launch of Sputnik in 1957 and the "discovery" of American poverty in the early 1960s opened another source of revenue. With the passage of the National Defense Education Act (1958) and the Elementary and Secondary Education Act (1965), federal subsidies rose to over $6 billion by 1975. Consolidated districts and wider tax bases raised the amount of local spending as well, but property tax revenues fell as a proportion of overall expenditures, from 64% to 46%, on average, by the 1970s (Kaestle & Lodewick, 2007).

The dual impetus for state and federal funding is noteworthy. On one hand, politicians intended to improve education for economic growth and national security, the sort of human capital investment associated with academic "excellence" that benefited all districts, regardless of wealth or student demographics. On the other hand, some funding programs were explicitly redistributive, compensating for poverty or deprivation in the name of "equity," and benefiting poor schools at the expense of wealthier ones. The question of whether state and federal resources targeted "excellence" or "equity"—and the degree to which they were to supplement or replace local funding—raised conflicts almost immediately. During the mid-20th century, as educational credentials became increasingly important for college attendance and middle-class jobs, connections tightened between home values and the perceived quality of local schools. Suburbs, in particular, promised good schools at low tax rates, but premised those advantages on the systematic exclusion of poor and non-White families. By the mid-20th century, then, local school districts were becoming bulwarks of economic and racial inequality. Homeowners in whiter, wealthier communities strenuously objected to the redistribution of their own resources. Whereas state and federal funding remained an acceptable means of modernizing schools across the board, attempts to equalize educational opportunity across district lines sparked a reactionary defense of local government and the material advantages that went with it.

Racism and White privilege were central to local control in the postwar era and continue to underlie many campaigns today. *Brown v. Board of Education* (1954) and subsequent cases targeting racial segregation continued two of the trends noted above: federal courts' willingness to protect minorities from discriminatory policies, and school districts' dependence on federal funding. With the passage of the Civil Rights Act (1964), judges and regulatory agencies imposed increasingly stringent orders on districts that refused to desegregate, and now could back those orders up by threatening to withhold federal funds. Throughout the South (and eventually in cities nationwide), White parents and district officials responded to these demands with noncompliance or various forms of evasion.

One of the most effective tactics was to replace explicit calls for segregation with more defensible appeals to "neighborhood schools," which relied on housing discrimination and gerrymandered attendance zones to maintain segregation. While there was a long history of children walking to local elementary schools, these appeals neglected to mention that by the 1960s most children already rode school buses between neighborhoods. In fact, for decades, students of color had often been bused *away* from their neighborhood schools—the original basis for the *Brown* litigation—while many White students were allowed to bus to other districts as their schools grew increasingly diverse. It was only when urban districts tried to redraw attendance zones or bus children for desegregation that White residents protested in defense of neighborhood schools. Their resistance suggests little commitment to localism as such, and instead an implicit commitment to racial segregation. In this context, local control became a catchphrase for a racist and inequitable status quo.

As White families fled urban neighborhoods and school districts, civil rights groups realized that meaningful desegregation could only be achieved through regional, interdistrict solutions—busing children not only within but between districts to achieve racial balance—and by the early 1970s, the boundaries between cities and suburbs seemed to be segregationists' last line of defense (Delmont, 2016; Ryan, 2010). However, the election of Richard Nixon in 1968 and the subsequent appointment of four conservative Supreme Court justices sharply revised the judiciary's commitment to equal educational opportunity and, in the process, inscribed the mythology of local control into constitutional law. In two landmark cases, the court rejected attempts to weaken district boundaries in pursuit of constitutional rights. *San Antonio v. Rodriguez* (1973) dismissed the claim that schoolchildren have a right to equal educational funding. "In an era that has witnessed a consistent trend toward centralization of the functions of government," wrote Justice Lewis Powell, "local sharing of responsibility for public education has survived . . . [due to] the depth of commitment of its supporters." Part of that commitment was a valid impulse "to devote more money to the education of one's [own] children" than to others' and to participate "in the decision-making process that determines how those local tax dollars will be spent." Centralizing school finance at the state level could threaten local autonomy, he contended, which would be an unacceptable attack on "local property taxation and control."

In *Milliken v. Bradley* (1974), the Court responded to an interdistrict busing plan in the same way. Chief Justice Warren Burger noted that "boundary lines may be bridged in circumstances where there has been a constitutional violation calling for inter-district relief," but unless suburbs had actively segregated their schools, he ruled that "district lines may not be casually ignored or treated as a mere administrative convenience." "Substantial local control of public education in this country is a deeply rooted tradition," Burger concluded. In principle, these cases asserted the value of local school government. In practice, they solidified district boundaries and increased the comparative inequalities between them. For those inclined to dismiss local control as a cynical falsehood—a fig leaf for racism and exclusion—this is its most significant aspect and its ongoing legacy: a narrowly transactional vision of citizenship, in which voters invoke local democracy only to preserve antidemocratic arrangements (Driver, 2018).

The self-serving and reactionary myths that underlie many calls for local control do not invalidate localism in all cases. There are many valid criticisms of state and federal educational policy and many praiseworthy examples of community participation in education. For instance, there have been multiple movements for self-determination in African American, Native American, and Hispanic communities, which see community control of schools as a prerequisite for social justice. Some supporters have characterized charter schools as a new form of localism, restoring the responsiveness, legitimacy, and civic energy that have been lost as traditional school districts have grown increasingly bureaucratic. Both urban and rural areas have begun to experiment with "community school" models, in which schools have again become sites of organizing, public meetings, and social services. Some parent groups have opposed state curricular standards and standardized testing regimes that they find overbearing. For all of their ugliness, even recent debates around textbook selection and schools' handling of race, gender, or sexuality have renewed interest in local policymaking, raising legitimate questions about parents' rights and professional prerogative, and reminding citizens on all sides of the responsibilities of collective self-government (Ewing, 2018; Rickford, 2016; Theobald, 1997; Todd-Breland, 2018). Whatever position one takes on local policymaking, it is important to do so honestly and consistently, without relying on slogans stripped of any substantive meaning. If one wants to weigh the merits of localism in any particular case, the first thing to do is to ask, local control *for what* or *for whom*? Well-meaning people can differ over acceptable answers to those questions, but in doing so they must move past platitudes and say what they mean.

REFERENCES

Balogh, B. (2009). *A government out of sight: The mystery of national authority in nineteenth-century America*. Cambridge University Press.

Brown, E. (2017, July 20). DeVos tells conservative lawmakers what they like to hear: More local control, school choice. *Washington Post*. Retrieved from https://www.washingtonpost.com/local/education/devos-tells-conservative-lawmakers-what-they-like-to-hear-more-local-control-school-choice/2017/07/20/fb97015e-6d5c-11e7-9c15-177740635e83_story.html

Brown v. Board of Education, 347 U.S. 483, 74 S. Ct. 686, 98 L. Ed. 873 (1954).

Delmont, M. F. (2016). *Why busing failed: Race, media, and the national resistance to school desegregation*. University of California Press.

Driver, J. (2018). *The schoolhouse gate: Public education, the Supreme Court, and the battle for the American mind*. Pantheon Books.

Ewing, E. (2018). *Ghosts in the schoolyard: Racism and school closings on Chicago's South Side*. University of Chicago Press.

Kaestle, C. F., & Lodewick, A. E. (Eds.). (2007). *To educate a nation: Federal and national strategies of school reform*. University Press of Kansas.

Laats, A. (2015). *The other school reformers: Conservative activism in American education*. Harvard University Press.

Meyer v. Nebraska, 262 U.S. 390 (1923).

Milliken v. Bradley, 418 U.S. 717 (1974).

Neem, J. (2017). *Democracy's schools: The rise of public education in America*. Johns Hopkins University Press.

Northwest Ordinances. (1787).

Pierce v. Society of Sisters, 269 U.S. 510 (1925).

Rickford, R. J. (2016). *We are an African people: Independent education, Black power, and the radical imagination*. Oxford University Press.

Ryan, J. (2010). *Five miles away, a world apart: One city, two schools, and the story of educational opportunity in modern America*. Oxford University Press.

San Antonio v. Rodriguez, 411 U.S. 1 (1973).

Scribner, C. F. (2016). *The fight for local control: Schools, suburbs, and American democracy*. Cornell University Press.

Steffes, T. (2012). *School, society, and state: A new education to govern modern America, 1890–1940*. University of Chicago Press.

Theobald, P. (1997). *Teaching the commons: Place, pride, and the renewal of community*. Westview Press.

Todd-Breland, E. (2018). *A political education: Black politics and education reform in Chicago since the 1960s*. University of North Carolina Press.

West Virginia Board of Education v. Barnette, 319 U.S. 624 (1943).

Zimmerman, J. (2009). *Small wonder: The little red schoolhouse in history and memory*. Yale University Press.

CHAPTER 5

The Myth of Industrial-Era Classrooms

Sherman Dorn

In 2010, U.S. secretary of education Arne Duncan told his audience at the American Enterprise Institute, "Our K–12 system largely still adheres to the century-old, industrial-age factory model of education." Eight years later, his successor Betsy DeVos told the same audience, "The vast majority of learning environments have remained the same since the industrial revolution, because they were made in its image." Duncan and DeVos were invoking the modern version of an old metaphor comparing schools with factories. Here is Alvin Toffler in his 1972 book *Future Shock*:

> Mass education was the ingenious machine constructed by industrialism to produce the kind of adults it needed. . . . the whole idea of assembling masses of students (raw material) to be processed by teachers (workers) in a centrally located school (factory) was a stroke of industrial genius. The inner life of the school thus became an anticipatory mirror, a perfect introduction to industrial society. (Toffler, 1984, p. 400)

To Toffler, what mass education in the United States accomplished was subtle training of children into the habits and life of a worker. Toffler was joined almost half a century later by Duncan and DeVos in framing current mass education as an explicit and intended design, but without Toffler's concern that the main task of education was socialization into work's drudgery.

What Duncan, DeVos, Toffler, and others get right about the history of school organization is the dominance of a common structure, a collection of age-graded classrooms, each with a single teacher and students close in age. With some important exceptions, for 2 centuries the single-teacher, age-graded classroom practice has been the norm in every American school larger than a single, small class (see Zimmerman, this volume, on the myth of the little red schoolhouse). What they got wrong are the timing and the reasons for the remarkable stability of the single-teacher, age-graded model.

COMPETITION AND ACCOMMODATION, NOT DESIGN

Schools with single-teacher, age-graded classrooms were not the result of explicit *design* in the era of mechanized industrialization so much as they developed in *competition* with alternative models in the early 1800s. The true factory-model schools of the early 19th century were the creation of British reformer Joseph Lancaster, and the failure of his model set the stage for the dominance of one-teacher classrooms in large schools. To Lancaster, the way to organize mass education in growing cities was to make it possible for a single adult to supervise dozens or hundreds of students in a single large room. Lancaster's ideal school divided children into small groups, and for each group one student would serve as the group's monitor, teaching that small group in a dedicated section of the class. Leading all of these group monitors would be the head monitor, another student who was high achieving by the judgment of the sole adult in the room, the school's supervising and only teacher. Out of this system of grouping and monitors came Lancaster's name for his model, the monitorial school.

In the early 19th century, the monitorial school became the official model in many American cities (Kaestle, 1973). In each case, the model was unpopular with parents and teachers, and city schools turned to its less-factory-like alternative, the hiring of multiple teachers to run their own classrooms. In Baltimore, for example, the city government started a school system in 1829 with four monitorial schools, each a rectangular box 45 feet wide and 78 feet long (Johnson, 1994). But the monitorial model quickly failed as student attendance was too inconsistent; a school could not rely on a set of students to be available as monitors every day. In addition, parents complained that monitors were being used as unpaid workers for the school, rather than spending their time learning. Principals quickly turned to whole-class recitation, using monitors to help keep order rather than teach, and by 1839, the Baltimore school system officially abandoned the monitorial model and hired assistant teachers to run their own classrooms.

These single-teacher classrooms with whole-group instruction are now the norm, and as town and city school systems grew in the 19th century, they became more segregated by age (or age-graded). But age-graded, single-teacher classrooms have not had a true monopoly. The single-teacher, age-graded classroom as the building block of formal schooling has regularly faced alternative models, if in small numbers of classes: outdoor schooling, open-plan schools, and models of collaborative teaching that promote the inclusion of students with disabilities in general classrooms. Outdoor schooling has existed in several forms, from open-air tuberculosis classrooms (e.g., Ellis, 2019) to camp-like settings that have served as alternative school settings (e.g., Hobbs, 1982). Where they have existed, they have been exceptions to the norm of single-teacher age-graded classes, a form of safety valve that a bureaucratic school system could use to house (and separate out) the chronically ill or the misbehaving.

In the 1960s and 1970s, some schools were built to accommodate beliefs that schooling should involve far less rigidity of pedagogy. These open-plan schools either had accordion-like movable walls like the middle school that I attended in Orange County, California, or large open areas that could theoretically accommodate up to 100 students. Inspired by the British open-classroom movement, the American version married discussions of teacher-centered pedagogy with ideas about school architecture. But as Larry Cuban (2004, 2023) argued, both the open-plan schools and the larger open-classroom movement were too fragile to survive politically in the face of concerns in the 1970s about disorder and academic progress in schools. By the time I attended Lincoln Middle School in 1976, those flexible accordion walls divided each building into eight classrooms, never moving, never fulfilling their promise; the one-teacher-per-classroom norm had resumed its position.

By the 1990s, a collaborative teaching or co-teaching model developed out of the open-classroom movement in the 1960s and 1970s, and it became the template for a general co-teaching model for inclusive education of students with disabilities (Thousand et al., 2007). In 1994, the National Center for Educational Restructuring and Inclusion reported a study of districts with more inclusive settings for students with disabilities, as nominated by state superintendents or education commissioners. Co-teaching was a prominent model in those schools—still age-graded but with more than one teacher in a classroom. Over the following decades, the practice of co-teaching for inclusive purposes spread, with a variety of approaches (e.g., Solis et al., 2012). There is no official national source of data on the prevalence of co-teaching, but the co-teaching model is now clearly identified with inclusive practices, as more than 60% of students with disabilities spend at least 80% of their school time inside a general classroom rather than in separate classes or schools (National Center for Education Statistics, 2022).

Single-teacher classrooms replaced monitorial schools, became age-graded, and survived to the present with minimal challenge, not because they were a rigid legacy of industrialization but because they were flexible. They could be standardized for construction and used in any size school. (One could view the long history of school architecture as a story of aggregating standard units to fit the ideology of the day; Weisser, 2006.) The single-teacher, age-graded classroom can thus accommodate changes in the purpose of schooling. As Powell et al. (1985) argued, American schools have often responded to challenges by incorporating new programs as add-ons rather than through systemic change. The single-teacher classroom is the architectural embodiment of this accommodation principle.

The accommodation principle is in plain view in thousands of schools around the country. There are many physical structures in modern schools that appeared in the 20th century, after the age-graded classroom with a single teacher established its foothold: laboratory classes, shop classes, gymnasiums, and school theaters. As Rudolph (2019) describes, the most prestigious science instruction in American K–12 schools shifted from textbook study to laboratory study around the turn of the 20th century, and the ideal instruction then required laboratory equipment. At the same time, the evolution of tracking streamed groups of students into entirely separate curricula such as vocational classes, and this growth of tracking created pressures for schools to purchase equipment for shop classes. The gymnasium and school theater are different types of structures that are larger and multipurpose, often inviting groups of teachers and larger groups of students to use each space. Unlike the open-plan school, all of these classroom variations have become part of the standard architecture of schools, though they each vary in important ways from a modular classroom with its several dozen desks and a place for a (single) teacher at the front. The story of the 20th century is not the rigid adherence to a single-teacher, age-graded classroom but the accommodation of change within limits, just so long as the most common classroom has similar dimensions and organizational roles.

More generally, beyond the single-teacher age-graded classroom, the tendency for teaching practices to remain stable and shift slowly has two deeply rooted causes and related illusions. One root is the conservative nature of teaching as a profession, in the small-c sense of the word conservative (Lortie, 1975). Teachers and administrators wrestle with competing and sometimes contradictory expectations, expectations that have grown over the decades. As a result, practitioners are averse to major changes in practice. That aversion does not mean that school practices have remained stagnant, but that change has often been incremental, and what used to be considered dramatic change, such as the use of chalkboards or primary-grade "activity centers," have been incorporated into school routines so gradually that we forget they were once radical proposals (Cuban, 1993). School practices have changed—but in retrospect, the biggest changes no longer appear revolutionary.

The second root of stable teaching practices is a broader aversion to change but at a society level: We define some things as essential to a "real school" because of common experience (Metz, 1989). Real schools have letter grades. Real schools have textbooks, spelling tests, and cursive handwriting. Real high schools have football teams. David Tyack and Larry Cuban (1995) called these hidden, settled assumptions the "grammar of schooling," akin to the way that our practical use of language contains common expectations. And in the same way that languages shift but still have norms, school practices can simultaneously shift and also keep the perception that real schooling is clearly defined. There can be a political cost for school systems that break the hidden grammar of schooling. In short, it is not generally obsolescence that makes older practices stick around. It is as often a general cultural expectation of what schools are and can be that limits what schools do. The result is the type of accommodation around the edges that Powell et al. (1985) described.

THE HISTORY OF THE INDUSTRIAL METAPHOR

Against this nuanced history, the factory-model myth appeals to today's politicians for two reasons. First, as Audrey Watters (2015) has noted, it is a shorthand justification for education reform. We need to change schooling now because current educational practices are obsolete, and "industrial-era classroom" and "factory model of education" are convenient slurs. The second and related appeal is metaphorical. The myth of industrial-era classrooms has evolved out of attempts over the decades to find usable metaphors for mass education. Since the development of large school systems in the late 19th century, both educators and their social critics have attempted different comparisons with other large organizations (Dorn & Johanningmeier, 1999). One metaphor was military, which John Dewey used in 1896: "There must be some schools whose main task is to train the *rank and file* of teachers—schools whose function is to supply *the great army* of teachers with *the weapons of their calling* and direct them as to their use" (p. 353; emphasis added).

But the dominant comparison in the Progressive Era was between schools and businesses, and that metaphorical way of discussing schooling has persisted over more than a century. Schools have long been criticized for not being *enough* like businesses, and it is far more recently that major school critics have said that they look too much like businesses, of any era. In the early 20th century, school critics thought city school systems were inefficient, too closely tied to local politics. In Philadelphia, for example, the city was divided into 41 wards in 1900, roughly corresponding to neighborhoods, and there was an elected school board for each ward. The city's politics revolved around the wards, with the city's parties organized to elect its neighborhood leaders to positions in the wards. In 1903, four members of the 28th Ward school board were convicted of soliciting bribes from the ward's teachers. The outrage was followed by proposals to make the city's schools run more like businesses. In 1905, the state legislature abolished the ward school boards and replaced the city school board with one member from each ward. Replacing the 41-member school board tied to the city's ward politics was a smaller board appointed at-large by the city's judges—something very much like a corporate board of directors (Issel, 1970; Nash, 1943). But cities did not need a bribery scandal for school critics to push for more corporate-style school governance. The criticism of schools as not businesslike enough was common in the early 20th century, as was the conversion of school boards from large elected bodies to smaller, appointed boards (Tyack, 1974).

Today, politicians like Arne Duncan and Betsy DeVos have kept the metaphor but reversed the argument: In the 21st century, for those using the industry metaphor, schools should be *less* like businesses, or less like the types of businesses that operate as factories. As Larry Cuban (2014) argued, people debate their values through the metaphor, which "stems from the century-old disputes over what purposes schools serve in a capitalist democracy. This age-old question is seldom openly debated and too often has been lost in the rhetoric and metaphors used by reformers over the past century." From a historical perspective, one should not be surprised at the new use of an old metaphor: Schools are like the factory type of business, and while that once was a goal, now we think that it is bad.

Part of the reason why the industrial metaphor has survived for a century is the way we talk about education and the economy. Since the Second World War, and especially since the early 1980s, politicians and school reformers have repeatedly argued for the value of schooling in providing economically useful skills, skills that high school and college graduates use in the workplace, and skills that will support national economic goals. In this view, education is an investment in the future, a way to build human capital. This human-capital argument is the most recent version of the desire for schools to solve major social problems, or what Grubb and Lazerson (2004) called the education gospel. (See Beatty's chapter, this volume, for how the broad utopian wish for schooling has shaped debates over preschool education.) And that economic goal has kept alive the metaphor that compares schools with industry.

SCHOOLING AND THE ECONOMY: A MORE USEFUL HISTORICAL PERSPECTIVE

A subtle error in the industrial-era myth points the way to a more useful historical understanding of schooling and its relationship with the economy. A hidden assumption of the industrial-era myth is that there is one type of factory, one thing we can call industrialization that shaped schools. But industrialization has been a complicated, multiphase process, and what a factory looked like in an 1860 shoe town in Massachusetts was nothing like a car assembly plant of 1960 Detroit, let alone biological and pharmaceutical labs in Maryland today. There have also been waves of regionalized deindustrialization, shifting the weight of much economic activity away from towns in the late 19th century and large cities in the late 20th century. These economic changes have occurred on a different clock from changes in school practices (also see Cuban, this volume).

Instead of judging schools by how well they match the cadence of economic change, we can reasonably assess how well they change in ways immediately important to students and families. We could worry about how quickly schools follow economic trends, or about how quickly they follow improving knowledge about how children learn and develop. Historically, they have not, but not because of a mythical industrial design of classrooms. While 19th-century urban schools decided between monitorial and running a school with multiple classrooms and teachers, most American school students faced rough treatment by teachers in rural schools. One-room schoolhouses had regular practices of their own, separate from the questions of mass education: individual student recitation of texts, physical punishment of students, and the occasional beating of an unpopular teacher by unhappy students (Finkelstein, 1974). Among those pushing for incipient bureaucracy in 19th-century schools, including those who are most closely associated with early age-graded classrooms, those early systematizers were probably most inclined to humanize schooling, make it less humiliating (Katz, 1971). No matter the form or decade, 19th-century schooling was dominated by the impulse to insist on memorization and for teacher control of the class environment. None of this started with or was predicated on economic changes.

Later in the 19th century, more schools talked about preparing students for jobs in an explicit way—and in doing so, school systems reinforced and created new ways of dividing and providing unequal education to students, by tracking and by limiting opportunity in ways clearly discriminatory by social class, sex, and race. The most common application of the philosophy of industrial education was to remove academic subjects from the curriculum for Black Southerners. As the longtime head of the Hampton Normal and Agricultural Institute, Samuel Chapman Armstrong preached the virtues of industrial education, and his protégé, Booker T. Washington, did the same as head of the Tuskegee Institute during an era when Black Southerners were excluded from industrial jobs and increasingly disfranchised during the start of the Jim Crow era (Anderson, 1988). At least for students at Hampton and Tuskegee, and the students of their graduates, industrial-era education often meant an incomplete education under the pretense that it better prepared them for jobs they were not allowed to have.

The deeper history of economic rhetoric in school reform is one of broken promises and displaced structures. The true factory model of classroom was the early 19th-century monitorial school, but its replacement by single-teacher, age-graded classrooms could be just as stultifying and humiliating, and likewise with one-room schoolhouses. Vocational education in the era of mechanized industrialization became a mechanism and excuse for tracking and unequal opportunities.

The persistence of certain practices such as single-teacher, age-graded classrooms is important, absolutely. But it is not the result of some imaginary factory model. The problem with age-graded classrooms and isolated teachers is not the era in which they arose—nobody is complaining about books as "Reformation-era education"—but the constraints that they impose, as much on the professional growth and support of teachers as anything else. But the myth exists because teaching and schooling is risk-averse, and because we argue based on metaphors: schools as factories, teachers as armies, schools as malls. The change in the factory metaphor is telling (Schools should be *more* like factories! No, they should be *less* like factories!). And in the end, the explanation of the long-term pattern is different from the claim that we are somehow stuck in an industrial-era system. Knowing the accurate history frees us from the idea that schools cannot change. They can, and we are not the first generation to try. Nor will we be the last.

REFERENCES

Anderson, J. D. (1988). *The education of Blacks in the South, 1865–1935*. University of North Carolina Press.

Cuban, L. (1993). *How teachers taught: Constancy and change in American classrooms, 1890–1990* (2nd ed.). Teachers College Press.

Cuban, L. (2004). The open classroom: Were schools without walls just another fad? *Education Next, 4*(2), 68–71.

Cuban, L. (2014, May 8). *Schools as factories: Metaphors that stick*. Retrieved from https://larrycuban.wordpress.com/2014/05/08/schools-as-factories-metaphors-that-stick/

Cuban, L. (2023, March 28). *Will "open classrooms" return?* Retrieved from https://larrycuban.wordpress.com/2023/03/28/will-open-classrooms-return/

DeVos, B. (2018). *Prepared remarks by U.S. Education Secretary Betsy DeVos to the American Enterprise Institute*. Retrieved from https://www.ed.gov/news/speeches/prepared-remarks-us-education-secretary-betsy-devos-american-enterprise-institute

Dewey, J. (1896). Pedagogy as a university discipline I. *University [of Chicago] Record, 1*, 353–355.

Dorn, S., & Johanningmeier, E. V. (1999). Dropping out and the military metaphor for schooling. *History of Education Quarterly, 39*(2), 193–198. Retrieved from https://doi.org/10.2307/370038

Duncan, A. (2010, November 17). *The new normal: Doing more with less*. Retrieved from https://www.ed.gov/news/speeches/new-normal-doing-more-less-secretary-arne-duncans-remarks-american-enterprise-institute

Ellis, J. (2019). *A class by themselves? The origins of special education in Toronto and beyond*. University of Toronto Press.

Finkelstein, B. (1974). The moral dimensions of pedagogy: Teaching behavior in popular primary schools in nineteenth-century America. *American Studies, 15*(2), 79–89. Retrieved from http://www.jstor.org/stable/40644043

Grubb, W. N., & Lazerson, M. (2004). *The education gospel: The economic power of schooling*. Harvard University Press.

Hobbs, N. (1982). *The troubled and troubling child*. Jossey-Bass.

Issel, W. (1970). Modernization in Philadelphia school reform, 1882–1905. *Pennsylvania Magazine of History and Biography, 94*(3), 358–383.

Johnson, W. R. (1994). "Chanting choristers": Simultaneous recitation in Baltimore's nineteenth-century primary schools. *History of Education Quarterly, 34*(1), 1–23. Retrieved from https://doi.org/10.2307/369226

Kaestle, C. F. (Ed.). (1973). *Joseph Lancaster and the monitorial school movement: A documentary history*. Teachers College Press.

Katz, M. B. (1971). From voluntarism to bureaucracy in American education. *Sociology of Education, 44*(3), 297–332. Retrieved from https://doi.org/10.2307/2111995

Lortie, D. C. (1975). *Schoolteacher: A sociological study*. University of Chicago Press.

Metz, M. H. (1989). Real school: A universal drama amid disparate experience. *Politics of Education Association Yearbook, 4*(5), 75–91.

Nash, C. R. (1943). The history of legislative and administrative changes affecting the Philadelphia public schools, 1869–1921 [PhD Dissertation], Temple University.

National Center for Education Statistics. (2022). Percentage distribution of school-age students served under Individuals with Disabilities Education Act (IDEA), Part B, by educational environment and type of disability: Selected years, fall 1989 through fall 2021. In *Digest of Education Statistics* (table 204.60). Author. Retrieved from https://nces.ed.gov/programs/digest/d22/tables/dt22_204.60.asp?current=yes

National Center for Educational Restructuring and Inclusion. (1994). *National study on inclusion*. City University of New York, Graduate School and University Center. Retrieved from https://eric.ed.gov/?id=ED375606

Powell, A. G., Cohen, D. K., & Farrar, E. (1985). *The shopping mall high school: Winners and losers in the educational marketplace*. Houghton Mifflin.

Rudolph, J. L. (2019). *How we teach science: What's changed, and why it matters*. Harvard University Press.

Solis, M., Vaughn, S., Swanson, E., & McCulley, L. (2012). Collaborative models of instruction: The empirical foundations of inclusion and co-teaching. *Psychology in the Schools, 49*(5), 498–510. Retrieved from https://doi.org/10.1002/pits.21606

Thousand, J. S., Nevin, A. I., & Villa, R. A. (2007). Collaborative teaching: Critique of the scientific evidence. In L. Florian (Ed.), *The Sage handbook of special education* (pp. 417–428). Sage.

Toffler, A. (1984). *Future shock* (Reissue ed.). Bantam.

Tyack, D. B. (1974). *The one best system: A history of American urban education*. Harvard University Press.

Tyack, D., & Cuban, L. (1995). *Tinkering toward utopia: A century of public school reform*. Harvard University Press.

Watters, A. (2015, April 25). *The invented history of "the factory model of education."* Retrieved from http://hackeducation.com/2015/04/25/factory-model

Weisser, A. (2006). "Little red school house, what now?" Two centuries of American public school architecture. *Journal of Planning History, 5*(3), 196–217. Retrieved from https://doi.org/10.1177/1538513206289223

Part II

MYTHS OF PROGRESS AND DECLINE

CHAPTER 6

The Myth of Declining Student Behavior

Judith Kafka

Student misbehavior in school is a perennial concern. At times of social upheaval and/or reform, however, public commentators, policymakers, educators, and school administrators are particularly likely to evoke a mythical yesteryear, when teachers taught, students listened, and educators' authority was sacrosanct. We hear today that efforts to reduce school suspensions and other forms of punitive discipline have led to students being "permitted to run roughshod over any adult who gets in their way" (Frankel & Buck, 2022, para.11). Such claims are not new; they echo complaints from earlier eras that because of "progressive" educational reform, pupils were running "riot over the teacher and over each other" (Melby, 1955, p. 36). When popular outrage over apparent student indiscipline is on the rise, critics often express concern for what they perceive is a loss of teachers' traditional authority. "Remember when cursing out a teacher was a very big deal?" a New York City educator wrote in 2019. "Well, now it's just Tuesday" (McGeever, 2019, para. 3). President Ronald Reagan sounded a similar alarm in the 1980s, bemoaning teachers' loss of disciplinary power. Teachers could no longer "teach," according to Reagan, "because they lack the authority to make students take tests, hand in homework, or even quiet down their class. In some schools, teachers suffer verbal and physical abuse" (quoted in CCHR, 1984, p. 2).

These statements all suggest that there was a time in our nation's history when student insubordination, if it occurred at all, was swiftly and efficiently eliminated because teachers were able to exert control over their students and classrooms. In truth, however, students' willingness to both subvert and openly defy teachers' authority is part and parcel of our nation's long history of education. Forms of student rebellion, misbehavior, and indiscipline have varied across time and place, as have teachers', schools', and broader society's responses. Yet "teaching" has always included behavioral and moral training, and teachers' classroom authority has always been subject to negotiation and contest (Kafka, 2011, 2016; Scribner & Warnick, 2021). This chapter debunks the myth of a golden age of student compliance and subordination in the United States through an examination of the history of student indiscipline and disorder in 19th- and early 20th-century schooling. It demonstrates that student misbehavior, while not universal, has nonetheless been historically omnipresent across all kinds of settings—rural and urban, elite and poor, segregated White, Black, and Indigenous, and so on. Moreover, the history of student indiscipline and outright defiance suggests that we are unlikely to produce safe and orderly classrooms through increasingly draconian means of control evoked from false memories of the past. Instead, teachers, administrators, and concerned citizens may be better off developing disciplinary systems and structures that acknowledge and honor student agency and autonomy, while still prioritizing school safety and student learning.

UNDISCIPLINED AND UNINSTRUCTED: STUDENT BEHAVIOR IN ANTEBELLUM SCHOOLING

Teachers have struggled to manage student behavior since even before the establishment of what we today call public schools. In fact, a central purpose of the "common" schools of the early 19th century, which were tax-supported institutions usually open and free to all White children in the area, was to ensure that the nation's next generation would develop the strong moral character and work ethic needed to maintain a successful economy and democracy. Schools and teachers were charged with this task because the largely Protestant elite believed that most American parents were unable to fulfill this duty at home. As a writer in the *Common School Journal* explained in 1841, teachers "must rub off" the proverbial "rust" their students acquired at home in order to replace their parents' suspect mores and values with those better suited for an emerging free market economy (as cited in Katz, 1968, p. 304).

The Need for Control

In the growing cities of the 19th-century Northeast and Midwest, where newly arrived immigrants and rural migrants fueled prosperity while raising moral panic among the elite, concern about student behavior in school was often compounded by local leaders' clear disdain for the children they sought to educate (Kaestle, 1983). The Boston school committee report from 1857–58, for example, described its city's students as "undisciplined, uninstructed, often with inveterate forwardness and obstinacy, and with the inherited stupidity of centuries of ignorant ancestors," and enjoined teachers to transform such youth "from animals into intellectual beings" (as cited in Katz, 1968, p. 120). In Brooklyn, New York, a newspaper editorial justified the city's "wise system of public schools" as a means of protecting society from the "crime and wickedness" that would surely emerge in the absence of government-provided education ("The Truant Institution," 1857, p. 2).

City leaders' belief in the transformative possibility of schooling was primarily aimed at White children of the poor—immigrant and otherwise. However, in localities where common schools were also accessible to Black children (usually in segregated institutions), White leaders' assumptions about the need for behavioral training and moral intervention was extended to Black youth as well. Thus in 1863, a Brooklyn school committee member heralded a Black principal's competence based on the "good order and credible appearance of the children" at his "Colored" school (Board of Education, 1863, p. 2). Students' behavioral compliance was not assumed in the antebellum era; it was to be acquired by educators through whatever means they could muster.

Thus, 19th-century teacher manuals were full of advice on how educators could maintain control over large groups of unruly youth. While "obedience" and "subordination" were frequent watchwords, the amount of attention school leaders paid to explaining *why* complete deference to teachers' authority was necessary (anything less would result in teachers losing all power in the classroom), and the lengths to which they went to articulate the best means of achieving such subservience (corporal punishment was popular although many reformers condemned the practice), suggests that compliance was hardly a given (Mann, 1872; Orcutt, 1871; Payson, 1816; Taylor, 1835; Wayland, 1835).

Student Indiscipline

The historical record on how students *actually* behaved in antebellum schools and classrooms is far from comprehensive, but much of what scholars have documented makes clear that instances of student resistance and rebellion were common, and that teachers often felt their authority was tenuous at best (Finkelstein, 1989; Scribner, 2023). This was true across contexts—including urban and rural common schools; Sunday schools run by churches; private academies and colleges; Black-operated and supported schools for Black children (mostly in the North); *escuelitas*, or small (and sometimes not-so-small) community-based schools run for and by Mexican Americans (mostly in the Southwest); and schools for Native American children, which included both day and boarding schools, run by missionaries, the U.S. federal government, and/or Native Americans themselves.

In the mostly White common schools of early 19th-century America, while teachers were hired by town committees and often boarded with local families, they nonetheless were on their own when it came to maintaining order in the schoolhouse. As Joseph Kett (1977) notes, teachers "could not point consistently to any source of authority beyond themselves. . . . The school was theirs, to be 'kept,'" and they weren't always successful in doing so (p. 48). Thus, Vermont Superintendent of Schools complained in 1849 that "insubordination and rebellion of scholars" was "encouraged by their *parents at home*" and that school committees did nothing to support the teachers for fear of alienating important community members. Sometimes students' misbehavior was more than teachers were willing to bear; teachers quitting their posts midyear would often result in school closures. Horace Mann, Massachusetts's first secretary of the board of education, reported in 1843 that older boys had successfully forced at least 300 schools in the state to close over the course of 5 years by chasing away their teachers (both sources quoted in Tyack & Hansot, 1990, p. 66).

Older boys in particular often presented behavioral challenges to teachers during this period. On the one hand, they regularly left school just when they seemed to most need "instruction and restraint," in the words of a Sunday school official (quoted in Kett, 1977, p. 131). On the other hand, older boys could be just a few years younger (or on occasion even older) than their teachers, rendering corporal forms of punishment difficult to implement (Finkelstein, 1989; Kett, 1977). In fact, the threat of unmanageable older boys was one of the cudgels opponents used to argue against the feminization of the teaching force in the mid-19th century. A superintendent in Rhode Island, for example, argued in 1855 that women teachers would not be able to maintain order with unruly older boys, just as they would not be able to "manage a vicious horse or other animal, as a man may do" (Blount, 1998, p. 19). Conversely, proponents of women as teachers argued that women's "very delicacy and helplessness" was what allowed them to tame previously unmanageable youth (Tyack and Hansot, 1990, p. 68).

Sometimes student rebellion during the antebellum era could be quite violent. Memoirs and reporting from the period are full of tales of White students physically harming their teachers. Sometimes an individual student would respond to an act of corporal punishment in kind; other times students as a group reportedly threw their teachers down hills, or pushed them into fires, through frozen lakes, and so on (Finkelstein, 1975; Scribner, 2023; Zimmerman, 2009). At times these violent rebellions were part ritual. In some regions, students regularly took part in the practice of "barring out" or "turning out" their teachers—a tradition in which teachers were expected to force their way into the school while students tried to keep them out. If unsuccessful, teachers could offer a bribe such as treats or vacation time in exchange for entry. These events were usually a combination of ceremony and playacting, with parents and community members often cheering on the schoolchildren. Yet some instances turned quite extreme, especially when teachers refused to yield to students' demands and/or when students were armed with swords, guns, or other weapons that caused serious injury, or, in some cases, even death (Finkelstein, 1975; Greenough, 1999; Kephard, 1925; Kett, 1977; Williams, 1873; Zimmerman, 2009).

While much of the documentation of student indiscipline from the antebellum era is about White schoolchildren and their teachers, disruptive, disrespectful and otherwise disobedient student behavior was not an exclusively White phenomenon. In schools for Black children in the urban North, for example, which were often created, funded, and operated independently by Black communities because their children were excluded from the nominally "public" schools their tax dollars helped to support, Black teachers at times complained of their struggles to maintain control in the classroom. As one such teacher wrote in a story published in 1832: "There have been times when my spirit has been bowed, as it were to the earth by the unkind behaviour of children" (cited in Baumgartner, 2019, p. 184).

Similarly, Native American students who attended day and boarding schools established by their own Indigenous nations could also be disobedient and challenge the authority of their teachers. In schools established by the Creek Nation's government, for example, some students rejected English-only rules, even though their parents had sent them to school to become proficient in English. Some Creek students also ran away from their boarding schools, or attended day schools only sporadically, undermining the established schedule and policies and frustrating their teachers and school leaders (Steineker, 2016).

Student indiscipline and rebellion was also part of the schooling experience at some of the nation's most elite educational spaces during the antebellum era. In early high schools, for example, which were attended by only a select few—mostly middle class but sometimes a small number of poor youth—during this period, teachers regularly recorded acts of misbehavior (National Center for Educational Statistics, 1993, Table 8; Reese, 1995). Even though high school students were not considered "ruffians or ne'er-do-wells," they nonetheless were cited for behaviors ranging from talking without permission and giggling, to cursing, running in the classroom, and general insubordination (Reese, 1995, p. 192). Moreover, college students—who were almost exclusively White, relatively affluent teenage sons of the professional and upper classes in the antebellum era—often openly defied and challenged their instructors during this period (Geiger, 2000; Horowitz, 1988; Novak, 1977). Even Thomas Jefferson, who hoped to avoid such conflicts at his beloved University of Virginia, was not spared this indignity. Late in his life, Jefferson was forced to contend with violent student rioting at the school; one of the perpetrators was reportedly his own great nephew (Pangle & Pangle, 1993).

In most of the nation, school attendance, where accessible, was voluntary in the antebellum era—or at least up to parents. In places where compulsory education *did* exist, rules requiring youth to attend school were rarely enforced (Hutt, 2012; Kafka, 2023; Steffes 2012). This context likely contributed to teachers' struggles to maintain control in their classrooms, as they had no laws or officials to support their efforts. Yet even when compulsory education became normalized in the late 19th and early 20th centuries, students continued to challenge, contest, and even reject teachers' authority.

A FRAGILE HOLD: CLASSROOM CONTROL IN LATE 19TH- AND EARLY 20TH-CENTURY SCHOOLING

Post-Civil War America saw the development of the bureaucratic "one best system" of public education in most of the nation's northern and western cities (Tyack, 1974), growth of the district school model across much of rural United States, and an expansion of universal education in the South (Anderson, 1988; Reese, 2005; Steffes, 2012). Even as school attendance became more common, however, and the legitimacy of schooling as an extension of state authority more widely accepted, teachers' struggles to control student behavior persisted.

Student Insubordination in Late 19th-Century Schools

Compulsory education laws may at times have added to students' (and often their families') rejection of teachers' authority, as now even youth who would rather not be in school were nonetheless required to attend (Kafka, 2023; Steffes, 2012). Schools and teachers confronted an array of acts of student resistance, rebellion, and general indiscipline in the postbellum period, and the structures and tools available to them for response often seemed inadequate to the task. The board of education in Brooklyn, New York, for example, in 1867 listed student behaviors that could result in suspension from school: "defacing, or in any way injuring or damaging the school property, or . . . gross misconduct, using obscene or profane language. . . ." Yet even those who appeared "hopeless" were to be barred from the city's schools for no more than 6 months, after which they could return (Board of Education of the City of Brooklyn, 1867, pp. 21–22). At a time when students tended to attend school for less than 4 months a year, these suspensions were far less consequential than they would be today (National Center for Educational Statistics, 1993, p. 27).

Fifteen years later, the limits of educators' authority in the face of student insubordination were underscored when the parents of 15-year-old Emma Walker pressed charges against her school principal after he beat her with a rattan for refusing to read aloud during a superintendent's examination. In his defense, the principal explained that while in the past he had merely suspended the child for obstinacy and defiance, in this instance he felt the whipping was warranted "as the girl's conduct lowered the percentage of the school" on the exam ("A Little Trick," 1883, p. 4). While public commentators and board of education members agreed that a child's refusal to read on command was a punishable offense, they also maintained that so, too, was the principal's use of corporal punishment, which had officially been banned from the city's schools. That in this instance both the child and principal were Black, and the incident in question occurred at a designated "Colored" school, shaped the context in which this battle of wills took place, and likely influenced its portrayal in the local White newspaper. At the same time, however, Emma Walker's refusal to comply with her principal's directive, and his evident frustration and feelings of ineffectiveness in the face of her repeated acts of insubordination, were not uncommon across settings or contexts.

Teachers in institutions like the Freedpeople's schools in the South and *escuelitas* in the Southwest—two forms of schooling that provided an education to children from racially/ethnically oppressed groups who were routinely excluded from White schools—likely expected a degree of parental support when attempting to control student behavior, and undoubtedly they often received it (Goetz, 2020; Walker, 2000). Yet students misbehaved nonetheless. In the South, where Black families post–Civil War often established Freedpeople's schools on their own or with philanthropic and/or governmental aid, student opposition to teachers' authority was not unusual—despite Black parents' often considerable financial and political support for the schools (Anderson, 1988). On the one hand, as Heather Williams (2005) writes, sometimes student defiance included, somewhat charmingly, refusal to leave school at the end of the day and appealing for shorter vacations. But teachers also described less endearing acts of indiscipline, such as: "Neglect of school work, stubbornness, impudence, lateness, and talking in class" (p. 147). Although teachers of the Freedpeople's schools—Northern and Southern, Black and White—often reported winning over their students and creating order in their classrooms through a combination of inviting pedagogy and firm rules, many nonetheless complained of stubbornly disruptive students, some of whom, even on expulsion, would hang "round the schoolhouse, to the constant annoyance of the teacher and the demoralization of the school" (quoted in Butchart, 2010; Williams, 2005, p. 148).

Student Behavior at the Turn of the Century

The turn of the 20th century was a period of broad educational reform in the United States, during which educators were increasingly called on to acknowledge students' agency and organize their schools and classrooms to better meet children's needs and interests (Reese, 2005; Tyack, 1974). Journalists like Joseph Rice and reformers like John Dewey criticized teachers' systems of oppressive behavioral control, in which students were required during recitations to literally "toe the line" by standing "on the line, perfectly motionless, their bodies erect, their knees and feet together, the tips of their shoes touching the edge of a board in the floor" (Rice, 1893, as cited in Tyack, 1974, p. 55). At the same time, however, teachers were also often painfully aware of the precarity of their classroom control. Kate Rousmaniere (1997), for example, details the many strategies New York City teachers employed during this period in an effort to maintain order—from corporal punishment and humiliation to bribery and negotiation. One teacher recalled challenging a student to a spitball competition in an effort to win his compliance; others reported paying large boys in their classes to help keep things under control.

One might expect to have found greater student compliance in residential institutions like boarding schools imposed on Native American children by the U.S. government and state- and city-operated reform and truant schools. Both types of settings were notorious for their harsh and punitive conditions, which at times led to serious illness, injuries, and/or death; the boarding schools for Native American youth also overtly sought to strip children of their cultures and familial ties. Yet even in these "total institutions" (Goffman, 1968), youth often enacted explicit acts of disobedience and resistance—ranging from continuing to use their home languages, to coordinated acts of vandalism and arson, refusal to work, physical assault of adults, and running away (Adams 1995; Agyepong, 2018; Child, 1998; Lomawaima, 1994; Morris, 2022; Warren 2010). This was true in highly regimented and punitive institutions and in those that sought a softer, more familial model of behavioral training. State inspectors at the Howard Colored Orphanage and Industrial School in Kings Park, New York, for example, were perplexed in 1917 to find that "nothing resembling military discipline prevails at the institution; the children freely go about their work and play." According to the inspectors, this leniency led to behavioral offenses including "stealing, running away to the village, insubordination, and coming late to school," yet there was "no authorized method of punishment," and minimal records of discipline were maintained (Department of Public Charities, 1917, pp. 51–52). The inspectors recommended implementing a more formal system of "privileges and rewards" to address the institution's "discipline problem" (p. 11).

As in earlier periods, it's also clear that adults tolerated, if not outright celebrated, some student misbehavior at the turn of the 20th century—especially in White settings. Stovey (2021) explains that in small midwestern towns, for example, school leaders and the broader community viewed some degree of "tomfoolery" from area high school students as "an aspect of life to be both enjoyed and accepted" (p. 181). Jon Zimmerman (2009), in his book on American nostalgia for the one-room schoolhouse, notes that in the postbellum era, "writers added a strong dose of romance to the battle between master and student, which came to symbolize the liberty and vitality of a long-lost rural America" (p. 65).

Not all forms of student resistance were limited to the classroom during this period. In Chicago, for example, students staged a walkout and school boycott in 1902 in response to a centralized and harsh new grading system (Murphy, 1990). Similarly, in 1917, Jewish students in New York City openly revolted against educational reforms they viewed as discriminatory, by conducting protests and boycotts (Ravitch, 1974; Weiner, 2010). Students could also be destructive in their acts of rebellion. As Campbell Scribner (2023) details, school vandalism, arson, and other forms of property destruction were quite common in the early decades of the 20th century, as students at times registered their dislike and distrust of schools by destroying them—sometimes with human casualties.

CONCLUSION

Student misconduct, insubordination, defiance, and general indiscipline have been a part of schooling since its inception, and educators' authority to address such behaviors has always been contested. What *has* sometimes varied across time, place, and context—even on occasion within individual schools and classrooms—is how educators, administrators, and the general public have responded to student disobedience and misconduct. While misbehaving students have at times been met with strict and swift punishment, historical evidence going back centuries demonstrates that such practices did not guarantee student compliance or effectively shore up teachers' authority. Rather than heed calls for increased punishment in schooling, then, perhaps we as a nation would be better served working to develop school disciplinary systems and structures that *assume* student agency and seek to harness it in service of a safe and supportive learning environment.

REFERENCES

A little trick. (1883, December 12). *Brooklyn Daily Eagle*, 4.
Adams, D. W. (1995). *Education for extinction: American Indians and the boarding school experience, 1875–1928*. University Press of Kansas.
Agyepong, T. E. (2018). *The criminalization of Black children: Race, gender, and delinquency in Chicago's juvenile justice system, 1899–1945*. The University of North Carolina Press.
Anderson, J. D. (1988). *The education of Blacks in the South, 1860–1935*. University of North Carolina Press.
Baumgartner, K. (2019). *In pursuit of knowledge: Black women and educational activism in antebellum America*. New York University Press.
Blount, J. (1998). *Destined to rule the schools: Women and the superintendency, 1873–1995*. State University of New York Press.
Board of Education. (1863, August 5). *The Brooklyn Daily Eagle*, 2.
Board of Education of the City of Brooklyn. (1867). *Manual of the Board of Education of the City of Brooklyn*. City of Brooklyn Board of Education: Manual and

Course of Study [Records of the New York City Board of Education, Series 2], New York City Municipal Archives.

Butchart, R. (2010). *Schooling the freed people: Teaching, learning, and the struggle for Black freedom, 1861–1876*. University of North Carolina Press.

Cabinet Council on Human Resources (CCHR) Working Group on School Violence/Discipline. (1984). *Disorder in our public schools: Report to the President*. Department of Education. Retrieved from https://eric.ed.gov/?id=ED242016

Child, B. J. (1998). *Boarding school seasons: American Indian families, 1900–1940*. University of Nebraska Press.

Department of Public Charities, Bureau of Institutional Inspection, City of New York. (1917). *Report of the general inspection of the Howard Orphanage and Industrial School*. [Howard Orphanage and Industrial School collection, Box 1, folder 17], Schomburg Center for Research in Black Culture.

Finkelstein, B. (1975). Pedagogy as intrusion: Teaching values in popular primary schools in nineteenth-century America. *History of Childhood Quarterly, 2*(3), 349–375.

Finkelstein, B. (1989). *Governing the young: Teacher behavior in popular primary schools in nineteenth-century United States*. Falmer Press.

Frankel, G., & Buck, D. (2022, November 25). School discipline: How tolerating misbehavior hurts students. *National Review*. Retrieved from https://www.nationalreview.com/2022/11/how-tolerating-misbehavior-hurts-students/

Geiger, R. L. (Ed.). (2000). *The American college in the nineteenth century*. Vanderbilt University Press.

Goetz, P. M. B. (2020). *Reading, writing, and revolution: Escuelitas and the emergence of a Mexican American identity in Texas*. University of Texas Press.

Goffman, E. (1968). *Asylums: Essays on the social situation of mental patients and other inmates*. Penguin.

Greenough, J. P. (1999). *Resistance to the institutionalization of schooling in the antebellum southern Highlands* [Doctoral dissertation, University of California, Berkeley].

Horowitz, H. L. (1988). *Campus life: Undergraduate cultures from the end of the eighteenth century to the present*. University of Chicago Press.

Hutt, E. (2012). Formalism over function: Compulsion, courts, and the rise of educational formalism in America, 1870–1930. *Teachers College Record, 114*(1), 1–27.

Kaestle, K. (1983). *Pillars of the republic: Common schools and American society, 1780–1860*. Hill and Wang.

Kafka, J. (2011). *The history of "zero tolerance" in American public schooling*. Palgrave Macmillan.

Kafka, J. (2016). In search of a grand narrative: The turbulent history of teaching. In D. Gitomer & C. Bell (Eds.), *Handbook of research on teaching* (5th ed., pp. 69–126). American Educational Research Association.

Kafka, J. (2023). Growing up together: Brooklyn's Truant School and the carceral and educational state, 1857–1924. *Journal of Urban History, 49*(5), 974–994. Retrieved from https://doi.org/10.1177/00961442221142053

Katz, M. (1968). *The irony of early school reform: Educational innovation in mid-nineteenth century Massachusetts*. Beacon Press.

Kephard, I. L. (1925). Barring-out the teacher. In A. E. Martin & H. H. Shenk (Eds.), *Pennsylvania history as told by contemporaries* (pp. 392–396). The Macmillan Company.

Kett, J. (1977). *Rites of passage: Adolescence in America 1790 to the present*. Basic Books.

Lomawaima, K. T. (1994). *They called it Prairie Light: The story of Chilocco Indian School*. University of Nebraska Press.

Mann, H. (1872). *Annual reports on education* [esp. the *Seventh annual report, and remarks on the seventh annual report of the Hon. Mann, secretary of the Massachusetts Board of Education*] Lee and Shepard.

McGeever, J. B. (2019, March 13). How "suspension schools" smash the "school-to-prison pipeline." *New York Post*. Retrieved from https://nypost.com/2019/03/13/how-suspension-schools-smash-the-school-to-prison-pipeline/

Melby, E. (1955, November 27). Five fallacies about modern education. *The New York Times Magazine*, 13, 36–42.

Morris, W. H. (2022). "The eye of the juvenile court": Report cards, juvenile corrections, and a Colorado street kid, 1900–1920. *History of Education Quarterly*, 62(3), 312–336. Retrieved from https://doi.org/10.1017/heq.2022.22

Murphy, M. (1990). *Blackboard unions: The AFT and the NEA, 1900–1980*. Cornell University Press.

National Center for Educational Statistics. (1993). *120 years of American education: A statistical portrait*. Government Printing Office.

Novak, S. J. (1977). *The rights of youth: American colleges and student revolt, 1798–1815*. Harvard University Press.

Orcutt, H. (1871). *The teacher's manual: Containing a treatise upon the discipline of the school, and other papers upon the teacher's qualifications and work*. Thompson, Brown and Company. (Original work published 1858)

Pangle, L. S., & Pangle, T. (1993). *The learning of liberty: The educational ideas of the American founders*. University of Kansas Press.

Payson, T. (1816). *Address delivered before the associated instructors of Boston and its vicinity, on their anniversary, October 10, 1816*. John Eliot.

Ravitch, D. (1974). *The great school wars: A history of the New York City public schools*. Basic Books.

Reese, W. J. (1995). *The origins of the American high school*. Yale University Press.

Reese, W. J. (2005). *America's public schools: From the common school to "No Child Left Behind."* Johns Hopkins University Press.

Rousmaniere. K. (1997). *City teachers: Teaching and school reform in historical perspective*. Teachers College Press.

Scribner, C. F. (2023). *A is for arson: A history of vandalism in American education*. Cornell University Press.

Scribner, C. F., & Warnick, B. R. (2021). *Spare the rod: Punishment and the moral community of schools*. University of Chicago Press.

Steffes, T. (2012). *School, society, and state: A new education to govern modern America, 1890–1940*. University of Chicago Press.

Steineker, R. F. (2016). "Fully equal to that of any children": Experimental Creek education in the antebellum era. *History of Education Quarterly*, 56(2), 273–300. Retrieved from https://doi.org/10.1111/hoeq.12183

Stovey, P. (2021). Books, basketball, and order of the fish: Youth culture in Midwest, small-town high schools, 1900–1930. In K. P. Steele (Ed.), *New perspectives on the history of the twentieth-century American high school* (pp. 169–203). Palgrave Macmillan.

Taylor, J. O. (1835). *The district school: Or national education* (3rd ed.). Carey, Lea and Blanchard.

The truant institution and its advocates. (1857, October 23). *Brooklyn Daily Eagle*, 2.

Tyack, D. (1974). *The one best system: A history of American urban education.* Harvard University Press.

Tyack, D., & Hansot, E. (1990). *Learning together: A history of coeducation in American public schools.* Yale University Press.

Walker, V. S. (2000). Valued segregated schools for African American children in the South, 1935–1969: A review of common themes and characteristics. *Review of Educational Research, 70*(3), 253–285.

Warren, K. C. (2010). *The quest for citizenship: African American and Native American education in Kansas, 1880–1935.* University of North Carolina Press.

Wayland, F. (1835). *The elements of moral science.* Cooke and Company.

Weiner, M. F. (2010). *Power, protest, and the public schools: Jewish and African American struggles in New York City.* Rutgers University Press.

Williams, H. (2005). *Self-taught: African American education in slavery and freedom.* University of North Carolina Press.

Williams, J. S. (1873). *Old times in West Tennessee.* W. G. Cheeney.

Zimmerman, J. (2009). *Small wonder: The little red schoolhouse in history and memory.* Yale University Press.

CHAPTER 7

The Myth of Faulty City Schools

John L. Rury

Writing in *The Atlantic* 5 years ago, journalist Alia Wong noted that Americans "frequently harbor negative associations with the term urban, and by extension, 'inner city' communities and institutions, such as schools" (Wong, 2018). Although focusing on the present, it was an observation with a lengthy history, and easily could have been made decades earlier. The popular 1954 novel (and later movie) *Blackboard Jungle* offered a bleak view of an urban high school and the "juvenile delinquents" attending it (Hunter, 1954). Seven years later, James B. Conant, a former Harvard president and ambassador to Germany, published a slim book titled *Slums and Suburbs*, which highlighted the growing disparity in school resources in central cities and their adjoining communities (Conant, 1961). By then the inferiority of big city schools was becoming conventional wisdom. It wasn't long before many such institutions became generally known as places to avoid, hotbeds of misbehavior, and deficient academic standards. Families with the resources to do so began leaving the cities in large numbers, leading to the advent of yet another widely used term: "white flight" (Rury, 1999).

By the time Wong was writing about the "stigma" of urban schools, in that case, the presumed superiority of suburban schools had been long established, and growing social and economic diversity had become evident in certain outlying locations too. But even though some city education systems have improved, they still provoke negative connotations for many parents, especially when considering schools for their children (Badger & Quealy, 2017). This is especially true of Whites, who tend to favor suburban institutions and their adjacent communities, which typically have far fewer poor and minority residents than central cities. In fact, these attitudes have existed long enough that many Americans would be quite surprised to learn that urban schools were once considered to be the very best, and that many today continue to serve their diverse constituencies quite effectively. Despite the historical loss of many affluent students, most of them White, these institutions continue to be productive for their often disadvantaged clientele, providing pathways for the pursuit of many dreams and better lives (Rury, 2005).

WHEN URBAN SCHOOLS PREVAILED

Big cities have long suffered problems of inequality, poverty, and sociocultural conflict, but they also have been centers of wealth and educational excellence, with institutions reflecting a range of opportunities for fostering student success. Given their greater population, financial resources, and local demand for educated workers, the nation's larger cities originally invested in large public high schools, which trained legions of office workers, teachers, municipal employees, and aspiring lawyers and doctors. As such, these institutions became ladders of social mobility for many sons and daughters of European immigrants, providing pathways out of the blue-collar working class to secure a middle-class lifestyle. Smaller numbers of non-White students also attended such institutions, often on a segregated basis, and secondary education sometimes helped them as well, although on a far less consistent basis. If the idea that public schools could uplift children of destitute origins was a myth, it was likely grounded in the experiences of these largely White urban youth (Fass, 1989; Tyack, 1974).

Throughout much of the 20th century, urban high schools were much larger than their counterparts in smaller towns or the countryside, offering a wider range of course offerings and better facilities than outlying institutions. City school districts typically paid better too, so they generally employed the top teachers, at least with regard to educational credentials and experience. And their size and superior resources often meant that city schools could field stronger athletic teams as well, adding to their popular appeal. For decades up through the 1950s, many of these institutions more than held their own against their suburban and rural counterparts (Rury, 2020).

Urban advantages extended to other dimensions of schooling as well. Analysis of census data indicates that teenagers living in cities in 1940 had a considerably higher likelihood of finishing high school than their suburban peers, possibly because of the greater availability and appeal of their secondary institutions. It also seems that youth living in cities at that time had somewhat higher social and economic status than teens in many suburbs. By and large, suburban communities in many parts of the country often were small towns or even open countryside. Compared to the vibrant and exciting setting that larger cities offered, these communities could seem quite dull and isolated. But this was a situation that soon would change rather dramatically (Saatcioglu & Rury, 2012).

RISING SUBURBAN ADVANTAGE

The clear benefits that many suburban schools convey today may seem quite natural, but these institutions did not always enjoy their current status. Their advantages were the result of a number of historical forces that transformed metropolitan landscapes across the country, beginning in the highly urbanized Northeast. A key factor was the rise of near universal automobile ownership and construction of highways connecting center cities to outlying communities, along with commuter rails and other such accommodations. Beset by urban housing shortages and encouraged by policy choices that built new roads and ensured cheap gasoline, Americans began exiting to newly opened developments on the fringes of urbanized areas. Between 1940 and 1960, the country's suburban population grew nearly 30 million, more than twice the growth of central cities. The trend gained momentum from there, and by 1980, only 40% of the country's metropolitan population lived in central cities, with a substantial majority in surrounding suburbs (Jackson, 1987; Teaford, 2006).

Migrants from big cities were disproportionately young, married, and upwardly mobile. They also were overwhelmingly White. These were families that could afford suburban housing and stay-at-home moms to make multiple children and their husbands' daily commuting workable. They were drawn to these new burgeoning communities by the prospect of neighbors just like them, while ethnic and racial minority families were systematically excluded. And as these families moved to suburbia, the populations of the country's central cities became older, poorer, and darker in complexion (Duany et al., 2000).

New schools became a major attraction of the suburbs, and as these outlying communities grew they made educational institutions a selling point for prospective residents. This was the baby boom era, and ambitious suburbanites were keen to give their children the best possible education, contributing to a lively competition among outlying school systems (Dougherty, 2008). More affluent suburbs attracted college-educated migrants, contributing to heightened interest in schooling. The result was rapid growth and substantial investment in new facilities, staffed with many veteran teachers, quickly creating the impression that suburban schools were far superior to their aging urban counterparts. This was a principal theme of Conant's book in 1961, and the metropolitan changes it highlighted only became more pronounced in the decades to follow (Rury, 2020).

The contemporary suburban school advantage, in that case, was the result of a particular set of historical circumstances, which made it possible for millions of urban dwellers to move to the edges of metropolitan America. The result was schools that benefited from their affluent clientele, registering graduation rates and test scores that were higher than the urban schools that many left behind (Saatcioglu & Rury, 2012). The cities they were abandoning were changing at the same time, partly due to a migration of a different sort. The rise of suburban schools, in that case, were just one dimension of the monumental changes that occurred at the time. To get the complete picture, it's necessary to look at what happened back in the urban core.

THE URBAN GHETTO AND ITS SCHOOLS

While relatively affluent white families flocked to suburbs, impoverished African Americans began leaving the rural South in greater numbers to seek new opportunities, mainly in big cities. In the decades following the start of the Second World War, nearly five million African Americans migrated from the South to northern and western states, taking up residence mainly in large urban centers. Most were relatively young, quite poor, and unskilled in terms of nonagricultural employment. Drawn by the prospect of jobs in the robust postwar economy, they settled in established Black communities such as New York's Harlem or Chicago's South Side, and similar districts elsewhere. Barred from most other neighborhoods, Black families crammed into these densely populated areas, straining the existing housing stock as well as city services—and schools. This pattern of migration had started decades earlier, but reached new heights during the 1950s and 1960s. Abetted by mechanized cotton farming and the longstanding southern racial repression, migration had a transformative impact on urban life. It also held profound educational implications (Goldsmith & Blakely, 1992; Kantor & Brenzel, 1993).

One consequence of this migration was a growing problem of segregated and overcrowded schools, resulting in large classes, double-shift instructional schedules, and fatigued staff and facilities. As a result, the prevailing narrative of urban education began to feature elements of crisis: crumbling buildings, underqualified teachers, poorly prepared students, political turmoil, and racial conflict (Rury & Mirel, 1997). Following the *Brown* decision, the notion that separate schooling was inherently unequal became deeply ingrained in the national consciousness, and the very idea of largely Black schools became seen as inherently problematic. These issues were early points of conflict between community activists and urban school officials during the 1950s and 1960s. Almost from the start, there was a vivid perception that Black schools were inferior to those serving White children in the major cities (Burkholder, 2021).

Early clashes over the quality of schooling for Blacks drew attention to problems in nearly all areas of their lives. Social scientists invented new terminology to describe Black students, calling them "disadvantaged" or "culturally deprived," although both terms eventually became controversial. In fact, Black students often lagged behind their White counterparts, especially in high schools. Those who had fallen behind in earlier grades, or who had not received a solid foundation, were at an obvious disadvantage. Given this, it was hardly any wonder that the Black "dropout" rate was considerably higher than the corresponding White rate, at least to start with (Martinez & Rury, 2012; Rury & Hill, 2012).

Even so, there were success stories in Black education during this period, most of which are not well known. One is the growth of secondary attainment among African American youth. Their high school graduation rates increased at a pace faster than their White peers during this era, but especially after 1960, when perceptions of an urban school crisis began to register. It was a record of improvement that occurred when social and economic conditions in the big cities often grew worse. Just how or why this happened is not altogether clear, but it suggests that inferences drawn from the past may need to be occasionally reexamined, especially as new information becomes available and new questions are posed about both past and present (Rury, 2009).

The secondary attainment levels of African American youth grew most dramatically prior to 1960, partly a function of initially low southern graduation rates, but they continued to improve in the following decades. During these years, the national gap between Black and White high school graduation rates closed appreciably. Tellingly, this disparity declined just as dramatically in the central cities. These developments belied theories of cultural deprivation that held Black students less capable of success in school. As a number of studies have demonstrated, when background conditions of poverty and family structure were statistically controlled, Black youth actually exhibited higher likelihood of graduation than Whites. A bit later, data from the National Assessment of Educational Progress (NAEP) showed that African American achievement in both reading and mathematics increased dramatically between 1971 and 1988, eventually closing the gap with White scores by 50%. These represented remarkable improvements in African American academic performance, at the same time that the city schools serving most Black students were labeled scholastically inferior and disorderly (Rury, 2009; Rury & Hill, 2012).

Many factors contributed to these changes, of course. Education was a major focal point of federal anti-poverty initiatives, starting in the mid-1960s, and Title I and other programs directed additional resources to urban schools. While these funds often failed to fully offset declining local revenues, they did provide new support for students most in need. In addition, a wide range of educational programs were sponsored by private foundations, community organizations, and corporate partner programs. While many were episodic, their impact was probably greatest in urban centers, and they contributed to the impression that new levels of attainment were possible (Kantor & Lowe, 1995). African American college enrollments also began to increase, fueled in part by a greater willingness to admit Black students, and this provided an incentive for many to succeed in high school. A Black middle class was emerging, as new employment opportunities opened as well. Altogether, it was a time of excitement and new horizons. Contrary to the popular perceptions, higher levels of educational attainment, so long denied to African Americans, began to appear at a historically new scale (Kim & Rury, 2007).

Despite problems often associated with urban education that started during the postwar era, there was reason to be quite positive about changes in Black schooling in major cities. Even where integration largely failed and persistent racial differences in educational achievement existed, ever larger numbers of Black youth were making their way through the schools, and a sizable African American middle class was emerging as a result. These were developments that contradicted the problematic reputation that urban schools acquired during the age of suburbanization, despite the many challenges they faced.

CONCLUSION

It is commonplace today to hear comments that postal zip codes are good indicators of social inequality, including the quality of schools. But the foregoing discussion suggests that such generalizations are not always trustworthy and may not apply well to the past. Suburban schools began to exhibit many advantages over their urban counterparts during the 1950s, but city schools still operated as powerful engines of social mobility for African Americans historically denied access to education. While graduation rates and test scores remained higher in suburban districts, urban schools closed much of the gap in the decades following 1960. This general process of convergence on such measures became less consistently evident after 1990, when conditions of concentrated poverty and associated problems grew even worse in central cities, but in many cases the urban schools continued to provide opportunities to their students (Rury & Hill, 2012; Wong, 2018).

Recent research by Stanford University's Sean Reardon and other educational researchers has demonstrated that city schools often outperform suburban institutions in the *growth* of their students' achievement, as measured by test scores. Suburban schools may exhibit higher scores overall, but they often contribute less advancement to their largely affluent students. The matter of which institutions are better from an educational standpoint, in that case, remains an open question, as it was in the past. If the object of schooling is growth, after all, it appears that many urban institutions continue to do an exemplary job. While they may not raise all of their underprivileged clientele to the same level as well-heeled suburban students, they often help to close the gap considerably. And these accomplishments go unacknowledged far too often, contributing to the urban legend of educational failure (Reardon, 2019).

REFERENCES

Badger, E., & Quealy, K. (2017, December 5). How effective is your school district? A new measure shows where students learn the most. *The New York Times*. Retrieved from https://www.nytimes.com/interactive/2017/12/05/upshot/a-better-way-to-compare-public-schools.html

Burkholder, Z. (2021). *An African American dilemma: A history of school integration and civil rights in the North.* Oxford University Press.

Conant, J. B. (1961). *Slums and suburbs: A commentary on schools in metropolitan areas.* Signet Books.

Dougherty, J. (2008). Bridging the gap between urban, suburban and educational history. In J. Reese & J. L. Rury (Eds.), *Rethinking the history of American education* (pp. 245–259). Palgrave Macmillan.

Duany, A., Plater-Zyberk, E., & Speck, J. (2000). *Suburban nation: The rise of sprawl and the decline of the American dream.* North Point Press.

Fass, P. S. (1989). *Outside in: Minorities and the transformation of American education.* Oxford University Press.

Goldsmith, W. W., & Blakely, E. J. (1992). *Separate societies: Poverty and inequality in U.S. cities.* Temple University Press.

Hunter, E. (1954). *The blackboard jungle: A novel.* Simon and Shuster.

Jackson, K. T. (1987). *Crabgrass frontier: The suburbanization of the United States.* Oxford University Press.

Kantor, H., & Brenzel, B. (1993). Urban education and the "Truly Disadvantaged": The historical roots of the contemporary crisis, 1945–1990. In M. B. Katz (Ed.), *The underclass debate: Views from history* (pp. 366–402). Princeton University Press.

Kantor, H., & Lowe, R. (1995). Class, race, and the emergence of federal education policy: From the new deal to the great society. *Educational Researcher, 24*(3), 4–11.

Kim, D., & Rury, J. L. (2007). The changing profile of college access: The Truman Commission and enrollment patterns in the postwar era. *History of Education Quarterly, 47*(3), 302–327.

Martinez, S. L. M., & Rury, J. L. (2012). From "culturally deprived" to "at risk": The politics of popular expression and educational inequality in the United States, 1960–1985. *Teachers College Record, 114*(6), 1–31.

Reardon, S. F. (2019). Educational opportunity in early and middle childhood: Using full population administrative data to study variation by place and age. *RSF: The Russell Sage Foundation Journal of the Social Sciences, 5*(2), 40–68.

Rury, J. L. (1999). Race, space, and the politics of Chicago's public schools: Benjamin Willis and the tragedy of urban education. *History of Education Quarterly, 39*(2), 117–142.

Rury, J. L. (2005). Introduction: The changing contours of urban education. In J. L. Rury (Ed.), *Urban education in the United States: A historical reader* (pp. 1–16). Palgrave Macmillan.

Rury, J. L. (2009). Attainment amidst adversity: Black high school students in the metropolitan North, 1940–1980. In K. Wong & R. Rothman (Eds.), *Clio at the table: History and educational policy* (pp. 37–58). Peter Lang.

Rury, J. L. (2020). *Creating the suburban school advantage: Race, localism, and inequality in an American metropolis.* Cornell University Press.

Rury, J. L., & Hill, S. A. (2012). *The African American struggle for secondary schooling: Closing the graduation gap.* Teachers College Press.

Rury, J. L., & Mirel, J. E. (1997). The political economy of urban education. *Review of Research in Education, 22*, 49–110.

Saatcioglu, A., & Rury, J. L. (2012). Education and the changing metropolitan organization of inequality: A multilevel analysis of secondary attainment in the United States, 1940–1980. *Historical Methods, 45*(1), 21–40.

Teaford, J. C. (2006). *The metropolitan revolution: The rise of post-urban America.* Columbia University Press.

Tyack, D. B. (1974). *The one best system: A history of American urban education.* Harvard University Press.

Wong, A. (2018, December 12). Parents are biased against even quality "urban" schools. *The Atlantic.* Retrieved from https://www.theatlantic.com/education/archive/2018/12/urban-schools-white-parents/577843/

CHAPTER 8

The Myth of American School Decline

David A. Gamson

Just before the pandemic, 55% of adults responding to a national survey said that schools were worse today than when they were students (Phi Delta Kappan, 2018). This belief reflects years of headlines stressing the seeming sag of scores on national standardized tests (Berliner & Glass, 2014). Business leaders and politicians regularly bemoan what they perceive as lackluster scholastic results. As one observer put it, "today's American public education is still lagging behind its own past as well as its international competitors" (Go, 2011, p. 72). In this view, American students were once well-versed in the academic basics and well-behaved in their classrooms; they were once held to high academic expectations, which they met, and they attended schools that were well-run by well-educated, well-respected teachers and administrators. School reformers often use the misdiagnosis of educational problems to push for policies that they say will put America back on top. But when not based on a firm understanding of the school system's strengths and weaknesses, such reforms are a waste of precious time and resources, if not patently harmful.

That the narrative of school decline is a myth becomes evident when we examine the significant changes and improvements to schools and curricular materials over the past century. Today's schools have shortcomings, certainly, and are not what they yet could be, but schools are also demonstrably better than they were in decades past, in several ways. Curricula are much richer than they once were; graduation rates are higher than ever; and—before the pandemic—scores on national assessments had risen over recent decades. The myth of school decline is sustained in part by a nostalgic perception that the nation's schools once existed in a state of grace from which they have now fallen. This chapter first reviews claims that tout the tale of school declension. I next remind readers that to insist that schools were once better than they are today is to assume that schools were once of high quality for all students, something that historically is far from accurate. Then I offer historical evidence demonstrating that over the past 100 years, American schools—far from teaching less over time—have in fact taught more content to more students in increasingly useful and robust ways. However, to say that schools have improved over time is not to say that American schools are without problems and challenges, nor is it to say that American schools are currently the best versions of what they can be. American schools face significant problems today, weaknesses often caused by sources outside of schools.

CLAIMS OF DECLINE

Industry leaders and politicians are fond of scolding the public schools. One of the most insistent detractors of public education over the past couple of decades has been Microsoft founder Bill Gates, who regularly depicts American public schools as "obsolete" and incapable of preparing students either for rigorous college coursework or for the modern technological workforce (Gates, 2005, 2016). Gates laments that American students have allegedly become the laggards in the international contest for high academic achievement. Compared to other countries like Singapore, Finland, and South Korea, he insists, "we do much worse for our students as a whole." Yet in his view this was not always the case: "in the 1960s," he says, American schools "were the best across the board. Even in the 1970s we were the top in most things. It's in the last 20 years that the U.S. has moved to pretty near the bottom of the rich countries' statistics for math, reading, science" (Gates, 2010).

Whether consciously or not, journalists also advance the declension narrative, regularly broadcasting negative news on student test scores. Indeed, Americans have become accustomed to headlines announcing dreary assessment results for American students: "U.S. Students Still Lag Globally in Math and Science," ran one *New York Times* headline in 2012 (Rich, 2012). "U.S. High Schoolers Drop Further Behind Global Peers in Math, Study Finds," reported the *Washington Post* in 2016 (Heim, 2016). The curriculum has been "dumbed down," says one commentator, claiming that American schools undertook a "decades-long flight from learning" (Sykes, 1996, p. 9). And *Forbes* magazine evokes the image of the one-room schoolhouse, not as a relic of the pedagogical past but as a laudable "vision for the future" (Busteed, 2020). (Also see Zimmerman chapter, this volume.)

Politicians or policymakers exploit these fears of decline, usually for the purpose of pushing pet solutions. For example, in March 2018, then-Secretary of Education Betsy DeVos, a longtime advocate for market-driven educational schemes, infamously posted a tweet with a picture of two classrooms. One classroom was decades old, the other more recent. Both images featured "traditional" classrooms—students sitting at their desks, eyes focused on the teacher. "Does this look familiar?" DeVos inquired. "Students lined up in rows. A teacher in front of a blackboard. Sit down; don't talk; eyes up front. Wait for the bell. . . . Everything about our lives has moved beyond the industrial era. But American education largely hasn't" (DeVos, 2018). (Also see Dorn chapter, this volume, for a discussion of the myth of the industrial-era classroom.) DeVos intended her critique to serve as a rallying point for school choice advocates, but it backfired. Hundreds of teachers tweeted back pictures of their own students learning in a wide variety of creative classroom arrangements.

DeVos and Gates and many other advocates for various reforms such as charters, vouchers, cyber-schools, or overly stringent accountability mechanisms use this discourse that the nation's schools have declined, stagnated, or become obsolete. Only if they can convince American citizens that "all else has failed" can they press forward with their own reforms that dramatically undermine core foundations of the American school system.

GOOD SCHOOLS FOR WHOM? NEVER A GOLDEN AGE IN EDUCATION

Were schools really better in the 1970s, the 1950s, the 1930s, or the 19th century, as critics have contended? Hardly. First, in those supposed golden ages, schools never served everyone. During the 19th-century Common School Movement—the era of the one-room schoolhouse—enslaved children in the South were prohibited from getting an education at all, and other minoritized children were often excluded from public schools. After the Civil War, African Americans made progress in their campaign for common schools, but as Reconstruction ended in the late 1870s, politically powerful Whites curtailed further expansion of common schools in general and for Black children in particular (Anderson, 1988, p. 148) through violent means and Jim Crow laws.

As historian James Anderson (1988) points out, Black students in the South were deprived of the benefits of common schooling until *after* the first third of the 20th century and even then were only begrudgingly and incompletely allowed access to public school funds by the southern White policymakers who held the purse strings. Worse yet, explains Anderson, the most oppressive feature of southern schooling was the fact that local governments supported the secondary education of Whites but refused to create high schools for Black youth. The few Black high schools that did exist were mostly located in urban districts. Almost all southern rural communities, and half of those in cities, failed to provide public high schools for Black children, reflecting the opposition of the vast majority of White Southerners to Black secondary education (Anderson, 1988, p. 186).

Throughout the first half of the 20th century, and well past the 1954 *Brown v. Board of Education* Supreme Court decision, severe segregation persisted in most public schools—in both the North and South (see Rias chapter, this volume). The majority of segregated schools lacked adequate facilities, textbooks, classroom space, and numbers of instructors. Throughout the first three-quarters of the century, the percentage of school-aged African American youth enrolled in school trailed the enrollment rate of White children (Rury & Hill, 2015), and not until the early 1970s did school-aged White and Black youth enroll in schools in equal proportions (roughly 90%) (National Center for Education Statistics, 1993, p. 14). It is little wonder, then, that Black adults were *less* likely to say that schools had gotten worse over time in the *Phi Delta Kappan* poll mentioned at the opening of this chapter (60% of Whites say that school is worse today vs. 40% of Black respondents). Nostalgia for the educational past is mostly a White, middle-class exercise.

EVIDENCE OF SCHOOL IMPROVEMENT

"No other people ever demanded so much of schools and of education as have the Americans," the historian Henry Steele Commager noted in 1951 (cited in Schrag, 2007, p. 15A). In the nearly three-quarters of a century since, Americans have demanded even more; and educators have answered. Schools have dramatically increased access; expanded course offerings; educated waves of immigrants coming to our shores; introduced special education and mainstreaming; provided needed mental health counseling and other social services; fed breakfast and lunch to millions of students; offered an enlarged array of extracurricular activities; and taught students about the dangers of alcohol, tobacco, drugs, and unsafe driving. It is therefore not surprising that they might periodically seem to struggle to accomplish all that is demanded of them.

Given the wide array of responsibilities they have been given, test scores are not the only metric by which schools should be judged. Nonetheless, observers are often keyed into test scores as the primary measure of school quality. Until the pandemic, which caused scores to drop across the board in all subjects, test scores on national assessments had risen over the past half-century. The most reliable and consistent long-term measure of student achievement is the National Assessment of Educational Progress (NAEP), a nationally representative assessm.ent of what American students know and can do in subjects such as mathematics and reading. One type of assessment is called the long-term-trend NAEP, which tracks the performance of students ages 9, 12, and 17. The long-term-trend NAEP shows *improvement across all age groups in both reading and math* (National Center for Education Statistics, 2023). There are other indicators that we can point to. High school completion rates—students who finish in 4 years—have risen, from 79% in 2011 to 87% in 2020 (National Center for Education Statistics, 2021). Given the variety of social factors that can negatively impact student achievement—childhood poverty being one of the most significant—it might be said that the schools are doing remarkably well. Although the childhood poverty rate showed pre-pandemic declines, some 11 to 12 million children still live in poverty in this country.

CURRICULUM IMPROVEMENTS

In their disparagement of public school quality, critics have targeted both the math and reading curriculum, arguing, for example, that the math curriculum has become overly "fuzzy," focusing too heavily on inquiry approaches to learning and, supposedly, abandoning instruction in basic math facts and procedural skills (Cavanagh, 2009; Schoenfeld, 2004; Schwartz, 2023). Criticisms of American reading textbooks have been equally fierce (Pearson, 2004); the University of Virginia's E. D. Hirsch Jr. (2009, p. 42) asserted that English language arts has been a "cognitive wasteland." However, without empirical analyses that document and detail curricular shifts, changes, or consistencies over the past century, educators and researchers are unable to counter (or confirm) charges that schools have weakened or watered down the rigor of school textbooks. Therefore, much of our understanding of curricular change has relied on lore and conjecture.

These myths can have serious consequences. For example, the alleged deterioration of textbook quality served as an explicit justification for the creation of the 2010 Common Core State Standards (CCSS). "While the reading demands of college, workforce training programs, and citizenship have held steady or risen over the past fifty years or so," the Standards authors contended, "K-12 texts have, if anything, become less demanding" (Common Core State Standards Initiative, 2010, p. 2). Where did the idea of less demanding curricula come from?

The CCSS relied heavily on a study from 1996 (Hayes et al., 1996), claiming to find "precipitous declines" in average sentence length and vocabulary level in reading textbooks (Common Core State Standards Initiative, 2010, p. 3). After analyzing portions of elementary, middle, and high school textbooks published between 1919 and 1991, Hayes et al. (1996) argued they detected a "pervasive decline in the difficulty" of these schoolbooks (p. 489). However, several historical misunderstandings embedded in this study skewed their results. For example, in their assessment of pre–World War I reading textbooks—which they found to be "very difficult"—the researchers relied on the well-known *McGuffey's Eclectic Readers*. Of course these reading passages were very difficult, the historian responds: The literary selections in the McGuffey's are essentially compilations of adult reading materials cut and pasted for younger readers (Sullivan, 1994). Moreover, unlike textbooks most of us are familiar with today, late 19th- and early 20th-century readers were designed for the purposes of elocution, not comprehension. In other words, children were *not expected* to understand what they read; instead, they were examined on how well they could read the text aloud, in the tradition of declamation (Mathews, 1966; Pearson, 2009).

Curious about claims of curricular decline, I worked with colleagues at Penn State to investigate the changes to both the reading and the mathematics curricula over the course of the 20th century. We collected a broad sample of elementary-grade mathematics and basal reading textbooks published over the past century that could accurately represent the textbook market. Employing the concept of "cognitive complexity," we examined how challenging reading texts and math problems were for the students who used these materials in their classrooms (Baker et al., 2010; Gamson et al., 2013). These were large studies, involving nearly 450 textbooks in total, and not all the conclusions can be detailed here, but I will highlight some of the key findings.

In reading, we focused on 3rd- and 6th-grade texts. Our findings showed a distinctly different pattern of historical shifts in text complexity than the declines reported by the authors of the CCSS. That said, our measures showed that *there was* a decline in the complexity of 3rd-grade reading texts in the early decades of the century, but the clear and compelling story is that the difficulty of reading textbooks increased steadily after the 1940s. Sixth-grade texts were much more stable, but rather than declining, they too show notable increases after the 1940s. Put simply, our findings offer compelling evidence that the complexity of *reading textbooks, at least at the 3rd- and 6th-grade levels, has either increased or remained noticeably consistent over the past three-quarters of a century* (Gamson et al., 2013). It is clearly inaccurate for the CCSS authors to offer the blanket condemnation that school reading texts have "trended downward in difficulty in the last half century."

Even more so than reading, the changes to the math curriculum, as evidenced in elementary textbooks across the century, demonstrate a massive increase in the amount of content and complexity. Let's start with a curious fact about mathematics in the early grades: In the first decades of the 20th century, most experts believed that their young students shouldn't be exposed to mathematics before the 2nd or 3rd grade, the idea being that children first had to learn to read (Wentworth, 1907). In other words, during the years that their cognitive functions were rapidly developing, children were exposed to little or no math content at all. Not surprisingly, studies at the time showed that the later students started, the harder it was for them to catch up. In the 1930s and 1940s, mathematics instruction was still often withheld until the second half of the 1st grade. Not until the 1950s and 1960s did 1st-grade textbooks become standard, containing increasingly more math content in the decades that followed.

In the first third of the century, the arithmetic content for the older elementary grades was usually highly repetitive and time-consuming, but not particularly cognitively challenging. Before the 1960s, reasoning content was rare; textbooks still relied heavily on algorithms and rote procedure. As the century progressed, however, younger and younger children received more and more math content; at the same time, the early grades curriculum enlarged and improved dramatically, slowly moving beyond basic arithmetic skills into more advanced dimensions of mathematics, such as decimals, percents, and ratios. Starting in the mid-1970s, there was a rapid pushdown of advanced material into earlier and earlier grades. Statistics, probability, and data analysis—topics once reserved for high school—found their way into elementary grades by end of century. By 1975, kindergarteners used textbooks that covered 10 different content areas, and by the 1990s, kindergarten textbooks covered more content and more pages than had 2nd-grade textbooks of the 1930s. Arithmetic textbooks averaged just 87 pages in the early 1900s, but by the end of the century, elementary math textbooks had an average of 330 pages (Baker et al., 2010).

What is true of mathematics and reading i.s also true of other disciplines. Students today benefit from a wide array of curricular materials that are savvier and more sophisticated than in decades past. Any comparison of textbooks of today with those of 50 years ago yields remarkable differences in content, scope, sequence, and coverage. Today, school texts are more cognitively challenging than they have ever been.

CONCLUSION

To say that schools today are *better* than they once were is *not* to deny current realities. Schools today face a range of daunting circumstances beyond recent pandemic learning loss, including increased segregation, child poverty, inequitable funding, inadequate facilities for many students, and the growing achievement gap between the country's wealthiest and poorest children (Reardon, 2013). Many of these challenges are not of the school's creation. Research in recent decades has demonstrated the precise social factors that negatively impact student learning. These studies help explain why American students lag on some international indicators of student achievement at the same time that they point the way to larger social changes that include family health and economic security programs that can have a positive effect on student outcomes (Cutright & Fernquist, 2014).

If policymakers and school reformers operate on the belief that today's schools are worse than they once were, it sends the wrong message and misdirects us toward solutions that are sure to waste valuable resources. Nostalgia makes for bad educational policy.

REFERENCES

Anderson, J. D. (1988). *The education of Blacks in the South, 1860–1935*. University of North Carolina Press.

Baker, D., Knipe, H., Collins, J., Leon, J., Cummings, E., Blair, C., & Gamson, D. (2010). One hundred years of elementary school mathematics in the United States: A content analysis and cognitive assessment of textbooks from 1900 to 2000. *Journal for Research in Mathematics Education, 41*(4), 383–423. Retrieved from https://doi.org/10.5951/jresematheduc.41.4.0383

Berliner, D. C., & Glass, G. V (Eds.). (2014). *50 myths & lies that threaten America's public schools: The real crisis in education.* Teachers College Press.

Busteed, B. (2020, November 7). Why the one-room schoolhouse is a vision for the future, not just a relic of the past. *Forbes.* Retrieved from https://www.forbes.com/sites/brandonbusteed/2020/11/07/why-the-one-room-schoolhouse-is-a-vision-for-the-future-not-just-a-relic-of-the-past/

Cavanagh, S. (2009, March 13). Re-examining a math skirmish. *Education Week.* Retrieved from https://www.edweek.org/teaching-learning/re-examinining-a-math-skirmish/2009/03

Common Core State Standards Initiative. (2010). *Common Core State Standards for English language arts & literacy in history/social studies, science, and technical subjects; Appendix A: Research supporting key elements of the standards.* Retrieved from www.thecorestandards.org/assets/Appendix_A.pdf

Cutright, P., & Fernquist, R. M. (2014). Cross-national differences in academic achievement: Why the United States lags behind other rich nations. *Sociological Focus, 47*(2), 71–83. Retrieved from https://doi.org/10.1080/00380237.2014.883803

DeVos, B. (2018, March 6). *Does this look familiar?* Retrieved from https://twitter.com/BetsyDeVosED/status/971161379179843584

Gamson, D. A., Lu, X., & Eckert, S. A. (2013). Challenging the research base of the Common Core State Standards: A historical reanalysis of text complexity. *Educational Researcher, 42*(7), 381–391. Retrieved from https://doi.org/10.3102/0013189X13505684

Gates, B. (2005). *Prepared remarks by Bill Gates, co-chair, 2005 National Education Summit on High Schools.* Bill & Melinda Gates Foundation. Retrieved from https://www.gatesfoundation.org/ideas/speeches/2005/02/bill-gates-2005-national-education-summit

Gates, B. (2010). *Bill Gates on what's wrong with public schools* [Interview]. Retrieved from https://macleans.ca/general/bill-gates-in-conversation/

Gates, B. (2016). *I love this cutting-edge school design.* Gatesnotes.Com. Retrieved from https://www.gatesnotes.com/Why-I-Love-This-Cutting-Edge-School-Design

Go, M. H. (2011). Saving public education. *State & Local Government Review, 43*(1), 72–76. Retrieved from https://www.jstor.org/stable/41303177

Hayes, D. P., Wolfer, L. T., & Wolfe, M. F. (1996). Schoolbook simplification and its relation to the decline in SAT-verbal scores. *American Educational Research Journal, 33*(2). Retrieved from https://journals-sagepub-com.ezaccess.libraries.psu.edu/doi/abs/10.3102/00028312033002489

Heim, J. (2016, December 6). U.S. high schoolers drop further behind global peers in math, study finds. *The Washington Post*, A.13. Retrieved from https://www.proquest.com/docview/1845907513/abstract/227B56E90F144348PQ/26

Hirsch, E. D. (2009). *The making of Americans: Democracy and our schools.* Yale University Press.

Mathews, M. M. (1966). *Teaching to read, historically considered.* University of Chicago Press.

National Center for Education Statistics. (1993). *120 years of American education: A statistical portrait.* U.S. Department of Education, Office of Educational Research and Improvement.

National Center for Education Statistics. (2021). *Digest of educational statistics; table 219.46 public high school 4-year adjusted cohort graduation rate*. Retrieved from https://nces.ed.gov/programs/digest/d21/tables/dt21_219.46.asp

National Center for Education Statistics. (2023). *Student groups and trend reports—Long-term trends NAEP*. National Center for Education Statistics. Retrieved from https://nces.ed.gov/nationsreportcard/ltt/

Pearson, P. D. (2004). The reading wars. *Educational Policy, 18*(1), 216–252. Retrieved from https://doi.org/10.1177/0895904803260041

Pearson, P. D. (2009). The roots of reading comprehension instruction. In S. E. Israel & G. G. Duffy (Eds.), *Handbook of research on reading comprehension* (pp. 3–31). Routledge.

Phi Delta Kappan. (2018). The 50th annual PDK poll of the public's attitudes toward the public schools. *Kappanonline.Org, 100*(1). Retrieved from https://kappanonline.org/the-50th-annual-pdk-poll-of-the-publics-attitudes-toward-the-public-schools/

Reardon, S. F. (2013). The widening income achievement gap. *Educational Leadership, 70*(8), 10–16.

Rich, M. (2012, December 11). U.S. students still lag globally in math and science, tests show. *The New York Times*. Retrieved from https://www.nytimes.com/2012/12/11/education/us-students-still-lag-globally-in-math-and-science-tests-show.html

Rury, J. L., & Hill, S. A. (2015). *The African American struggle for secondary schooling, 1940–1980: Closing the graduation gap*. Teachers College Press.

Schoenfeld, A. H. (2004). The math wars. *Educational Policy, 18*(1), 253–286. Retrieved from https://doi.org/10.1177/0895904803260042

Schrag, P. (2007, September 9). Schoolhouse crock: 50 years of blaming America's educational system for society's woes. *Journal Gazette, The (Fort Wayne, IN)*, 15A. Access World News. Retrieved from https://infoweb.newsbank.com/apps/news/document-view?p=AWNB&docref=news/11BD2AF28C9498A8&f=basic

Schwartz, S. (2023, July 13). California adopts controversial new math framework. Here's what's in it. *Education Week*. Retrieved from https://www.edweek.org/teaching-learning/california-adopts-controversial-new-math-framework-heres-whats-in-it/2023/07

Sullivan, D. P. (1994). *William Holmes McGuffey: Schoolmaster to the nation*. Fairleigh Dickinson University Press; Associated University Presses.

Sykes, C. J. (1996). *Dumbing down our kids: Why America's children feel good about themselves but can't read, write, or add*. St. Martin's Griffin.

Wentworth, G. (1907). *New elementary arithmetic*. Ginn.

CHAPTER 9

The Myth That U.S. Schools Were Desegregated in 1954

Hope C. Rias

Many Americans believe that schools in the United States were desegregated in 1954 after the *Brown v. Board of Education* decision. Preservice teachers whom I teach are often shocked to learn of *Liddell v. Board of Education* (1979) in which Liddell, parent of a child in the St. Louis schools, successfully showed that Black children were repeatedly denied access to predominantly White schools, almost two decades after *Brown*. In 1972, when Minnie Liddell sued the St. Louis School Board for racial discrimination, she was met with resistance. White St. Louisans were insistent that school desegregation was resolved in the 1950s and that all parents now had the choice to live in communities with good schools. Segregation, they claimed, was a matter of personal choice (Rias, 2014, pp. 121–122). Even the National Association for the Advancement of Colored People (NAACP) initially refused to work with Liddell. They were certain that the fight for school desegregation had been won and settled nationally (Rias, 2014).

The district court found that Liddell's claims were credible, and she did eventually receive NAACP support. Liddell's lawsuit led to the creation of one of the nation's largest desegregation programs in the nation. It began in 1980, more than 35 years after *Brown*. The myth that school desegregation occurred in 1954 is enduring. The *Brown* ruling was made at the federal level; however, since schools are locally managed, school districts were tasked with creating and enforcing their own desegregation plans. When they refused, a series of nuanced court battles were necessary to ensure compliance.

In 1954, Thurgood Marshall successfully argued before the U.S. Supreme Court that racial segregation in public schools violated the U.S. Constitution. The Court agreed. The first *Brown v. Board of Education* (1954) case established that separate schools were inherently unequal. School segregation violated the 14th Amendment of the U.S. Constitution that assured equal protection of the law to every citizen. Advocates for school desegregation rejoiced. Support from the U.S. Supreme Court meant that desegregation was no longer a lofty goal but federal law. Many believe that this ruling was the single most important Supreme Court decision of the 20th century.

The Myth That U.S. Schools Were Desegregated in 1954

While the Court ruling was significant, it did not end school segregation. This chapter addresses the myth that *Brown v. Board of Education* (1954) ended school segregation in the United States.

Although Marshall had successfully argued his case before the Supreme Court, he was concerned that school leaders would not comply with the Court's ruling unless they were compelled to do so. Marshall appealed to the Supreme Court a second time. To facilitate desegregation, he asked the Court to set a compliance date for schools to desegregate. The Court declined. Interpreting the law was the Court's mission; enforcing it was not. While the Court would not mandate a compliance date, they ruled that desegregation should occur "with all deliberate speed" (*Brown v. Board of Education II*, 1955).

Marshall was right in his concerns over how long school districts would take to comply with the new mandate. After *Brown v. Board of Education*, school districts employed numerous techniques to avoid school desegregation. Southern states organized massive and often violent resistance to school desegregation. Northern states engaged in less overt methods to avoid desegregation. While some school districts desegregated, others circumvented the law for decades. In Washington, D.C., Black students were desegregated without incident. Several western states passed legislation to combat discrimination in public schools. They included Washington, California, Arizona, New Mexico, North Dakota, Montana, Colorado, and Wyoming.

WIDESPREAD RESISTANCE TO *BROWN*

Resistance to the *Brown* ruling was easier to identify in states where violence was used as the primary method of resistance. *Brown* was met with massive resistance in the southern states of Alabama, Louisiana, Virginia, Texas, Georgia, and Mississippi (Franklin, 2021, pp. 35–36). Missouri and other border states exercised resistance that was harder to identify. Border states were states that lay between northern and southern states that fought against each other in the Civil War. Border states (Missouri, Delaware, Kentucky, Maryland, and West Virginia) crafted unique racial policies that discriminated against Blacks, often nonviolently. The lack of racial violence often led Whites to believe that equality existed. Nowhere in the country was *Brown* welcomed with open arms; discrimination, however, was hard to recognize in states that were not marked by racial violence as its primary form of resistance. The Delaware constitution, for example, prohibited racial discrimination but also allowed segregated schools (Franklin, 2021, p. 36). In Delaware, White residents resisted the desegregation attempt of 11 Black high school students when they tried to enroll in a White high school in Milford.

Although Delaware schools began desegregating at the elementary level, there was opposition at the high school level. There was no Black school in Milford, Delaware, so school officials began to enroll Black students in the local White school in 1954. Parents complained and White attendance fell daily. Death threats were directed at every member of the school board. Each member resigned. To avoid further conflict, Milford schools closed for 2 weeks. When they reopened, other White communities around Delaware protested school desegregation. The Black teens who had been enrolled in Milford High School were disenrolled and were sent to Jason High School, a Black school that was 16 miles away (Franklin, 38). Attorneys for the "Milford Eleven" continued to fight in court for their right to attend local public schools. In 1967, President Lyndon Johnson threatened to withhold federal funds from schools that were segregated, and the threat of losing federal funding was the impetus for Delaware schools to finally dismantle school segregation (The Education Trust, 2019; Franklin, 2021, p. 38).

Various strategies were used to avoid desegregation. In Little Rock, Arkansas (1958), and Prince Edward County, Virginia (1959), local leaders chose to close public schools rather than enroll Black students with Whites (Green, 2015). Public monies in the form of vouchers were sometimes provided to White families to help offset the cost of private schools where segregation might be easier to maintain. The argument that parents should have a choice was often the reason given for school districts' defiance of *Brown*. When White parents could not persuade schools to continue segregation in their local districts, they voted with their feet. White families moved to the suburbs where they would have access to all-White communities. White flight from desegregated communities became the ultimate expression of parental choice. It left schools resegregated, and new strategies had to be employed to force compliance with *Brown* (Rias, 50).

In addition to school closures, school districts employed numerous other strategies to avoid compliance with *Brown*. "Intact busing" was employed in St. Louis, Missouri. When a Black school was overcrowded, the Black children and their teacher would be bussed to a White school each morning. The whole class would use a separate classroom and have lunch and recess apart from the White students. In effect, this so-called intact busing allowed for segregation within a host school, intact referring to the school system's design to keep the bussed students grouped "intact" (i.e., segregated) as they proceeded class by class through the school day. The *Brown v. Board of Education* ruling intended for Black students to be enrolled in White schools if there was room. Rather than enroll Black children, intact busing allowed children to stay enrolled at their overcrowded, underfunded school and simply borrow facilities at a White school daily (Rias, 2019, p. 60). The practice of intact busing raises questions about desegregation opponents who claimed not to support desegregation because busing was too expensive. Schools were willing to pay to bus Black children to maintain segregation, but when desegregation proponents proposed busing as a tool for desegregation, opponents then raised cost as a prohibitive issue (Rias, 2019, p. 67).

Another strategy used to avoid desegregation was the misuse of color-blind data. School districts could be sued for violating the law if plaintiffs could prove the existence of segregation. Schools began erasing racial data from rosters, maintaining segregation without documenting it. This strategy was utilized by St. Louis Public Schools for 6 years after the *Brown* decision (Rias, 2019, p. 53). Contemporary educators might question why racial data is collected in modern times. It is to ensure that discrimination is not happening. Color-blindness was used as a tool of segregation. If no one could identify the race of the students who were allowed to attend public schools, then there could be no lawsuit. Collecting racial data allows for transparency.

Another tactic used to avoid school desegregation was the funding of newly built schools in Black communities. One key argument in *Brown v. Board of Education* was that separate was inherently unequal. Although that decision should have been the final edict, many who opposed racial integration imagined ways to eliminate the inequality of schools while still maintaining segregation. Local segregationists advocated for the building of new schools in Black communities to relieve overcrowding that would otherwise force Black students to enroll in White schools. If Blacks had their own newly constructed schools, perhaps they would be satisfied to stay in their own communities rather than enroll in White schools with better resources.

LOCAL ACTIVISM TO ENFORCE COMPLIANCE WITH *BROWN*

While education historians have worked to document desegregation history and the impact of *Brown v. Board of Education*, new scholarship highlights local activism in communities where authorities worked to avoid desegregation even after *Brown*. Vanessa Siddle Walker and V. P. Franklin have recently published work that highlights local efforts to dismantle school segregation after many school districts around the country refused to comply with *Brown*.

When school districts defied *Brown*, grassroots activists drew on a long history of school advocacy. Miles Horton had founded the Highlander Folk School in the 1930s in Monteagle, Tennessee, to train Blacks to be organizers and peaceful protesters. Legendary educator Septima Clark, who trained at Highlander, became a leader in the efforts to train Blacks to advocate for themselves. The Highlander Folk School offered training sessions in which community members would learn about their rights and how to advocate for themselves. In 1957, the Highlander Folk School became the first Citizenship School that trained people to vote and to act when their rights were disregarded (Walker, 2018, p. 4).

In response to continued segregation, local activists sued for the right to send their children to public schools. Perhaps the best-known example of local advocacy occurred in Little Rock, Arkansas, in 1957 when activist Daisy Bates, the president of the Arkansas State Conference of the NAACP, guided nine students through a strategic plan to desegregate Central High School. In 1955, the school board in Little Rock agreed to a slow implementation of desegregation that would begin in the fall of 1957. Initially, Arkansas governor Orval Faubus prevented the nine Black students from entering Central High School. In response, President Dwight Eisenhower federalized the Arkansas National Guard and ordered them to escort the Black students into the school (Franklin, 2021, p. 44). With the help of the federal government, nine Black students integrated Central High School for the remainder of the school year. In the fall of 1958, however, Faubus used his power to close all public high schools in Little Rock so that no one would attend desegregated high schools. Faubus intended to redirect school funds to private schools where he could maintain segregation (Gordy, 1997, p. 429). When the 8th U.S. Circuit Court of Appeals blocked Faubus's plan, Little Rock was left without public high schools for a year. Historians refer to this as "the lost year." In 1959, high schools in Little Rock reopened, and desegregation finally occurred (Gordy, 1997, p. 442; Green, 1998).

After Little Rock, lawsuits were filed around the country against school districts that defied *Brown*. In 1958, *Aaron v. Cooper* was filed in response to Arkansas governor Faubus, who resisted school desegregation. The lawsuit called for the elimination of obstacles to school access (*Aaron v. Cooper*, 1958). In Charlotte, North Carolina, in 1971, James Swann and nine other families sued the Charlotte-Mecklenburg School Board. The lawsuit forced the district to consider transportation that would aid desegregation (*Swann v. Charlotte-Mecklenburg Bd. Of Education*, 1971). In 1973, *Keyes v. School District No. 1, Denver, Colorado* was the first lawsuit after *Brown* that involved a western school district. The Supreme Court ruled that de facto segregation (practiced but not codified into law; see Erickson & Highsmith chapter, this volume) required remedies. *Keyes* established that even northern districts that did not have explicit laws banning desegregation (de jure segregation) were still responsible for the equal protection of all children. The practice of segregation, even if not codified by law, must be remedied. The ruling made it possible for more discreet forms of segregation to be dismantled in court (*Keyes v. School Dist. No. 1, Denver*, 1973). Like Denver, St. Louis schools used discreet, nonviolent methods to maintain segregation.

ST. LOUIS AS A MICROCOSM OF THE UNITED STATES

In St. Louis and the surrounding counties, numerous techniques were employed to avoid compliance with *Brown*. In 1954, the St. Louis Board of Education wrote a desegregation plan that went largely ignored. The use of tactics such as color-blind data, intact busing, and newly built segregated schools were clever, nonviolent, and far subtler than the violent clashes that occurred in the South. As a result, St. Louis and the surrounding county schools did not see widespread desegregation until 1983. These nuanced acts of resistance against *Brown* required equally creative strategies to force compliance with the law. Desegregation activists had to continually revise their strategies to oppose each newly implemented plan to maintain segregation. It took nearly 30 years for St. Louis Public Schools and the surrounding county schools to comply with *Brown*.

Liddell v. Board of Education (1979) was the lawsuit that eventually dismantled school segregation in St. Louis. Minnie Liddell lived on the segregated Northside where there were too few schools to accommodate the population. Liddell's eldest son, Craton, had been bussed and transferred to various schools to alleviate overcrowding. Liddell formed grassroots alliances to help lobby the school board to create better school conditions for Black children. Liddell, with help from the Concerned Parents Alliance, boycotted St. Louis schools for 6 weeks, recruiting parents of 450 children to withhold them from school (Rias, 2019, p. 96). Northside children could easily have been bussed to predominantly White schools in other parts of the city, but the district responded by building one new Northside school. Although Liddell's son would be allowed to attend the newly built school, other Northside children would have to attend school in a formerly condemned building. Liddell sued the school district (*Liddell v. Board of Education*, 1979).

In response to her lawsuit, the district court issued a consent decree that would allow St. Louis Public Schools to avoid trial or the admission of wrongdoing. Judge James Meredith found that while there were numerous factors that created segregation, school leaders participated in the practice. Judge Meredith ruled that schools in St. Louis must take actions to desegregate public schools. Beginning in September 1980, 4,400 White students and 3,400 Black students would be bussed for the purpose of desegregation (Heaney & Uchitelle, 2004, p. 93).

In 1980, poor health led Judge Meredith to resign, and a new judge took the case. To address White flight that aided suburban school segregation, the new district court judge, William Hungate, offered suburban public schools the opportunity to desegregate on a voluntary basis beginning in September 1981. When only five schools volunteered, Hungate offered a harsher alternative: He threatened to merge the St. Louis city school system with all 23 suburban public school districts and to appoint a special administrator who would oversee the collective funds of the newly merged districts if they did not create a workable desegregation plan (Heaney & Uchitelle, 2004, p. 118). A series of appeals were filed but the decision was again upheld in appellate court. With the fear of a countywide merger of 23 school districts looming, suburban school officials slowly began working toward acceptance of a desegregation plan.

In 1983, a three-part settlement was reached. First, 15,000 Black students would be transferred from city to suburban schools. Second, racially balanced magnet schools would be created in the city in hopes of drawing suburban students to specialized city schools. Finally, predominantly Black city schools would receive remedial and compensatory funds to offset the drastic population decline (Heaney & Uchitelle, 2004, p. 122). The court formed the Voluntary Interdistrict Coordinating Council, with Susan Uchitelle appointed as the head. She, along with a team of others, devised a plan that would allow for desegregation of St. Louis suburban schools.

CONCLUSION

Although *Brown v. Board of Education* (1954) was impactful, it did not lead to the immediate end of school segregation. School districts around the country found ways to circumvent the law, in some cases for decades. When Thurgood Marshall asked the Supreme Court to assign a deadline for compliance with desegregation, the Court refused. Local activism and numerous court hearings were necessary to force schools to comply with the law. The decades-long strategies that school districts employed to circumvent school desegregation proved that Marshall's fears were accurate. The Supreme Court ruling that school segregation violated the Constitution set the stage for decades of lawsuits in local school districts around the country. Plaintiffs who sued their school districts were supported by judges who found school districts to be in violation of the Constitution. The Supreme Court's ruling was necessary, but local activists had to fight to ensure that the Constitution was upheld in local school districts.

REFERENCES

Aaron v. Cooper, 261 F.2d 97 (8th Cir. 1958).
Brown v. Board of Education, 347 U.S. 483, 74 S. Ct. 686, 98 L. Ed. 873 (1954).
Brown v. Board of Education, 349 U.S. 294, 75 S. Ct. 753, 99 L. Ed. 1083 (1955).
The Education Trust. (2019, May 17). Segregation, integration, and the Milford 11. Retrieved from https://edtrust.org/extraordinary-districts/special-edition-segregation-integration-and-the-milford-11/
Franklin, V. P. (2021). *The young crusaders: The untold story of the children and teenagers who galvanized the Civil Rights Movement*. Beacon Press.

Green, A. A. (1998, September 27). Little Rock's "lost class" of 1959 recalls turbulent year. *Arkansas Democrat-Gazette*. Retrieved from https://www.arkansasonline.com/news/1998/sep/27/little-rocks-lost-class-1959-recalls-turbulent-yea/

Green, K. (2015). *Something must be done about Prince Edward County: A family, a Virginia town, a civil rights battle*. Harper.

Gordy, S. (1997). Empty classrooms, empty hearts: Little Rock secondary teachers, 1958–1959. *The Arkansas Historical Quarterly, 56*(4), 427–442. Retrieved from https://doi.org/10.2307/40027889

Heaney, G. W., & Uchitelle, S. (2004). *Unending struggle: The long road to an equal education in St. Louis*. Reedy Press.

Keyes v. School Dist. No. 1, Denver, 413 U.S. 189, 93 S. Ct. 2686, 37 L. Ed. 2d 548 (1973).

Liddell v. BD. OF ED., CITY OF ST. LOUIS, ETC., 469 F. Supp. 1304 (E.D. Mo. 1979).

Rias, H. (2014). *Interview with Kimberly Norwood*.

Rias, H. (2019). *St. Louis school desegregation: Patterns of progress and peril*. Palgrave Macmillan.

Swann v. Charlotte-Mecklenburg Bd. of Ed., 402 U.S. 1, 91 S. Ct. 1267, 28 L. Ed. 2d 554 (1971).

Walker, V. S. (2018). *The lost education of Horace Tate: Uncovering the hidden heroes who fought for justice in schools*. The New Press.

CHAPTER 10

Reframing the Myth of School Reform Failure: Clocking School Change

Larry Cuban

One well-worn myth about American education that cyclically appears is that school reforms have failed again and again (Ravitch, 2020). New elementary school reading or math programs, for example, pop up year after year to improve students' performance. Yet these programs slowly fade away and new ones replace them. Over decades, teachers have experienced again and again a "New Math" and a "New Social Studies." Time-worn and popular, however, do not make the myth true. In this chapter, I argue that the concept of "reform failure" has to be reframed historically. Examining school reform over a longer time span to render a judgment about success or failure often produces a complex picture of the life and death of a school reform.

Consider the case of "open space" schools during the 1960s and 1970s. Often labeled a "failure" (Kirk, 2017; Trejos, 2001), open space schools is an exemplar of how tricky it is to judge whether a reform is indeed a success or failure. Open space schooling refers to the interior architecture of the school where large, medium, and small spaces can be used to accommodate large-group, small-group, and independent work by students and teachers. Often confused with open space schools are "open education" and "open classrooms." Although these pedagogical reforms are linked, they are independent of one another. Open education surged in popularity in the late 1960s as a British import of progressive ways of teaching primary- and upper-grade children through small-group and independent work combined with student decision-making in choosing "learning centers" in which they would visit during the school day. The role of the teacher was closer to a coach and guide rather than delivering teacher-directed lessons, using textbooks, administering quizzes and exams, and assigning nightly homework. Many advocates of "open education" also promoted open space schools to get rid of the age-graded school, thus linking the two reforms (Cuban, 2004).

WERE OPEN SPACE SCHOOLS A REFORM FAILURE?

Instead of self-contained, four-walled classrooms of about 900 square feet holding one teacher and 25 students that opened into long hallways, school boards hired architects to design schools without walls with large open spaces—sometimes called pods—where teams of teachers would teach groups of multi-age children, collaborate with one another, and come up with innovative lessons that would engage students and sustain academic achievement.

The newly designed physical structure would alter traditional age-graded schools in organizing students (e.g., multi-age groups rather than separating students by age), how teachers worked together (e.g., more team teaching rather than a solitary teacher assigned to a separate classroom), and how they taught the required curriculum by tailoring instruction and learning to the differences among students in abilities and their needs (e.g., small groups, individual work, and crossing subject boundaries with thematic units rather than whole-group instruction, textbooks, homework, and tests). Student-centered teaching, not the familiar teacher-centered lesson, would become the norm, open space reformers assumed ("Student-Centered Learning," 2018).

Open space architecture and enthusiasm for innovative grouping of children, teaching, and learning customized to individual students spread rapidly across the United States. The District of Columbia schools, for example, spent $163 million in the 1970s to build 17 open space schools. In the same decade, Arlington County (VA) spent $25 million to convert 13 traditional schools into open space facilities. Montgomery County (MD) spent $32 million to build 21 open space schools, and Fairfax County (VA) spent $48 million on 13 buildings that combined both open and closed space (Libit, 1995; Valente, 1979). Yet within a decade, teachers and administrators in these open space schools had put up partitions and built walls to restore self-contained classrooms. By the end of the 1980s, open space schools were a prime example of a seemingly "failed" reform (Tanforan, 2022). I served as superintendent in the Arlington (VA) Public Schools between 1974 and 1981. I visited schools and classrooms a few days each week, and by the end of my first year, I noticed that in at least a half-dozen open space elementary schools built in the late 1960s and early 1970s, partitions made of bookcases, newly installed accordion separators, and plastered walls had been erected to re-create separate classrooms for K–6 teachers.

Fast-forward to the 3rd decade of the 21st century. Open space architecture in brand new buildings and refurbished older buildings has reappeared. Fueled by the ubiquity of computer devices and rhetoric about new technologies in practice such as "blended learning" and "personalized instruction," new schools have been erected that have flexible space—common areas for clusters of classrooms, small conference rooms, and space for individual students to read and do worksheets and write. Multiple-sized spaces have returned in many buildings for both students and teachers to use new technologies in daily lessons. These new spaces again promised that teachers would shift from traditional teacher-centered lessons to student-centered ways of teaching that differentiated instruction and involved children and youth in daily activities (Drummond, 2017; Horn, 2015).

Does this historical recounting of the once innovative open space architecture in schools in the late 1960s mean that it was a "success" for a brief moment in time—a shooting star—but eventually "failed" because walls and self-contained classrooms returned by the 1980s? Or have open space schools "succeeded" in that some district school boards and superintendents—there are over 13,000 in the United States—have rediscovered the virtues of teaching and learning in open space buildings but now have adapted buildings to the technological context of the 21st century?

This example of a once highly touted school reform disappearing and returning raises serious questions about the time scale policymakers, researchers, and practitioners use to judge reform "success" and "failure." In this chapter, I reframe school reform as looking at different clocks to revise the concept of reform "failure" to include *when* such a judgment is made.

CLOCKS?

In some upscale hotels over the registration desk, clocks show times across the globe. Different time zones alert travelers to what time it is in the city they wish to call. There are such clocks for school reform also. These clocks record the different speeds of reform talk, policy adoption, what happens in classrooms, and what students learn. Were these clocks in public view, policymakers, administrators, practitioners, and researchers would see that changes in policy talk and action have occurred but at different speeds, some far too slow for impatient reformers to notice. Framing reform as being recorded by different clocks gives a glimpse into the myth of reforms constantly "failing."

The myth of failure, of course, has a history. It is anchored in commission reports (e.g., National Commission on Educational Excellence, 1983), books (e.g., Ravitch, 2020), and studies (e.g., Hess, 1998) over the last century that document flurries of curricular, organizational, and instructional reforms. The myth also comes from the feverish rhetoric of entrepreneurial reformers who see failure everywhere in order to sell their particular product (e.g., "personalizing learning," charter schools). Yet the hyped policy talk, books, and documents seldom distinguish between major reforms that have stuck such as coed schooling, kindergartens, comprehensive high schools, and desegregated schools and those that have disappeared (e.g., educational radio and television, the platoon school). Historians and thoughtful observers, however, have learned that school reform has a series of clocks that move at different speeds.

MEDIA TIME

This is the fastest reform clock of all, ticking every day and week. What is eye-grabbing and controversial registers on the media clock. Tweets, Instagram, blogs, newspaper and TV headlines document immediate events and opinion, shaping and legitimizing what policymakers put on school reform agendas. Condom distribution in high schools, for example, received strong media exposure as a school policy aimed at solving teenage pregnancies. Policymakers talk about online technologies that will revolutionize teaching and learning. In watching only the media clock, however, policymakers may wrongly conclude that what happens in one school in Arizona or New Jersey happens everywhere and that what is reported actually lasted beyond a few years.

POLICYMAKER TIME

This clock chimes every year campaigns for national, state, and local offices crank up to reelect incumbents or bring fresh faces to public posts. In some places, policymaker clocks tick faster when annual budgets or referenda come up for voter approval. To offer an example, federal and state policymakers have defined schools as an arm for the economy since the mid-1980s. Higher academic standards, copying corporate business practices, and advocating charters have been converted by top officials into campaign slogans. Presidents George H. W. Bush, George W. Bush, Bill Clinton, and Barack Obama between the early 1990s and 2016 have pushed for world-class standards, charters, and business-inspired reforms to raise students' performance. Policymaker time, then, runs on election cycles. "Failure" takes time. No Child Left Behind lasted nearly 15 years before it was replaced by the Every Student Succeeds Act (2015). Other clocks measure whether the overblown reform hype and adopted policies have actually been put into practice in schools and classrooms. Enter the bureaucratic time zone.

BUREAUCRATIC TIME

This clock records administrative actions aimed at putting policy decisions into practice. Often the hands of the faster media and slower policymaker clocks make a complete turn just as the bureaucratic clock passes the first hour. The lag between policymaker time and bureaucratic time occurs because of the complexity in converting federal, state, and district policies into feasible, clear procedures to guide principals and teachers who do the actual work of schooling. The bureaucratic clock chimes when new rules are announced, revised budgets presented, and increased departmental coordination occurs. An example of how the hands on the bureaucratic clock are reduced to a crawl can be seen in desegregation.

Brown v. Board of Education (1954) banned legally segregated schools. Studies have recorded the tortured progress of judicial policymaking as state governors and local school boards across the South wrestled both peacefully and violently with implementing the decision—a school reform—between the 1950s and 1980s. States and districts, prodded by federal court orders, slowly embraced open enrollment, busing, and other remedies for desegregating schools. Over time, district attendance boundaries were redrawn; schools were closed; magnet schools were opened. By the early 2000s, however, a half-century after the *Brown* decision, White flight from cities, growing Black urban ghettos, and the arrival of Asian and Latin American immigrants created de facto, not de jure resegregation in many urban, suburban, and rural districts.

Media, policymaking, and bureaucratic clocks, then, are seldom in sync. Important details that can spell the difference between "successful" and "failed implementation" take considerable time to craft and put into practice. Often political, demographic, and other nonschool factors create greater lag time between the clocks making judgments of "failure" premature.

PRACTITIONER TIME

If media time often looks like speeded-up Chaplinesque frames from 1920s films, then think of practitioner time as slow motion. One example should suffice. As computers spilled into schools during the 1980s, news media carried stories of an imminent revolution in teaching and learning. Districts bought devices like popcorn, placing them in classrooms and labs. In schools saturated with computers, some teachers were using machines for lessons a few hours a week. Even after media predictions of an impending revolution in teaching and learning, however, most teachers remained casual or nonusers.

By the early-1990s, in characteristic hastiness, media had already pronounced the "computer revolution" dead on arrival. That judgment was premature. Over decades, a slow growth in teacher use of computers has registered on the practitioner clock rather than the media's and policymakers' faster tick-tocks of months and a few years. With the ubiquity of tablets and laptops, computer devices are now in the hands of 1st-graders and Advanced Placement physics students. With the hyped-up push for "personalized learning" and online instruction (recall the massive and sudden shift to remote instruction during the COVID-19 pandemic in 2020), classroom devices have become as mundane in the nation's classrooms as the American flag and rows of desks facing whiteboards. "Failure?"

STUDENT LEARNING TIME

Lag times between different clocks is also evident when student learning is considered. Contemporary reformers want students to learn more, better, and faster. But the student-learning clock doesn't tick fast. It is very slow-moving. Because school-based learning cannot be separated from home-based learning, learning may show up years after formal schooling ended since children learn at different rates. Finally, school-based learning contains both intended and unintended effects. Most students, for example, learn to read, calculate, and write sufficiently to pass tests and leave school with credentials. But students learn much that goes untested: taking turns, handling anger in public situations, dealing with schoolyard bullies, not snitching, the rudiments of sex, and scores of other useful social knowledge and skills beyond the classroom curriculum. With all these caveats about the student time zone, how can this clock be read at all?

Think of two hands on this clock. The big hand marks teacher grades and the annual standardized paper-and-pencil tests taken periodically during the school year. As standardized tests have become primary means of estimating student academic performance over the last four decades, the big hand is noted most often by media and policymaker clock-watchers. When a new program is launched in a flurry of publicity, test scores are inspected swiftly to determine effectiveness. The second hand on this clock is much slower because of all the complications noted above. With the lag time of learning stretched over a student's school career and the difficulty of sorting out intended from unintended effects, the second hand creeps across the face of the clock at a snail's pace and often goes unnoticed.

Reading different clocks may help travelers, but it is unclear how reformers knowing that there are separate ones for media, policymakers, administrators, practitioners, and student learning is practical. I offer two reasons why anyone interested in improving classrooms and schools across the United States should consider the metaphor of different clocks to get at the truth, not the myth, of failed school reform:

1. *Paying more attention to slower-paced clocks could shift public debate to substantial matters of classroom teaching and learning.*
The point of the tsunami of policy talk and attention given to charter schools, pay-for-teacher performance, and new technologies in recent years was to improve what happens between teachers

and students. Yet somehow that purpose got lost in the media and policymaker time zones. Because public attention was riveted on those fast-paced clocks, impatience with the slowness of bureaucratic, practitioner, and student-learning time led to premature and inaccurate judgments of reform failure.

2. *Those seeking school reform need to expect that important changes occur in slow motion.* The media clock is watched more closely by policymakers who respond to electoral cycles. The media clock not only identifies what policymakers ought to consider but also certifies that what is reported is legitimate and worthy of policy attention. Moreover, because fast-moving media clocks register more failures than successes—after all, a publicly funded flop will attract readers and viewers—reforms that get adapted and prove successful over time as recorded by the bureaucratic, practitioner, and student-learning clocks are less eye-catching, less newsworthy, and often overlooked.

Hence, concentrating on media time strengthens the belief that most school reforms fail. Policymakers come to assume that belief without fully questioning it. Public and practitioner faith in improving schools flags. Teachers and activist parents ask: What's the use of trying anything different? Such a belief corrodes professional and lay-reformer self-confidence and, worse, is inaccurate. Slower clocks have become seriously devalued by policymakers. But such slow-motion time counts far more for students and their teachers than the faster-paced, high-profile media time or election-driven policymaker time. Reformers need to heed the fact that the timeline of reform has no expiration date.

For these reasons, those committed to school improvement need to ignore the myth of failed reforms and pay attention to the many clocks that record the long journey toward school improvement.

REFERENCES

Cuban, L. (2004). The open classroom: Were schools without walls just another fad? *Education Next, 4*(2), 68–71.

Drummond, S. (2017, March 27). "Open schools" made noise in the '70s; now they're just noisy. *NPR.* Retrieved from https://www.npr.org/sections/ed/2017/03/27/520953343/open-schools-made-noise-in-the-70s-now-theyre-just-noisy

Every Student Succeeds Act, 20 U.S.C. § 6301 (2015). Retrieved from https://www.congress.gov/bill/114th-congress/senate-bill/1177

Hess, F. (1998). *Spinning wheels: The politics of urban school reform.* Brookings Institution.

Horn, M. (2015, June 29). Tear down this wall! A new architecture for blended learning success. *EdSurge.* Retrieved from https://www.edsurge.com/news

/2015-06-29-tear-down-this-wall-a-new-architecture-for-blended-learning-success

Kirk, M. (2017, April 27). Who thought "open classrooms" were a good idea? *Bloomberg*. Retrieved from https://www.bloomberg.com/news/articles/2017-04-27/the-debate-around-open-classroom-design

Libit, H. (1995, October 8). "Innovation" still besets some schools: 1960s trend to open space failed quickly. *Baltimore Sun*. Retrieved from https://www.baltimoresun.com/news/bs-xpm-1995-10-08-1995281062-story.html

National Commission on Educational Excellence. (1983). *A nation at risk: The imperative for educational reform*. Government Printing Office.

Ravitch, D. (2020). *Slaying Goliath: The passionate resistance to privatization and the fight to save America's public schools*. Knopf.

Student-centered learning. (2018, November 4). *Open Space Ed*. Retrieved from https://www.openspaceeducation.com/student-centered-learning/

Tanforan, V. (2022, March 24). Past and present: The legacy of Northgate's architecture. *Northgate High School Sentinel*. Retrieved from https://northgatesentinel.com/3514/feature/past-and-present-the-legacy-of-northgates-architecture/

Trejos, N. (2001, May 13). '70s open classroom fail test of time. *Washington Post*. Retrieved from https://www.washingtonpost.com/archive/local/2001/05/13/70s-open-classrooms-fail-test-of-time/6385962e-f844-4d5b-9217-d680d451c85d/

Valente, J. (1979, December 11). Open space classes: Results doubtful? *Washington Post*. Retrieved from https://www.washingtonpost.com/archive/politics/1979/12/11/open-space-classes-results-doubtful/40c6e267-0287-4e56-89ca-d18ea82ef2c3/

Part III

MYTHS ABOUT TEACHERS

CHAPTER 11

The Myth That Good Teachers Are Born, Not Made

Kate Rousmaniere

Central to the age-old debate over what makes a good teacher is the myth of the "born teacher": the notion that good teaching requires an innate quality that some people have and others don't. We see this myth in popular Hollywood images of teachers such as *Dead Poets Society*, where the inspirational teacher is seemingly naturally talented, and someone who stands above and beyond the rest of the school (Heilman, 1991). The myth of the born teacher is harmful to education because it presents teachers' work as a simplistic act of personal charisma that does not require professional or academic knowledge. In addition, the myth relies on stereotypical assumptions about teachers' social identity, and overlooks the impact that social, economic and political contexts have on teachers' work. Teaching is complex work in a complicated organizational structure that requires skilled training and professional supports to address the needs of students and their families, and the demands of the organization. Teaching requires more than a natural inclination to inspire students, although such attributes are certainly helpful.

The myth of a native talent for a profession is not unique to teaching. There is a universal interest in identifying the source of particular ability among athletes, lawyers, scientists, surgeons, and business leaders. Why do some people seem to be particularly good at what they do? Is it a natural instinct? Were they born with such talent? Does training make a difference? A related debate has centered on the concept of personality traits: Are there certain personality characteristics—such as introversion or extroversion—that lead to success? Other popular "born-made" debates move beyond the nature of talent or expertise to questions about possible genetic predispositions for sexual and gender identity or the characteristics of evil and goodness (Goode, 2015; Wynn, 2006).

But the idea of the born teacher seems to be the most powerful and popular myth, interwoven in popular media, some traditional educational research, and common assumptions about the classroom, even as the working definition of a born teacher is not always clear. In these idealized images, the born teacher is not simply a talented instructor or intelligent person;

rather the mythical born teacher exhibits broader talents of communication, empathy, and "stick-to-itiveness" that they relay to students. Indeed, most depictions of a born teacher go far beyond the academic experience of instruction into less quantifiable measures such as inspiration, personal drive, and communication skills, often aligned with the idea that a teacher is not on the job but on a mission, and that they are naturally caring and giving people.

The myth of the born teacher posits that native abilities are especially needed in tough urban schools, where teachers are needed to inspire students to rise above their marginalized conditions and low self-esteem. In popular movies and TV shows about the specific challenges of city schooling, teachers are portrayed as relying on inspiration and a sense of calling to pull them through the frustrations of their working environment. In *Up the Down Staircase*, a novel published by Bel Kaufman in 1964 and released as a film three years later, Sylvia Barrett, a new teacher fresh out of graduate school is inspired to make change in an urban school where "the building itself is hostile: cracked plaster, broken windows, splintered doors and carved up desks, gloomy corridors, metal stairways, dingy cafeteria. . . . and an auditorium which has no windows." Still, Sylvia keeps her inspirational dream, admitting that at the end of an exhausting day, the one and only compensation of the job is "to make a permanent difference in the life of a child" (Kaufman, 1966, p. 143). And in *Abbott Elementary*, ABC's hit mockumentary sitcom about elementary school teachers in an urban school in the early 2020s, another new teacher is naturally inspired by the challenge of reaching seemingly hopeless students. "It's a calling," she says, adding that becoming a teacher was less of a personal choice and more of a predetermined path: "We do this because we're supposed to." Another Abbott Elementary teacher comments that teaching is like being on "a mission" (My No-Guilt Life, 2022).

In addition to their seemingly natural optimism and inspiration, the idealized teacher also dispenses homegrown wisdom, offering moral lessons of hard work and commitment, applying their own personal perception to motivate their students. In the Hollywood films *Stand and Deliver* (1988) and *Dangerous Minds* (1995), the inspirational teacher comes to class with practical, hands-on advice that belies their distance from students. "Knowledge counts but common sense matters," opines LouAnne Johnson in *Dangerous Minds,* while the math teacher in *Stand and Deliver* advises his inner-city students to reject the tough guy image of the local *barrio* because "tough guys don't do math. Tough guys fry chicken for a living." The implicit message here is that only a born teacher, someone with natural and instinctive communication skills, can not only survive but also make a positive impact in the lives of marginalized youth.

Most famously, in the 1989 film *Dead Poets Society*, an inspirational English teacher leads students to challenge the conservative boundaries of their traditional prep school through his unorthodox teaching methods in which he encourages his students to live their lives on their own terms, drawing on the Latin expression *carpe diem* ("seize the day"), and Walt Whitman's popular poem on leadership and bravery, "O Captain! My Captain!" The students learn poetry, but more importantly, they learn independence. Their dynamic teacher, notably acted by the improvisational comedian Robin Williams, teaches English and personal autonomy (Serey, 1992).

As with many inspirational teacher images, the classroom instruction in these scenarios is about both academic instruction and personal role modeling. The born teacher is portrayed as a naturally motivational individual as well as an educated person who can instruct academic content. It's not just that they know their academics, it's that they know how to relate to students. Accordingly, born teachers do not require academic qualifications or professional development—their talent is natural, individual, and instinctive, the result of individual, personal qualities, and not the result of teacher education or professional development (Burbach & Figgins, 1993).

The trope of the born teacher also holds for instructors in higher education. Like their peers in elementary and secondary schools, college professors are praised for their individual and personal talents in the classroom. It's the professor's unique personality or character in the college classroom that matters, and such qualities are considered to be "God-given" and not anything that can be taught. Accordingly, most college professors enter the college classroom with years of research experience but no instructional experience, and little to no emphasis on teaching in their evaluation and promotion processes. Indeed, even a century of extensive research on measuring college teaching and curricular effectiveness has led to little consensus on or attention to what makes for a good college teacher, and the evaluation of what makes for high-quality teaching ranks "among the greatest unsolved problems of academia" (Gelber, 2020, p. 156). In the professional norms of higher education, a professor's research and scholarly abilities are lauded and reviewed; their teaching is considered less significant and less worthy of review or training. And, significantly, effective college teaching is largely believed to be the result of personality or character and not anything that can be taught (Zimmerman, 2020).

Through the 1960s, because most institutions of higher education assumed that teaching skills came "naturally," few institutions offered professional support for developing professors' classroom skills. In the 1970s, in response to public critiques of higher education instruction, some institutions began to establish faculty development opportunities that offered support for effective teaching practices. A profession of faculty development began to emerge, reflecting a small but emerging understanding that teaching in higher education involved more than natural personality (Evers & Hall, 2009; Ouellett, 2010, pp. 5–6). Ironically, the rise of online teaching in higher education since the mid-1990s seems to have led to an acceleration of instructional support in the particular technical skills that are seen as necessary for online instruction (Mahmood, 2021; Orr et al., 2009; Ortlieb et al., 2020; Rios et. al., 2018). However, as in elementary and secondary education, the popular myth that good teaching is the result of individual character still holds, even if such talent is not always associated with the stereotypical "nutty professor." In the 1986 film *Back to School*, returning student Rodney Dangerfield comments that his eccentric professor played by the comedian Sam Kinison was a good teacher: "He really seems to care. About what? I have no idea."

Across levels of education, the concept of a born teacher has a long history. Indeed, the historical longevity of the myth of the born teacher offers some insight into both the popularity of the concept and its associated problems. The first "born teachers" were, and to a large extent remain, aligned with gender norms. In their larger campaign to change schooling from its harsh punitive origins to one based on new developmental psychology concepts, 19th-century American and European educators often argued that women had a "natural" tendency to be caring and nurturing teachers. Women teachers would be like a "mother made conscious" in what was seen to be their natural affection for children (Steedman, 1985).

Was it merely a coincidence that the argument for the hiring of "naturally caring" women teachers corresponded with the fact that women teachers could be paid less than men? And what about the stipulation, often held in local laws through the mid-20th century, that prohibited the hiring of married women, because, it was argued, women teachers' "innate" motherly tendencies in the classroom would only hold if they were not actual mothers or potential mothers (Ailwood, 2007; Carter, 2016)? So, too, were young women teachers preferred over older women teachers for what was identified as their natural energy and affection for youth (Rousmaniere, 2021).

If young unmarried women made the best and most "natural" teachers, the argument went, so did men make the best school administrators, acting in what was seen as their natural paternal capacity. The athletic, married man offered school districts a vision of the emotionally stable and heteronormative professional leader (Blount, 1999; Feuerstein, 2006; Rousmaniere, 2015; Strober & Tyack, 1980).

The assumption that good teachers were born with natural talents and instincts forced a question about the purpose of teacher education. In the early 1900s, newly founded teacher education departments in colleges of education faced this challenge and justified their work by assessing prospective teachers' individual personality traits to determine what types of people should be recruited and admitted to their programs. Such studies subjected the most intimate parts of a prospective teacher's life to systematic surveying and monitoring, as educational researchers probed aspiring teachers' family backgrounds, grades and behavior in school, physical and mental health, appearance, age, extracurricular activities, reading habits, hobbies, handwriting, and family relationships. Results confirmed what was already a popular belief: that good teaching required a "good attitude, a continually positive outlook, a generous spirit, selflessness, sympathy, judgment, self-control, enthusiasm, and the ability to overcome difficulties without complaint" (Rousmaniere, 1997, p. 130).

Such characteristics were not as neutral as researchers might have believed, since family backgrounds, accented speech, and physical appearance were all subject to discriminatory judgments. For example, school districts often held that a prerequisite characteristic for teaching was that teachers be physically "fit" and "able," thus requiring normative physical and cultural traits (Chmielewski, 2018; Rousmaniere, 2013). Those physical traits expanded into prohibitions against what was determined to be deviant sexuality and ethnic and racial identity, as well as advanced age (Collins, 2011; Rousmaniere, 2021). The concept of the born teacher thus opened the door to the prohibition of specific social identities.

With origins in the 19th century, the born teacher image has lasted well into contemporary times. An online search engine (google NGram Viewer) that charts the frequencies of a term found in printed sources published between 1500 and 2019 shows a height of published references to "born teacher" in the 1890s with a more recent rise of "born teacher" and "natural teacher" since the 1990s. This modern trend aligns with the modern conservative school reform movement that has tended to emphasize personal characteristics of virtue and morals, and a call for traditionally orderly schools where conformity to "standards" of behavior and good habits are stressed. The traditionalist advocacy of the independent, inspirational teacher was highlighted with the 1993 publication of then secretary of education William J. Bennett's *Book of Virtues* and, in 2001, President George W. Bush's presidential declaration of a National Character Counts Week. Such movements emphasized individual teachers' freedom and ability to be innovative as a way to allow their natural talent for teaching to emerge. The rise of popular online teacher inspiration quotes also reflects this contemporary interest in the individual, naturally talented teacher (Kelly-Gangi & Patterson, 2001).

There are a number of problems with the born teacher myth. For one thing, descriptions of a born teacher's attributes are often so broad as to include the qualities of successful employees in almost any profession, including a natural passion for learning, a naturally positive state of mind, flexibility, patience, creativity, work ethic, and love for human interaction. In addition, the myth of the born teacher presumes that there is a limited skill base to the occupation and that teachers do not need to continue to learn, thus minimizing the value of initial teacher education, ongoing professional development, or peer support in teacher organizations. If one believes that teaching talent is based on individual personality traits, then there is less faith that good teaching involves the development of pedagogical skills, or that a teacher's success may be impacted by the social and economic context of students' lives or the organizational context of schools (Dalton, 1995, 2010; Freedman, 1999; Trier, 2001).

Another problem with the myth of the born teacher is that the emphasis on teachers' distinctive personal characteristics distracts public attention from broader social and political forces that have impacted the work of the school. For this reason, a leading teacher education advocate has critiqued the belief that good teachers are born and not made as one of education's "most damaging myths" (Darling-Hammond, 2012, p. ix). Other scholars argue that the idea of the born teacher is a "nativist myth" that furthers Western cultural concepts of individualism and undermines a belief in teachers' ability to grow and change (Nalipay et al., 2022; Scott & Dinham, 2008). Aspiring teachers who believe that teaching talent is self-made further their reliance on their individual experience and not on developing critiques of social inequality or educational policy (Britzman, 1986).

Furthermore, educational researchers have disputed the popular adage that "good teachers are born, not made" with evidence that while natural personality traits matter in the identification of good teachers, an effective teacher also needs to be developed through skills training, academic coursework, and professional development. According to this research, teaching is complex work that needs complex preparation. Good teachers need to be both born *and* bred, and both innate characteristics and effective training lead to expertise in the classroom (Hambrick, 2016). For example, in his 2010 taxonomy of 49 cataloged teaching techniques, Doug Lemov argues that good teachers are not "born with special powers" but are artisans who have perfected the skills of the craft (Lemov, 2010, p. 14). And Max Malikow (2006) argues that:

> There is no such entity as a born teacher. However, by nature, some people possess a combination of personality characteristics that are conducive to effective teaching. Further, these characteristics have been enriched by a lifetime of favorable nurturing. Nevertheless, even the most genetically blessed teacher would benefit from a teacher education program. (p. 1)

The idea of teacher "dispositions," incorporated into teacher education degree programs and state licensure requirements in the late 20th century, also supports the idea that native talent is not all that it takes to be a good teacher. Dispositions are "the professional virtues, qualities, and habits of mind and behavior held and developed by teachers on the basis of their knowledge, understanding and commitments to students, families, their colleagues, and communities" (Sockett, 2006, as cited in Raths, 2007, p. 156). Under the teacher dispositions framework, a good teacher is the result of personal beliefs such as caring, fairness, honesty, responsibility, and social justice that are combined with learned practices such as punctuality, compliance with regulations, and professional appearance (Berliner, 2000; Cummins & Asempapa, 2013; Goe, 2007; McKnight, 2004; Thomas et al., 2012; Wayne & Youngs, 2003). A teacher's personal disposition combined with academic knowledge and professional development leads to good teaching.

In spite of such evidence that a good teacher is a combination of native inclination and acquired skills, lingering faith in the born teacher myth remains embedded in many contemporary understandings of teaching. This popular myth contradicts the lived experience of most teachers who understand that teaching is hard work that requires extensive academic and professional preparation and on-the-job supports.

REFERENCES

Ailwood, J. (2007). Mothers, teachers, maternalism and early childhood education and care: Some historical connections. *Contemporary Issues in Early Childhood, 8*(2), 157–165.

Berliner, D. (2000). A personal response to those who bash teacher education. *Journal of Teacher Education, 51*(5), 358–371.

Blount, J. (1999). Manliness and the gendered construction of school administration in the USA. *International Journal of Leadership in Education, 2,* 55–68.

Britzman, D. (1986). Cultural myths in the making of a teacher: Biography and social structure in teacher education. *Harvard Educational Review, 56*(4), 442–457.

Burbach, H., & Figgins, M. (1993). A thematic profile of the images of teachers in film. *Teacher Education Quarterly, 20*(2), 65–75.

Carter, P. (2016). From single to married: Feminist teachers' response to family/work conflict in early twentieth-century New York City. *History of Education Quarterly, 56*(1), 36–60.

Chmielewski, K. (2018). "Hopelessly insane, some almost maniacs": New York city's war on "unfit" teachers. *Paedagogica Historica, 54*(1–2), 169–183.

Collins, C. (2011). *"Ethnically qualified": Race, merit, and the selection of urban teachers, 1920–1980.* Teachers College Press.

Cummins, L., & Asempapa, B. (2013). Fostering teacher candidate dispositions in teacher education programs. *Journal of the Scholarship of Teaching and Learning, 13*(3), 99–119.

Dalton, M. (1995). The Hollywood curriculum: Who is the "good" teacher? *Curriculum Studies, 3*(1), 23–44.

Dalton, M. (2010). *The Hollywood curriculum: Teachers in the movies* (2nd ed.). Peter Lang.

Darling-Hammond, L. (2012). *Powerful teacher education: Lessons from exemplary programs.* John Wiley & Sons.

Evers, F., & Hall, S. (2009). *Faculty engagement in teaching development activities—Phase 1: Literature review.* Higher Education Quality Council of Ontario.

Feuerstein, A. (2006). School administration and the changing face of masculinity. *Journal of School Leadership, 16*(1), 4–33.

Freedman, D. (1999). Images of the teacher in popular culture. *Journal of Curriculum Theorizing, 15*(2), 71–84.

Gelber, S. M. (2020). *Grading the college: A history of evaluating teaching and learning.* Johns Hopkins University Press.

Goe, L. (2007). *The link between teacher quality and student outcomes: A research synthesis.* National Comprehensive Center for Teacher Quality.

Goode, E. (Ed.). (2015). *The handbook on deviance.* Wiley Blackwell.

Hambrick, D., et al. (2016). Beyond born versus made: A new look at expertise. *Psychology of Learning and Motivation, 64,* 1–55.

Heilman, R. (1991). Movies: The great-teacher myth. *The American Scholar, 60*(3), 417–423.

Kaufman, B. (1966). *Up the down staircase.* Avon.

Kelly-Gangi, C., & Patterson, J. (2001). *Celebrating teachers: A book of appreciation.* Barnes & Noble Books.

Lemov, D. (2010). *Teach like a champion: 49 techniques that put students on the path to college (K-12).* John Wiley & Sons.

Mahmood, S. (2021). Instructional strategies for online teaching in COVID-19 pandemic. *Human Behavior and Emerging Technologies, 3*(1), 199–203.

Malikow, M. (2006). Are teachers born or made? The necessity of teacher training. *National Forum of Teacher Education Journal, 16*(3), 1–3.

McKnight, D. (2004). An inquiry of NCATE's move into virtue ethics by way of dispositions (Is this what Aristotle meant?). *Educational Studies, 35*(3), 212–230.

My No-Guilt Life. (2022, January 15). *Not-so-scholarly quotes from Abbott Elementary on ABC.* Retrieved from https://noguiltlife.com/quotes-from-abbott-elementary/

Nalipay, M., et al. (2022). Are good teachers born or made? Teachers who hold a growth mindset about their teaching ability have better well-being. *Educational Psychology, 42*(1), 23–41.

Orr, R., Mitchell, R. W. S., & Pennington, K. (2009). Institutional efforts to support faculty in online teaching. *Innovative Higher Education, 34*(4), 257–268.

Ortlieb, E., McDowell, A., Stewart, O. G., Preschern, J., & Carhart, D. E. (2020). Towards a model for cultivating online learning communities. *Journal of College Academic Support Programs, 3*(1), 21–29.

Ouellett, M. L. (2010). Overview of faculty development: History and choices. In K. H. Gillespie, D. L. Robertson, & W. H. Bergquist (Eds.), *A guide to faculty development* (2nd ed., pp. 3–20). Jossey-Bass.

Raths, J. (2007). Experiences with dispositions in teacher education. In J. Raths & M. Diez (Eds.), *Dispositions in teacher education* (pp. 153–163). Information Age Press.

Rios, T., Elliott, M., & Mandernach, B. J. (2018). Efficient instructional strategies for maximizing online student satisfaction. *Journal of Educators Online, 15*(3). Retrieved from https://www.thejeo.com/archive/2018_15_3/rios_elliot_mandernach

Rousmaniere, K. (1997). Good teachers are born, not made: Self-regulation in the work of nineteenth-century American women teachers. In K. Rousmaniere, K.

Delhi, & N. De Coninck-Smith (Eds.), *Discipline, moral regulation, and schooling* (pp. 117–133). Routledge.

Rousmaniere, K. (2013). Those who can't, teach: The disabling history of American educators. *History of Education Quarterly, 53*(1), 90–103.

Rousmaniere, K. (2015). Looking at the man in the principal's office. In S. Terzian & P. Ryan (Eds.), *American education in popular media: From the blackboard to the silver screen* (pp. 195–217). Palgrave Macmillan.

Rousmaniere, K. (2021). Old teachers: A feminist research agenda. *History of Education, 50*(4), 501–516.

Scott, C., & Dinham, S. (2008). Born not made: The nativist myth and teachers' thinking. *Teacher Development, 12*(2), 115–124.

Serey, T. T. (1992). Carpe diem: Lessons about life and management from *Dead Poets Society*. *Journal of Management Education, 16*(3), 374–381.

Sockett, H. (Ed.). (2006). *Teacher dispositions: Building a teacher education framework of moral standards.* AACTE.

Steedman, C. (1985). "The mother made conscious": The historical development of a primary school pedagogy. *History Workshop Journal, 20*(1), 149–163.

Strober, M. H., & Tyack, D. (1980). Why do women teach and men manage? A report on research on schools. *Signs: Journal of Women in Culture and Society, 5*(3), 494–503.

Thomas, K., Bush, S., & Bucalos, A. (2012). Can it be fixed? The challenge of remediating problem dispositions and lessons learned. *AILACTE Journal, 9*, 34–48.

Trier, J. (2001). The cinematic representation of the personal and professional lives of teachers. *Teacher Education Quarterly, 28*(3), 127–142.

Wayne, A., & Youngs, P. (2003). Teacher characteristics and student achievement gains: A review. *Review of Educational Research, 73*(1), 89–122.

Wynn, S. (2006). Trait theory. In F. W. English (Ed.), *Encyclopedia of educational leadership and administration* (pp. 1029–1030). SAGE.

Zimmerman, J. (2020). *The amateur hour: A history of college teaching in America.* Johns Hopkins University Press.

CHAPTER 12

The Myth of Heroic Teachers in Special Education

Neil Dhingra, Joel Miller, and Kristen Chmielewski

"I want complete charge of her," Anne Sullivan tells Helen Keller's parents in the motion picture *The Miracle Worker* (1962). Hired by the Kellers to teach their blind and deaf 6-year-old daughter, Sullivan insists Helen be dependent on her for the very air she would breathe. Once Helen is separated from her reluctant family, Sullivan stoically endures wrestling matches and other violent acts to work a "miracle"—teaching Helen that everything in the world around her has a name. Helen becomes a sweet, well-groomed child who climbs into her teacher's lap. By the end of the film, Anne Sullivan and Helen Keller both sign "I love you." *The Miracle Worker* exemplifies the heroic teacher narrative: that a single teacher can achieve pedagogical wonders as they "connect" with seemingly unteachable students through wit and will of personality (Dalton, 2004, p. 23) and perhaps Christlike suffering (Burke & Segall, 2015).

William Gibson's original play (1957/2008) includes a performance note that Helen's "lips tremble" until at last emerges "a baby sound buried under the debris of years of dumbness" (p. 108). Cinematic Helen says, "Wah-wah." The historical Helen Keller did not need to speak. In real life, Sullivan did not believe that Helen's grasping that water has a "name" was miraculous. As Keller would later write, "the absence of a sense need not dull the mental faculties and does not distort one's view of the world" (Keller, 1914, p. 80; Leiber, 1996). In creating the heroic Sullivan, the film necessarily erased the real-life disabled Hellen Keller whose participation in the common good and contributing to public life as a lifelong socialist would be neither miraculous nor necessarily auditory (Nielsen, 2004). What the screenplay deems a "miracle" is thus mischaracterized for ableist, dramatic ends.

The presence of the heroic teacher myth in *The Miracle Worker* is unsurprising—mass media is one of the main ways in which teacher and school stereotypes are reproduced in popular culture (see Chapter 10 in this volume). The heroic teacher narrative is perhaps most misleading and damaging, though, with special education teachers and students with disabilities as characters. Based on other films, mostly documentaries, we suggest an available counternarrative in which teachers and *all* of their students are members of communities who discuss and deliberate with one another, directed to the common good—a good they might enjoy in relation to a town, soccer team, a summer camp, or the give-and-take of a classroom. In those communities, students with disabilities are not merely individuals but are seen as and retain the dignity of teammates and fellow classmates.

WHAT *THE MIRACLE WORKER* MEANT IN 1962

With exceptions like *The Miracle Worker*, disability is conspicuously absent from many popular narratives of schools and teachers, with almost no disabled students as main characters. (See, for example, the list of popular films on teachers cited in the Rousmaniere chapter, this volume.) The heroic teacher narrative is inherently and especially problematic with students with disabilities, and the counternarrative of an inclusive common good is often incompatible with this heroic-teacher narrative. The trope of the heroic teacher thus effectively erases disabled students.

Yet the heroic teacher narrative of Anne Sullivan and others remains appealing in part because of the optimism in reforms that provided access to public education for all students. Public schools were off-limits to disabled students through much of the 20th century (Osgood, 2005, 2008). Through the 1950s and 1960s, parents—voluntarily or coerced by state agencies—sent their disabled children to state hospitals and institutions (Grob, 1991), despite the beginning of the movement to stop state hospitals and institutions from being the primary setting for many disabled children. A public conception of disability as a medical condition commonly justified denials of educational opportunity, especially for disabled students who also carried marginalized race and ethnicity labels (Annamma et al., 2018; Artiles et al., 2016; Baynton, 2001; Porter, 2003). Advocates and activists had to work tirelessly before deinstitutionalization and then passage of the Rehabilitation Act and the federal special education law in the 1970s that finally established most of the current structure of special education processes (Carey et al., 2020; Ellis, 2019).

While special education law presently requires schools to craft individualized education programs (IEPs) with parents of disabled children, the process remains intimidating for those without resources (Ong-Dean et al., 2011). Working with disabled students is a source of apprehension for new teachers (Gately & Hammer, 2005; Idol, 2006; Lalvani, 2015). Thus, even after the past half-century's reforms, it is no surprise that popular culture might represent teaching students with disabilities as a heroic act of will rather than a skilled professional role.

The Miracle Worker appeared in theaters to popular acclaim in 1962 and won five Academy Awards in 1963, well before the major legal and policy victories of advocates. Nevertheless, the movie's heroic portrayal of Anne Sullivan came during the administration of John F. Kennedy (1961–1963), who endeavored to shift perspectives on the contemporary disability label of "mental retardation." Parents in the 1950s and 1960s often shared ways that medical professionals urged institutionalization, even for Kennedy's own sister, Rosemary. In the decade after the Kennedy administration, in landmark federal cases like *PARC v. Commonwealth of Pennsylvania* (1972) that fought the exclusion of disabled children from public schools, parent testimony documented how school administrators rejected parents' sending their children to school as disability preempted any "educability." On the one hand, the Kennedy administration and family attempted to normalize conversation about disability and move away from default institutionalization. On the other hand, the Kennedy administration also framed disability as a condition that might be cured—defining disability as a disease like polio. In a landmark address, President Kennedy "declared a new kind of war," calling "for an all-out attack on one of America's primary and heretofore neglected problems—mental retardation" (Rusk, 1961). For JFK, the country needed a heroic workforce to "seek out the causes of mental illness and of mental retardation and eradicate them" (Kennedy, 1961).

The contradictions in humanizing and also treating disability as a medical problem have persisted: In education, students with disabilities are included in the system of education but often conditionally, with fleeting possibilities of educational success. This complexity has shaped where and how the images appear of teaching students with disabilities: separate and heroic, like Anne Sullivan. When Ellen Handler Spitz writes, "A crucial element of the work is that it must occur apart from Helen's family" (2010, p. 113), the comparison of Sullivan's role is to that of child psychoanalysis, not school. The film may not be recommending the necessity of individual heroism but an ability to regulate emotional distance more characteristic of a therapist in a total institution than any real teacher in a local public school.

THE HEROIC TEACHER NARRATIVE BEYOND *THE MIRACLE WORKER*

The heroic-teacher narrative is misleading about teachers in general, as Kate Rousmaniere discusses in her chapter. As suggested by the difference between the historical Keller–Sullivan relationship and the film relationship, *The Miracle Worker* was the result of several creative choices, and not the only available portrayal of disability or how significant adults (including teachers) make a difference for disabled learners. One of the most celebrated recent cinematic examinations of disability is *Crip Camp* (2020), tellingly, a documentary whose footage dates from 1971, in which disabled youths are allowed to be themselves and participate in the common good in a decidedly—and necessarily—countercultural summer camp, *not* school (Dhingra et al., 2022). The adult counselors appear in the margins of the documentary, contributing to but not controlling camp life, which is characterized by inclusive group discussions led by the campers themselves. Yet *Crip Camp* remains an exception; the image of camp counselors or teachers enabling disabled students to fully participate in the common good of a school was and is elusive.

The Kennedy-era drama *A Child Is Waiting* (1963), which premiered with President Kennedy and Sargent and Eunice Shriver in the audience, returns to images of heroic Anne Sullivan-like teachers who inspire miracles of speech. Set in a fictionalized New Jersey mental institution, the film features a staff person, Jean Hansen, who must be more than a teacher. In search of meaning and not just a job, she establishes a maternal relationship with a silent and abandoned boy, Reuben. Under the tutelage of the stricter Dr. Clark, she has to learn to moderate (not eliminate) her love, lest it "denature" Reuben and prevent him from progressing as he must. Dr. Clark shows Jean the danger of their failing to educate Reuben in the form of a visit to a chaotic and crowded asylum that is Reuben's possible future, where he notes that some of the men had been sterilized like cattle. He declares, in Kennedyesque language, "It's not what you can do for these children, it's what they can do for you." Jean is finally able to get Reuben to progress through *speaking*, as he reads a poem at a pageant, which his father, who had abandoned him, regards as miraculous. The irony of *A Child Is Waiting* is that an earlier version of the film, directed by John Cassavetes, had focused more on the disabled children in cinema verité simply being, as Cassavetes said, "funny . . . human and warm," as opposed to being capable of dramatic progress in an enlightened institution with a heroic and mobilized staff (McCaffrey, 2019, p. 60). (The producer Stanley Kramer reedited Cassavetes's film; Cassavetes would disown *A Child Is Waiting*.)

This trope of the teacher having to be more than a teacher to enable their disabled students to participate in public through speaking proved long-lasting. Even in *Children of a Lesser God* (1986), in which Marlee Matlin as Sarah won the first Oscar awarded to a Deaf person, the teacher, James Leeds, becomes a lover, who desires not just that Sarah become more than the school's cleaning person but also that she *speak*, not least so she can say his name during lovemaking and share his love of Bach. The film ends with James and Sarah having to imagine a place "not in silence, not in sound" where they can be together, a utopia that has been evoked only through scenes of the characters being underwater (Spirko, 2013). Apparently, the real world remains necessarily limited for those who do not speak.

HEROIC TEACHER TROPES AND AN ABLEIST COMMON GOOD

Even without an emphasis on speech, the idea of working toward a common good in the classroom is present in classic films—such as *The Blackboard Jungle* (1955)—but the climaxes and denouements of these films are often subtly ableist and exclusionary of certain disability experiences (McCarthy, 2007; Perlstein, 2000). *The Blackboard Jungle* is remembered for its accuracy or exaggeration of juvenile delinquency, not disability (Golub, 2009). However and importantly, it culminates in nearly an *entire* classroom in a tough school supporting their teacher, including likely one student with a disability. That collective action supported Mr. Dadier as he finally confronts a gang leader student, Artie West. But why must West and a henchman be excluded from what Dadier deems "your classroom"? West earlier voiced his motivations: His bad behavior is a rational choice in bad circumstances, because if he commits crimes and is jailed, at least he will not be drafted (McCarthy, 2007). West is less than rational; he cannot imagine possibilities other than the constricting ones he has been given. Thus, he cannot do what Dadier asks of all his marginalized students—to "examine the story" they had been told, not least about themselves, and to "think for yourself."

When the entire classroom excludes West, an important role is played by a student who, Dadier was told, always grinned because he was an "idiot," but now wields an American flag in fervent defense of his teacher. Nevertheless, the politics of *The Blackboard Jungle* raises questions about the inclusivity of thinking for oneself. West was, a student tells us, "floatin' on Sneaky Pete wine," and the film fails to consider whether he experienced psychological or mental disorder (McCarthy, 2007) or abuse and sociopathy (Perlstein, 2000). In this film, then, we find implicit ableist limits excluding those who seem too difficult for "educability" from the common good.

The appearance of the common good in film has come primarily in the selective absence of disabled students, so disabled film characters historically have appeared in individualistic narratives of inspiration or tragedy. On one hand, there are characters like Auggie in *Wonder* (2017), a 10-year-old boy with a rare facial malformation who is trying to fit in at a private preparatory middle school. By film's end, Auggie has received a medal for inspiring others to be courageous and kind, doubtlessly the result of a heroic teacher in the form of his mother who had put her education, career, and dreams on hold to devote herself to her son's life and homeschooling. Like Anne Sullivan, in one scene, she grabs Auggie's arms after an outburst at the dinner table to force him to sit down, look at her, and reason through his anger. On the other hand, for other students with disabilities, there is the threat of removal from education and the common good—whether to the jail, where Artie West likely ends up, or to the asylums luridly shown in *A Child Is Waiting* and described by Anne Sullivan in *The Miracle Worker* as the fate awaiting a Helen Keller who never spoke. Some, but only some, disabled students, made capable by heroic teachers, can participate in the common good.

DOCUMENTARIES AND AN INCLUSIVE, IF ELUSIVE, COMMON GOOD

If heroic teacher films center individual charisma and the need for miracles, recent documentaries demonstrate it is possible to show teachers in other roles, especially collaboratively fostering the participation of marginalized students in the common good. For disabled students, though, this participation is sometimes shaped by defeats as much as dramatic denouement. Examples of this alternative are two documentaries focusing on Peter Gwazdauskas, a child with Down syndrome: the Oscar-winning *Educating Peter* (1992) and *Graduating Peter* (2001). In these documentaries, Peter is mainstreamed, first in a 3rd-grade Virginia classroom and then toward high school graduation. The plot features neither dramatic moments nor an obvious trajectory. *Educating Peter* openly shows challenges—Peter's 3rd-grade teacher, Ms. Collins, worries she "will not be there when something happens," as when Peter is shown shoving another student in the restroom, where she cannot be. Eventually, the entire class is involved in a discussion on incorporating Peter by collectively withholding attention for his misbehavior. As Ms. Collins notes, his classmates learn to "work better with him." While Peter participates more in class, the film is not an easy celebration of competence but rather "connectedness" with an entire classroom (Kliewer et al., 2015, p. 10) and culminates in Peter making friends with his classmates.

In *Graduating Peter*, an older Peter struggles, for as his mother says, "he has no way to express how he feels, that's the real problem." He is repeatedly shown alone and is medicated for depression at the end of 6th grade. "Peter continues to struggle with depression," the voice-over narration says as he enters senior year of high school. He finally discovers friendship as a soccer team manager, where he can both give and receive. On the team, the coach says, Peter reminds the soccer-focused high school athletes of "bigger issues." A teammate specifies what has been understood: Even if Peter has a different "future," he can still have a "successful life" and "fun living." As he speaks, the documentary editing shows Peter with his teammates at prom—they (and we) have learned that the common good is not bounded by conventionally described talent. This is a lesson that could not be communicated through his formal schooling alone, or to Peter and his fellow students as individuals.

In contrast with the fragile common good in Peter's life, the Peabody Award-winning documentary *Best Kept Secret* (2013) painfully shows the *absence* of the common good. *Best Kept Secret* follows Janet Mino, a dedicated special educator in Newark, New Jersey, and her class of autistic students. The class is graduating—Mino speaks of "falling off a cliff"—to become "consumers" of scarce social services. She fears placements that will not let them reach their potential and tirelessly looks for opportunities. At the film's end, one student is expelled from an already suboptimal adult care center; another is let go from a fast-food job; another splits his time between different places and recently started having seizures.

"I just hope it's enough," Mino says, and we learn she "hopes to start her own recreation and work program for adults with autism." To be a successful teacher, like Anne Sullivan, Mino must become much more than a teacher. And, perhaps, more than human: When a social worker colleague says she must learn "how to let go," this colleague is not a villain. Mino has no answer because here and now a single teacher, even a singularly self-sacrificing and caring one, almost a superhero, cannot be enough. The living, breathing heroic teacher cannot single-handedly replace "connectedness" and the camaraderie of a soccer team.

CONCLUSION

Good teachers do not create magical breakthroughs or perform miracles with students but instead take part in fostering an inclusive common good. This common good is politically resonant and fragile, and a good film about teachers remains honest about its realistic limits. Nevertheless, it has to include students with disabilities, as classic films tellingly find it hard to do, lest it become less than "common." Those who think carefully about the representation of teachers on-screen should actively encourage critical readings of classic films and place *The Miracle Worker*'s auditory miracle and heroic teacher and other mythical portrayals in juxtaposition with the available documentary counternarratives of complex teacher roles and the construction of the common good, such as the education needed to help Peter Gwazdauskas become a soccer team manager. This is how we might unlearn the myth of the heroic teacher and learn a better narrative about the common good, no matter how difficult to imagine because of the contradictory history and separated present of disability.

REFERENCES

Film References

Brooks, R. (Director). (1955). *Blackboard jungle* [Film]. MGM.
Buck, S. (Director). (2013). *Best kept secret* [Film]. Argot Pictures.
Cassavetes, J. (Director). (1963). *A child is waiting* [Film]. United Artists.
Chbosky, S. (Director). (2017). *Wonder* [Film]. Lionsgate.

Haines, R. (Director). (1986). *Children of a lesser god* [Film]. Paramount.
Newnham, N., & LeBrecht, J. (Directors). (2020). *Crip camp* [Film]. Higher Ground Productions.
Penn, A. (Director). (1962). *The miracle worker* [Film]. United Artists.
Wurzberg, G. (Director). (1992). *Educating Peter* [Film]. Direct Cinema Limited.
Wurzberg, G. (Director). (2001). *Graduating Peter* [Film]. State of the Art, Inc.

Print References

Annamma, S. A., Ferri, B. A., & Connor, D. J. (2018). Disability critical race theory: Exploring the intersectional lineage, emergence, and potential futures of DisCrit in education. *Review of Research in Education, 42*(1), 46–71.
Artiles, A. J., Dorn, S., & Bal, A. (2016). Objects of protection, enduring nodes of difference: Disability intersections with "other" differences, 1916 to 2016. *Review of Research in Education, 40*(1), 777–820.
Baynton, D. (2001). Disability and the justification of inequality in American history. In P. K. Longmore & L. Umansky (Eds.), *The new disability history: American perspectives* (pp. 33–57). New York University Press.
Burke, K. J., & Segall, A. (2015). Teaching as Jesus making: The hidden curriculum of Christ in schooling. *Teachers College Record, 117*(3), 1–27.
Carey, A. C., Block, P., & Scotch, R. (2020). *Allies and obstacles: Disability activism and parents of children with disabilities*. Temple University Press.
Dalton, M. (2004). *The Hollywood curriculum: Teachers in the movies*. Peter Lang.
Dhingra, N., Miller, J., & Chmielewski, K. (2022). *Crip Camp* and rethinking disability in the social studies classroom. *Social Education, 86*(3), 158–163.
Ellis, J. (2019). *A class by themselves: The origins of special education in Toronto and beyond*. University of Toronto Press.
Gately, S., & Hammer, C. (2005). An exploratory case study of the preparation of secondary teachers to meet special education needs in the general classroom. *The Teacher Educator, 40*(4), 238–256.
Gibson, W. (2008). *The miracle worker*. Scribner.
Golub, A. (2009). They turned a school into a jungle! How *The Blackboard Jungle* redefined the education crisis in postwar America. *Film & History: An Interdisciplinary Journal of Film and Television Studies, 39*(1), 21–30.
Grob, G. (1991). *From asylum to community: Mental health policy in modern America*. Princeton University Press.
Idol, L. (2006). Toward inclusion of special education students in general education. *Remedial & Special Education, 27*(2), 77–94.
Keller, H. (1914). *The world I live in*. Century.
Kennedy, J. F. (1961). Special message to the Congress on mental illness and mental retardation. *The American Presidency Project*. Retrieved from https://www.presidency.ucsb.edu/documents/special-message-the-congress-mental-illness-and-mental-retardation
Kliewer, C., Biklen, D., & Petersen, A. (2015). At the end of intellectual disability. *Harvard Educational Review, 85*(1), 1–28.
Lalvani, P. (2015). Disability, stigma and otherness: Perspectives of parents and teachers. *International Journal of Disability, Development and Education, 62*(4), 379–393.

Leiber, J. (1996). Helen Keller as cognitive scientist. *Philosophical Psychology, 9*(4), 419–440.

McCaffrey, T. (2019). *Incapacity and theatricality: Politics and aesthetics in theatre involving actors with intellectual disabilities.* Routledge.

McCarthy, K. E. (2007). Juvenile delinquency and crime theory in *Blackboard Jungle. Journal of Criminal Justice and Popular Culture, 14*(4), 317–328.

Nielsen, K. E. (2004). *The radical lives of Helen Keller.* New York University Press.

Ong-Dean, C., Daly, A. J., & Park, V. (2011). Privileged advocates: Disability and education policy in the USA. *Policy Futures in Education, 9*(3), 392–405.

Osgood, R. L. (2005). *The history of inclusion in the United States.* Gallaudet University Press.

Osgood, R. L. (2008). *The history of special education: A struggle for equality in American public schools.* Praeger Publishers/Greenwood Publishing Group.

Perlstein, D. (2000). Imagined authority: *Blackboard Jungle* and the project of educational liberalism. *Paedagogica Historica, 36*(1), 407–424.

Porter, R. (2003). *Madness: A brief history.* Oxford University Press.

Rusk, H. A. (1961, October 15). A new kind of war: President is lauded for urging all-out attack on problem of mental retardation. *The New York Times,* 65.

Spirko, R. C. (2013). "Better me than you:" *Children of a Lesser God,* deaf education, and paternalism. In T. Fahy & K. King (Eds.), *Peering behind the curtain: Disability, illness, and the extraordinary body in contemporary theater* (pp. 16–23). Routledge.

Spitz, E. H. (2010). To teach and to treat: Meditations on *The Miracle Worker. American Imago, 67*(1), 101–115.

CHAPTER 13

The Myth That Elementary Writing Instruction Is Recent

Joan M. Taylor

A long-recurring complaint about the absence of elementary writing instruction, defined as learning to compose original thoughts into written words, has persisted throughout the history of U.S. education and reverberated steadily. This century, several prominent spokespersons and publications have claimed that writing instruction was not present for young children prior to recent decades (Hawkins & Razali, 2012; National Writing Project & Nagin, 2003; Strickland et al., 2001). Historical artifacts in textbooks, journals, student samples, and memoirs, however, point to a far different account.

In the last years of the 20th century, elementary schools witnessed an upsurge of interest in writing instruction as "the writing process" approach (Ravitch, 2000) took hold throughout the United States and led to unprecedented teacher trainings and research. Newly inspired teachers guided young writers through a recursive process of prewriting, drafting, revising, and publishing as innovative materials and instruction flourished. Pioneering classrooms embraced writers' workshop approaches, contemporary children's literature as mentor texts, and scoring rubrics with student samples for comparisons, as well as new ideas about topic selection, sentence-combining practice, and grammar lessons embedded within writing instruction.

Nonetheless, 21st-century experts warned that writing continued to be *the neglected* R in an essential curriculum (National Commission on Writing for America's Families, Schools, and Colleges, 2003). This was followed by federal legislation with accountability and high-stakes writing assessments. With recent mandates for instruction and assessments in place, policymakers and the general public breathed a sigh of relief. *Now*, writing would finally be taught in elementary schools. However, this group of experts and policymakers was not the first generation to make these claims and assumptions.

COLONIAL WRITING INSTRUCTION AND ITS LATER CRITICS

The myth of the absence of writing instruction can be traced as far back as the opening days of the republic. Reviewing colonial American education, historian Cremin (1951) wrote, "Colonial schools had no blackboards or slates, so that the instruction in writing remained largely at the level of rote copying or imitation. That there was much connection of ideas, though, is to be strongly doubted" (p. 185). However, Benjamin Franklin (1749/1927) and schoolmaster Christopher Dock (1770/1908) were both urging the use of letter writing and peer response for young students. As its essential uses for business and personal dealings made letter writing the only means of long- and even short-distance communications, it necessarily required standard instruction and practice.

Through the late 18th and early 19th centuries, written composition was regularly a subject of general teaching advice. John Walker (1810) lamented, "Being engaged for several years in teaching young people a method of writing their thoughts on common subjects, I was desirous of availing myself of the labours of those who had gone before me; but was disappointed" (Walker, 1810, p. iii). He advised writing instruction begin "the moment young people can read fluently, and talk upon common subjects, that they may be enabled to write upon them; and nothing but habit is wanting" (p. iv).

Walker recommended multiple drafts and the importance of revision with teacher oversight. Using Walker's methods, young writers learned rules about sentence-combining, summarizing, expanding a topic, and using outlines for persuasive and expository texts, followed by hearing a classical mentor text read aloud and discussing how the rules were applied. After a second reading, students re-created the text from memory on the left side of a copybook, leaving the right side blank for future revisions.

He also offered student examples with suggested teacher comments. To the theme on "Make no more Haste than good Speed" (Walker, 1810, p. 246), a student wrote, "It may be well said, that in making too much haste we lose our time; for nothing can be more absurd than to hurry over a thing, and do it in an improper and bungling manner" to which Walker advised the teacher to direct the pupil's revisions with the following suggestion.

> It may be said, that in endeavouring to gain time by making too much haste; we lose time; for nothing can be more unfavorable to business than to hurry it over, and to do it in an improper and bungling manner. (p. 247)

Formal schooling was not the only means of acquiring writing instruction. Children's diaries and family memoirs from that era describe writing used to reinforce religious training through letters and summaries of sermons and readings (e.g., Earle, 1894; Mather, 1706/1911; Reynolds, 1712). At home and at school, children were learning the value of the written word as an accountability tool as well as the importance of revision, and relied on families and peers for feedback assistance.

Anna Green Winslow, in her diary accounts from 1771 to 1773, told how she received response on her writing from her father and mother based on her daily letter writing as well as from her aunt on her journaling (Earle, 1894). In an uncorrected March 26 entry, Anne related a sermon she heard the previous day and how her aunt had responded.

> Aunt has been up stairs all the time I have been writeing & recollecting this—so no help from her. She is come down now & I have been reading this over to her. She said she is glad I remember so much, but I have not done the subject justice. She sais I have blended things somewhat improperly—an interuption by company. (p. 51)

EARLY 19TH-CENTURY WRITING INSTRUCTION AND ITS LATER CRITICS

Likewise, those critical of early 19th-century writing instruction consistently claimed that it was missing from the elementary curriculum. Catharine Beecher (1874), in remarks endorsing instruction in her Hartford Seminary for young girls, stated, "The art of composition has seldom been made the subject of *instruction* in schools" (p. 38), and she offered evidence that this was not the case at Hartford. Nevertheless, literacy researchers Langer and Allington (1992) wrote, "In the 19th century, curriculum concerns in writing focused almost entirely on the college level, with minimal attention to its high school antecedents and almost no concern with elementary education" (p. 688).

When one looks for aspects of writing instruction and pedagogical advice that existed in the new republic during the first half of the 1800s, there is a developing sense of nationalism in American education. Modern American textbooks replaced older British ones, and a new U.S. school system was formulated. Common school advocates, Horace Mann and Henry Barnard were adamant in their support for elementary writing instruction. Like future writing instructors, Barnard (1841/1993), in his renowned *Connecticut Common School Journal*, recommended older pupils keep journals of daily occurrences and provided implicit endorsement for the youngest to write often on topics such as observations on their way to school or recently read lessons.

In her study of elementary composition textbooks for children, Schultz (1999) presented a variety of what she termed "first books" from the early 19th century, and not only documented their previously unrecognized existence, but furnished convincing evidence that these small books made illustrations more available as a heuristic for narrative and descriptive writing assignments. She also noted that unlike most previous composition textbooks, these first books (Brookfield, 1855/1866; Frost, 1839; Morley, 1838; Phippen, 1854) began with actual writing rather than rules and explanations. One of the books she studied, John Frost's *Easy Exercises in Composition*, encouraged students to forego any prewriting and simply "write freely and boldly, using expressions as suit his own feelings, and with his own understanding of the subject" (Frost, 1839, p. 58), thereby foreshadowing similar free-writing approaches in the 1920s.

The advent of teacher training institutions brought with it an influx of teaching textbooks, creating a more formal style of pedagogical guidance. In Jacob Abbott's (1833/1856) often reprinted book *The Teacher*, he urged that writing topics be related to student interests and personal events rather than abstract ideas, and suggested young learners examine their own communities' social issues to write about real events. Like some workshop practices today, he advised weekly reports on the state of the classroom and its progress, where student committees could suggest and write about areas of excellence, concern, and possible improvements for consideration by the entire class.

Predictably, as the whole-word method of reading instruction was gaining popularity, the whole-sentence system followed in writing instruction as described in Samuel S. Greene's (1848) popular text *First Lessons in Grammar*, where writers began with a complete thought and then expanded on it with words and phrases to extend the expression. Richard Green Parker's (1833) *Progressive Exercises in English Composition*, written expressly for beginners, also included sentence-combining activities with students deciding which revisions were most effective and engaging in practical lessons on conventions. Contemporary literary models of prose and poetry were interspersed, and in some cases writers were directed to revise or edit those examples. The book also offered prewriting advice that included steps in analyzing the topic, organizing the text, and composing; and it stressed exercise-based composition practice rather than rote memory in grammar exercises. Connors (1986), in a study of 19th-century textbooks, deemed Parker's text a seminal work in composition instruction, and explained how its pedagogy was subsequently reconstructed as a college exercise book, *Aids in English Composition*, to meet the growing needs of uninformed college teachers, thus suggesting elementary composition as a foundation for, rather than a younger sibling to, secondary composition instruction.

LATE 19TH-CENTURY WRITING INSTRUCTION AND ITS LATER CRITICS

The myth was also directed at those responsible for teaching elementary writing after the turbulent years following the Civil War, as once again earlier educators were accused by their successors of ignoring the subject. Rugg and Shumaker (1928), among the most vocal future critics, noted "only [in] our own new schools has the gap between the school and the growing child been closed" (p. 12). In addressing previous 19th-century practices in writing instruction, they observed,

> Writing when once begun in the primary grades, consisted of copying, reproducing, imitating—the content nearly always extraneous to the child's own personal experience. Writing was for the child a routine skill, not an opportunity to say what was on his mind concerning the things he did, the things he liked, the things he thought about. (p. 246)

Prominent secondary English professor and English education historian Arthur Applebee (2000) remarked, "During much of the 19th century, the teaching of writing focused on penmanship and little else. Later, writing instruction was often postponed until the middle and upper grades, when students have presumably achieved basic literacy in reading" (p. 90). Moreover, Burrows (1977) alleged there were few or no textbooks or instruction on elementary composition throughout the 1800s.

No textbooks? Really? Well no, not really. In the last half of the 19th century, George Quackenbos's *First Lessons in Composition*, issued in 1851, sold over 200,000 copies by 1888. Actually, there were many new and revised elementary textbooks that dealt directly with writing instruction. Previous *grammars* were being rebranded as *language* textbooks filled with oral and written composition instruction that integrated reading and writing. Some reading textbooks like *McGuffey's Eclectic Readers* were intentionally paired with grammar texts like *Pinneo's Primary Grammar of the English Language for Beginners* (Carr et al., 2005). Furthermore, while the continued debate over formal grammar instruction, especially the memorization and recitation of rules, stretched far into the 20th century, by the late 19th century it was being postponed until 6th grade, where it was embedded within composition instruction.

Eminent public figures like Edwin Sheldon who led the Oswego Movement and Colonel Francis Parker of child-centered Quincy Method fame sparked national attention for their instructional approaches with student writing that involved observations and experiences. Sheldon (1862/1871) offered step-by-step training for teachers in administering an object lesson based on Pestalozzian principles. Students, as a collaborative group, observed a commonplace item such as a sponge or an ear of corn, and after an inquiry-based discussion on its attributes and uses and a sharing of illustrative words, they were assigned to individually or collectively compose descriptions. The following is a popular textbook example.

1. List the parts of the following objects to be enumerated.

A ship.	A plough.	A clock.
A book.	A chair.	A carriage.
A house.	A tree.	An ear of corn.
A table.	A fence.	A sleigh.

2. Mention the uses of the same objects. A composition of several lines may be written on each, in describing the various uses, &c. (Weld, 1842/1852, p. 127)

In documenting Parker's Quincy school, biographer Leila Patridge noted that interspersed throughout the school day, children were directed to "talk with the pencil" about their experiences.

> One day the teacher holds a conversation of three or five minutes long—as time serves—with the children, concerning an object. The next day, or the day after that, whichever is most convenient, at some Busy-Work period, the teacher says to her pupils, "Write me all you can think of about"—that object. (Patridge, 1885, p. 425)

Children also regularly wrote about their experiences. In the following uncorrected example, a 3rd-year student wrote to the prompt "What I Did at Recess."

> First I went out. Then I went around the school. After that I went down to the pump where they were making ponds. I saw Tommy make a big pond. Then I came in. When I was coming in their was a boy lost his hat and had to go back after it. (p. 573)

Clearly, writing was a consistent function in their instructional day and was encouraged as a meaning-making activity as well as a form of communication.

Even practices similar to today's prewriting were part of the pedagogical traditions in writing instruction. Lilienthal and Allyn's (1862) *Things Taught: Systematic Instruction in Composition and Object Lessons*, popular well over a century ago, contained clear instructions to prewrite with outlines and questions, arrange ideas and compose first drafts, continue with revisions and editing, and conclude by finally reading their pieces aloud prior to submitting them to their teachers.

From a policy perspective, just prior to the 20th century, National Education Association's illustrious *Committee of Fifteen Report* recommended much practice in writing exercises and original composition in the elementary grades. "Daily from the first year the child will prepare some lesson or portion of a lesson in writing" (Harris et al., 1895/1969, p. 62). The report advised that written work from the 1st to the middle of the 5th year should include practice in letter writing, written reviews, reports of oral lessons, and paraphrases of literature in reading textbooks, as well as daily practice in writing about topics and adopting styles connected to content areas.

In addition to cross-curricular writing assignments, notable curriculum specialist W. W. Charters (1912) made the then-radical recommendation that lessons should include self-selected student topics of interest with value to the author as well as to the rest of the class, rather than assigned information written simply for the teacher. This was a clear departure from some previous practices, and it too was reintroduced and debated over the remainder of the century.

20TH-CENTURY WRITING INSTRUCTION AND ITS LATER CRITICS

Looking back a few decades, Berninger and Winn (2006) suggested that prior to the 1980s, writing instruction was not emphasized until secondary schooling. In referencing Hillocks (1986), they explained that due to the groundbreaking work of Donald Graves in the 1970s and 1980s, writing finally became part of elementary instruction. Distinguished English professor James Squire (2003), citing other highly respected researchers (Chall et al., 1977; Graves, 1978), concurred, "Indeed, not until the mid-1960s was composition stressed below the high school levels" (p. 3).

Their progressive predecessors from the early 20th century would have disagreed. Those educators were revising and restructuring curriculum and combining reading, writing, speaking, listening, spelling, grammar, and penmanship into the integrated language arts. As part of progressive reforms, student-written materials were suggested as replacements for standard reading textbooks, and language arts instruction was incorporated into other content areas such as history, geography, and nature studies (Goodykoontz, 1931; Hicks, 1932; Hosic, 1922; Whipple, 1920, 1934).

Child-centered education and socialized learning received a wide audience in the education community. Teachers became guides rather than instructors of writing and were advised to allow students to select their own topics based on personal experiences and interests (Hatfield, 1935; Holmes, 1936; Weeks, 1936). Democratically constructed class committees assumed responsibilities for writing projects and products. Prewriting activities were expanded as were peer reviews, termed *socialized corrections*, during various draft revisions. Student writing was published in class books, school newspapers, and local community news. According to education historian Larry Cuban (1993), it was progressive elementary rather than secondary teachers who more enthusiastically replaced teacher-centered, rote-memory, and lecture-style instruction with innovative teaching methods such as incorporating writing instruction into other content areas and units of study.

Young learners in at least some progressive schools, who were not yet able to write themselves, dictated their individual or group ideas to their teachers, and class experience stories were created at all grade levels. Observational studies and teacher memoirs from this era cite numerous instances where *class stories* in both urban and rural schools were adopted (Broening et al., 1939; Mika, 1976; Simpson, 1932; Smith, 1943). Later likenesses appeared in the *language experience approach* and *interactive writing lessons* within a community of writers.

In the mid-1920s, the creative writing movement, inspired by Hughes Mearns (1925) and his popular book *Creative Youth*, led to free-writing practices, a method reinvented from the 1800s and subsequently rediscovered in the 1970s. It encouraged independent, original thinking in children's writing, often in poetic form, and resulted in a flood of published student writing anthologies. Although this emphasis on creative self-expression led to some controversy on when and how much to disregard technical errors in favor of instilling personal inspiration, the vast majority of educators found correct conventions necessary for final copies after initial drafts had been generated from discussions or stimulated through directed activities. Myers (1996) has traced the writers' workshop model to a version that was commonly used in progressive classrooms during the first quarter of the 20th century. He also noted the shift in emphasis during this time, from product to process as a special focus of creative writing methods.

The written product, however, continued to be emphasized in new assessment experiments with the advent of the Hillegas-Thorndike and Harvard-Newton writing scales, which offered metrics and examples to quantify high school student writing proficiency. Elementary writing assessments (Breed & Frostic, 1917; Hudelson, 1923; Leonard, 1925; Van Wagenen, 1921) soon followed, and were analyzed, reinvented, replicated, and improved on for possible use. Several researchers (Guiler, 1926; Leonard, 1917; Van Wagenen, 1921; Willing, 1918) suggested analytically measuring the separate features of structure, content, and mechanics as separate values, thus anticipating the analytic-trait scoring method that would much later become a diagnostic tool for elementary writing teachers. While experts (Hosic, 1915; Scott, 1913) issued warnings of their possible misuse, the assessments were ultimately ignored by most busy teachers, though these evaluative tools were destined to resurface later in the century as an element of high-stakes testing in an era of accountability.

CONCLUSION

There are a number of possible reasons why each time period seems to have accepted the myth that elementary writing instruction was previously nonexistent, the most obvious being each era's recent and past experts cyclically criticizing its current neglect and thus concluding it was also absent in all earlier times. Prominent among the authorities were secondary and postsecondary education reformers who repeatedly noted a lack of proficiency in their incoming students and concluded basic instruction itself was missing in earlier grades. Administrators, curriculum writers, and publishers had little reason to doubt each era's authorities and promoted "new" practices for courses of study and textbooks.

Another contributing influence is the tendency for each generation to interpret the past through the lens of their present contexts and values, and that orientation to the present moment may have served as an expedient platform for viewing previous generations' ideas and experiences as inconsequential. In its wake, former methods could be unknowingly reinvented or possibly overlooked. Like multiple independent discoveries in the fields of math and science, new generations of literacy educators with similar teaching and learning circumstances used the same practical reasoning to come up with identical solutions, and in disregarding the past, believed their imitations were innovations.

The case can also be made that in striving for independence and agency, each generation sought to frame their recent writing instruction methods as unique by connecting them to novel tools of their time. With evolving educational landscapes and the introduction of new technologies, be they visual prompts, discussion venues, writing implements, or the most up-to-date publishing formats, the illusion of originality was solidified and parallel methods from the past ignored.

It is easy to predict, with advanced technologies and the advent of artificial intelligence (AI), there will be new arguments about the need to even teach writing, followed by even more accusations about the nonexistence of its instruction. While current research (Graham, 2019; Graham et al., 2012; MacArthur et al., 2016; Troia, 2009) is praiseworthy in defining how writing should be taught, it is not clear the instructional practices are actually new or will meet with universal acceptance any more than those preceding them.

Admittedly, some writing instruction at the elementary level may have been neglected and, like all past and present subjects, could have been better taught and was not available to all students; however, it *did* exist as a construct in remarkable ways. There is abundant evidence in historical documents, timeworn teacher and student textbooks, and selected personal memoirs. It was delivered by dedicated teachers through the established methods of their time; and significantly, those methods are not very different from today's research-based practices.

REFERENCES

Abbott, J. (1856). *The teacher: Moral influences employed in the instruction and government of the young. A new and revised edition.* Harper & Brothers, Publisher. (Original work published 1833)

Applebee, A. N. (2000). Alternative models of writing development. In R. Indrisano & J. R. Squire (Eds.), *Perspectives on writing: Research, theory, and practice* (pp. 90–110). International Reading Association.

Barnard, H. (1993). Third annual report, 1841. In G. Willis, W. H. Schubert, R. V. Bullough, C. Krindel, & J. T. Holton (Eds.), *The American curriculum: A documentary history* (p. 42). Greenwood Press. (Originally published in *Connecticut Common Journal*, 1841)

Beecher, C. E. (1874). *Educational reminiscences and suggestions.* J. B. Ford and Company.

Berninger, V. W., & Winn, W. D. (2006). Implications of advancements in brain research and technology for writing development, writing instruction, and educational evolution. In C. A. MacArthur, S. Graham, & J. Fitzgerald (Eds.), *Handbook of writing research* (pp. 96–114). Guilford Press.

Breed, F. S., & Frostic, F. W. (1917). A scale for measuring the general merit of English composition in the sixth grade. *Elementary School Journal, 17*(5), 307–325.

Broening, A. M., Falk, E. M., Hatfield, W. W., McEntyre, D. E., & Southwick, M. (1939). *Conducting experiences in English: A report of a committee of the National Council of Teachers of English, based on the contributions of 274 cooperating teachers of English.* Appleton-Century Company.

Brookfield, F. (1866). *First book in composition, for the use of schools. On an entirely new plan.* A. S. Barnes & Co. (Original work published 1855)

Burrows, A. T. (1977). Composition: Prospect and retrospect. In H. A. Robinson (Ed.), *Reading & writing instruction in the United States: Historical trends* (pp. 17–43). International Reading Association.

Carr, J. F., Carr, S. L., & Schultz, L. M. (2005). *Archives of instruction. Nineteenth-century rhetorics, readers, and composition books in the United States.* Southern Illinois University Press.

Chall, J. S., Conard, S. S., & Harris, S. H. (1977). *An analysis of textbooks in relation to falling SAT scores.* College Entrance Examinations Board.

Charters, W. W. (1912). *Methods of teaching: Their basis and statement developed from a functional standpoint* (3rd ed.). Row, Peterson & Company.

Connors, R. J. (1986). Textbooks and the evolution of the discipline. *College Composition and Communication, 37*(2), 178–194.

Cremin, L. A. (1951). *The American common school: An historic conception.* Teachers College, Columbia University.

Cuban, L. (1993). *How teachers taught: Constancy and change in American classrooms 1890–1990.* Teachers College Press.

Dock, C. (1908). A simple and thoroughly prepared school-management: Clearly setting forth not only in what manner children may best be taught in the branches usually given at school, but also how they may be well instructed in the knowledge of godliness. In M. G. Brumbaugh (Ed.), *The life and works of Christopher Dock: America's pioneer writer on education with a translation of* his works into the English language (pp. 90–156). J. B. Lippincott Company. (Original work published 1770)

Earle, A. M. (1894). *Diary of Anna Green Winslow: A Boston school girl of 1771.* Houghton Mifflin Company.

Franklin, B. (1927). *Proposals for the education of youth in Pennsylvania.* Harvard University Press. (Original work published 1749)

Frost, J. (1839). *Easy exercises in composition: Designed for the use of beginners.* W. Marshall & Co.

Goodykoontz, B. (1931). Some factors affecting the elementary English curriculum. *The Elementary English Review, 8*(1), 3–6.

Graham, S. (2019). Changing how writing is taught. *Review of Research in Education, 43,* 277–303.

Graham, S., McKeown, D., Kiuhara, S., & Harris, K. R. (2012). A meta-analysis of writing instruction for students in the elementary grades. *Journal of Educational Psychology, 104*(4), 879–896.

Graves, D. (1978). *Balance the basics: Let them write.* Ford Foundation.

Greene, S. S. (1848). *First lessons in grammar, based upon the construction and analysis of sentences; designed as an introduction to the "analysis of sentences."* Cowperthwait, DeSilver and Butler.

Guiler, W. S. (1926). Analysis of children's writings as a basis for instruction in English. *Journal of Educational Method: A Journal of Progressive Public Schools, 5,* 259–264.

Harris, W. T., Draper, D. A. S., & Tarbell, H. S. (1969). *Report of the Committee of Fifteen on elementary education.* Arno Press & The New York Times. (Original work published 1895)

Hatfield, W. W. (1935). *An experience curriculum in English: A report of the curriculum commission of the National Council of Teachers of English.* Appleton-Century-Crofts.

Hawkins, L. K., & Razali, A. B. (2012). A tale of 3 p's—Penmanship, product, and process: 100 years of elementary writing instruction. *Language Arts, 89*(5), 305–317.

Hicks, H. (1932). Classroom procedures in the elementary school. National Education Association of the United States. *Proceedings of the Seventieth Annual Meeting Held at Atlantic City, New Jersey, June 25–July 1, 1932, 70,* 438–440.

Hillocks, G., Jr. (1986). *Research on written composition: New direction for teaching.* National Conference on Research in English.

Holmes, E. E. (1936). Writing experiences of elementary children. *Elementary English Review, 13*(3), 107–111.

Hosic, J. F. (1915). The essentials of composition and grammar. In S. C. Parker (Ed.), *The fourteenth yearbook of the National Society for the Study of Education* (pp. 90–115). University of Chicago Press.

Hosic, J. F. (1922). An experiment in cooperation VI: Standards in composition. *Journal of Educational Method, 1*(6), 239–245.

Hudelson, E. (1923). English composition. Its aims, methods, and measurement. In G. W. Whipple (Ed.), *Part I, The 22nd yearbook, National Society for the Study of Education* (pp. 1–172). Public School Publishing Company.

Langer, J. A., & Allington, R. L. (1992). Curriculum research in writing and reading. In P. W. Jackson (Ed.), *Handbook of research on curriculum: A project of the American Educational Research Association* (pp. 687–725). Macmillan.

Leonard, S. A. (1917). *English composition as a social problem*. Houghton Mifflin.

Leonard, S. A. (1925). Building a scale of purely composition quality. *English Journal, 14*(10), 760–775.

Lilienthal, M. E., & Allyn, R. (1862). *Things taught: Systematic instruction in composition and object lessons*. Sargent, Wilson & Hinkle.

MacArthur, C. A., Graham, S., & Fitzgerald, J. (Eds.). (2016). *Handbook of writing research* (2nd ed.). Guilford Press.

Mather, C. (1911). *Diary of Cotton Mather: Volume 1 1681–1709*. Frederick Ungar.

Mearns, H. (1925). *Creative youth*. Doubleday Doran Company.

Mika, H. K. (Ed.). (1976). *Montana memories*. Montana Retired Teachers Association.

Morley, C. (1838). *A practical guide to composition, with progressive exercises in prose and poetry; embellished with cuts*. R. White.

Myers, D. G. (1996). *The elephants teach*. Prentice-Hall.

National Commission on Writing for America's Families, Schools, and Colleges. (2003, April). *The neglected "R": The need for a writing revolution*. Retrieved from https://eric.ed.gov/?id=ED475856

National Writing Project, & Nagin, C. (2003). *Because writing matters: Improving student writing in our schools*. Jossey-Bass.

Parker, R. G. (1833). *Progressive exercises in English composition* (3rd ed.). Lincoln and Edmands.

Patridge, L. E. (1885). *The "Quincy Methods" illustrated: Pen photographs from the Quincy schools*. E. L. Kellogg & Co.

Phippen, A. R. (1854). *The illustrated composition book: Containing directions, subjects and blank leaves for composition with original illustrations by Whiney, Jocelyn & Annin*. Henry W. Law.

Quackenbos, G. P. (1880). *First lessons in composition, in which the principles of the art are developed in connection with the principles of grammar; embracing full directions on the subject of punctuation; with copious exercises*. D. Appleton and Company. (Original work published 1851)

Ravitch, D. (2000). *Left back: A century of failed school reforms*. Simon & Schuster.

Reynolds, T. (1712). *Practical religion exemplify'd in the lives of Mrs. Clissold, and Mrs. Mary Terry: With their funeral sermons*. John Laurence at the Angel in the Poultry, and William Laurence at the Three Bowls in Rood Lane.

Rugg, H., & Shumaker, A. (1928). *The child-centered school: An appraisal of the new education*. World Book Company.

Schultz, L. M. (1999). *The young composers: Composition's beginnings in nineteenth-century schools*. Southern Illinois University Press.

Scott, F. N. (1913). Our problems. *English Journal, 2*(1), 1–10.

Sheldon, E. A. (1871). *A manual of elementary instruction, for the use of public and private schools and normal classes; containing a graduated course of object lessons for training the senses and developing the faculties of children*. Charles Scribner & Co. (Original work published 1862)

Simpson, M. E. (1932). Building an elementary school curriculum. *Educational Method: A Journal of Progressive Public Schools, 12*(2), 82–88.

Smith, E. E. (1943). Procedures for encouraging creative writing in the elementary school (Publication Number: 10101977) [Doctoral Dissertation, Northwestern University-Evanston, Illinois]. ProQuest Dissertations and Theses Global.

Squire, J. R. (2003). The history of the profession. In J. Flood, D. Lapp, J. R. Squire, & J. M. Jensen (Eds.), *Handbook of research on teaching the English language arts* (2nd ed., pp. 3–17). Lawrence Erlbaum.

Strickland, D. S., Bodino, A., Buchan, K., Jones, K. M., Nelson, A., & Rosen, M. (2001). Teaching writing in a time of reform. *Elementary School Journal, 101*(4), 385–397.

Troia, G. A. (Ed.). (2009). *Instruction and assessment for struggling writers. Evidence-based practices.* Guilford Press.

Van Wagenen, M. J. (1921). The Minnesota English composition scales; their derivation and validity. *Educational Administration and Supervision, 7*(9), 481–499.

Walker, J. (1810). *English themes and essays: Or, the teacher's assistant in composition; being a system of easy rules for writing exercises, illustrated by examples, adapted to the use of both sexes, at school: To which are added hints for correcting and improving juvenile composition.* J. T. Buckingham, Winter-Street.

Weeks, R. M. (Ed.). (1936). *A correlated curriculum: A report of the committee on correlation of the National Council of Teachers of English.* Appleton-Century.

Weld, A. H. (1852). *Weld's English grammar, illustrated by exercises in composition, analyzing, and parsing.* Sanborn & Carter. (Original work published 1842)

Whipple, G. M. (Ed.). (1920). *Part I: New materials of instruction prepared by the society's committee of new materials of instruction. The 19th yearbook of the Society for the Study of Education.* Public School Publishing Company.

Whipple, G. M. (Ed.). (1934). *The activity movement. The 33rd yearbook of the National Society for the Study of Education, Part II.* Public School Publishing.

Willing, M. H. (1918). The measurement of written composition in grades IV to VIII. *English Journal, 7*(3), 193–202.

CHAPTER 14

The Myth That Schoolteachers Take the Summer Off

Christine A. Ogren

"If a crystal ball could tell you the truth about anything, what would you want to know?" Arpi Meskimen asks Jayden Kwapis at the end of an episode of the NBC television comedy *Mr. Mayor* (Fey & Adams, 2021). Kwapis's offbeat answer, "Where do teachers go during the summer?" rests on the longstanding and widespread assumption that during the summer, teachers are entirely separated from their work in the schools. Without a trace of humor, a letter to the editor of the *Los Angeles Times* states this notion as a given. In response to an op-ed's argument that the public school system takes advantage of teachers, Gerry Swider (2018) of Sherman Oaks writes that although educators face "many challenges," they "have a vacation of two or three months every year." Adding, "That must be considered when evaluating teacher salaries," Swider also suggests that the long vacation justifies teachers' meager wages. Indeed, economist Michael Podgursky (2003) places "summers off" first on his list of reasons why education policymakers should not prioritize increasing salaries for teachers. The assumption that teachers do not work during the summer months has also contributed to their occupation's standing as less than fully professional. As Dan Lortie (1975) and John Goodlad (1990) note in their classic studies, teachers' short official work year contributes to their "special but shadowed social standing" and "not quite" professional status, respectively. However, even as schoolteachers do not have regular classroom responsibilities or receive paychecks for the summer months, that they take the summer entirely "off" from their professional roles is a misconception that discredits the many ways in which teachers contribute to the education system through their summer activities.

The modern school year with its long summer break resulted from 19th-century reforms that created public school systems with standardized procedures, including calendars (Gold, 2002). Nine-month sessions became the norm by the late 1870s, just as the teacher workforce became "feminized" (Clifford, 2014). School leaders, who were almost all men, instituted onerous controls on teachers' work and personal lives—including barring women teachers from marrying until well into the 20th century—in the interest of "professionalization," which really meant adherence to administrators' directives (D'Amico Pawlewicz, 2020). Paternalistic leaders even issued directions for how teachers should spend the summer on the premise articulated by the editors of *The Elementary School Teacher* in 1914: "Whatever might be the terms of the contract, teachers are in fact employed by the year" (Judd et al., 1914). A New York court sided with administrators in 1938 when it ruled, based on the recent rise of teacher tenure, that "No teacher has an inherent or statutory right to a vacation of two months or more" (*Juddson v. Board of Edu. of City of New York*, 1938). Teachers had their own ideas about how best to spend the summer as well as what it meant to be a professional educator, however, and they adapted administrators' prescriptions accordingly. Contrary to the myth that they simply take the summer off, teachers since the 1870s have used their summer activities to plant the seeds for a teaching force of broad-minded, worldly, independent professionals, to the ultimate benefit of their students and the schools.

Reformers' original intention in incorporating summer break into the school calendar was to allow students and teachers time to rest and recuperate—not, as Kenneth Gold explains in another chapter in this collection, to engage in farmwork. Administrators prescribed a summer of "quietude" to counteract the heavy tax that they believed teaching placed on teachers' physical and mental health; gender ideology at the time suggested that women teachers were especially vulnerable to nerve ailments and mental strain (Gold, 2002). An Iowa education journal described summer as "the season for *rest*, both physical and intellectual" ("What Shall We Do," 1878). Teachers may have agreed that rest was important—one emphasized teachers' need for "a vacation to recuperate their exhausted strength" (National Education Association, 1913, p. 240)—but they were seldom able to remain idle. While agriculture did not dictate the school calendar, rural teachers often labored in rigorous—and gender-specific—roles on the farms of their families of origin. Town and city teachers were equally active (Ogren, 2018), and administrators did not focus primarily on rest for long.

School leaders soon also encouraged—and, in many places, required—teachers to attend regional summer "institutes" (for which they usually did not receive compensation). Institutes convened for a few or several weeks in larger schools or other public buildings, and mainly focused on elementary and rural-school teaching methods and subject-matter knowledge. Evening lectures and slideshows also allowed teachers to deepen their understanding of the education system and to learn about various cultural topics. In Iowa, where over 20,000 teachers attended institutes each summer in the 1890s (Aurner, 1914, p. 180), one teacher complained anonymously that she had better uses for her time off than listening to "second and third rate home talent" drone on ("A Village School Ma'am," 1892). A teacher in neighboring Nebraska, on the other hand, relished opportunities at the institute in Alliance to socialize with other teachers and to attend art exhibits and concerts that were not available in the remote Sand Hills where she taught in a one-room school (Radke, 2000). In 1892, the institute in Knoxville, Tennessee, introduced White teachers to progressive methods of teaching reading and geography (Allison, 1983), while attendees of the "colored normal" in Mineola, Texas, passed a resolution thanking the principal "for the many noted lectures on school management and higher branches" ("News and Notes," 1892). With some support from the General Education Board, enrollment in summer institutes for Black teachers in the South grew from 5,000 in 1916 to over 23,000 in 1928 (Fairclough, 2007, p. 248). These Black—as well as a multitude of White—teachers left summer institutes with higher "regard [for] themselves as professionals" (pp. 319–320) and a stronger connection to the education system and the wider world.

The National Education Association (NEA) summer convention functioned as a sort of mobile, national institute, mainly for White teachers, beginning in the 1880s, and the meeting of the National Association of Teachers in Colored Schools (NATCS) did the same for Black teachers after its founding in 1903. (In the mid-20th century, each transformed into a teachers union and then they merged.) As professional associations, the NEA and NATCS facilitated classroom teachers' attendance at their summer meetings by arranging for inexpensive accommodations and reduced railroad fares; the NEA also promoted tourism in the region where the meeting took place. The 1887 NEA meeting in Chicago drew thousands of teachers from the Midwest and even 275 from Massachusetts (Gorton, 1889). Rural Minnesota teacher and future congressman Conrad Selvig (1951) was especially impressed with the "galaxy of great men and women"—including Harvard president Charles W. Eliot, John Dewey, and Carrie Chapman Catt—he heard speak at the 1902 NEA meeting in Minneapolis. "The world is not the same after one has been moved emotionally or broadened and lifted, intellectually, by a great speech," he later reflected (p. 48). Of a later Minneapolis meeting of the NEA, Portland, Oregon, teacher Nettie Rae Rankin (1928) wrote that one of the highlights was "meeting directly or indirectly with so many serious, intensely professional teachers, unselfish workers." Similarly, albeit on a smaller scale, the NATCS "Proceedings" for 1923 stated that the meeting had "brought educators from seventeen different states and the District of Columbia together to discuss and help solve matters as they relate to education." Attending these meetings most certainly enhanced teachers' work in the classroom.

Other organizations that were place-based also served as national institutes; the most prominent of these was Chautauqua Institution in western New York State. From the time of its founding in the 1870s, generations of teachers forged their professional identities at this "national podium" where middle-class Americans gathered to soak up culture and learn about social issues (Ogren, 2016). In the 1880s, future University of Chicago president

William R. Harper oversaw the summer school that operated within the larger institution, and the following decades saw the expansion of scholarships and low-cost or free accommodations for schoolteachers. They learned from famous scholars who taught in the summer school or presented public lectures, including Dewey, G. Stanley Hall, and Francis W. Parker; William James's 1896 lectures at Chautauqua on psychological principles related to education were later published as *Talks to Teachers* (James, 1899). Otis M. Shackelford (1911), a Black teacher in Missouri who spent three summers at Chautauqua in the 1900s, wrote that he left "strengthened intellectually, morally, and spiritually, and . . . endeavored to disseminate whatever of good I had learned, and thereby benefit the youths that chanced to fall under my guardianship" (p. 77).

Capitalizing on the market for summer teacher education, colleges and universities added summer sessions beginning in the 1890s. With enrollments of close to 300,000 teachers nationwide by the mid-1920s, summer sessions replaced summer institutes. Dean Raymond Walters (1926) of Swarthmore College described the teachers as "invaders [who] stream across the Yard at Harvard; they file from Teachers College to the Library at Columbia . . . they sit on the Oak Knoll at Minnesota; in the cool of the evening they stroll along the serpentine brick walls that Thomas Jefferson built at the University of Virginia" (p. 60). An advertisement in the NATCS *Bulletin* for the summer quarter at Tuskegee Institute (1929) was addressed "To the ambitious teacher who wants to keep up," while in the NEA *Journal*, an ad for George Washington University (1925) promised, "A sojourn in the Nation's Capital forms a background for both teaching and citizenship," and another for the University of Denver (1936) touted "lectures on today's social, economic, and educational problems" along with "planned recreation in snow-capped Rockies."

State governments and private foundations provided some scholarship support, but teachers still had to make financial sacrifices in order to attend summer sessions. They did so not only to fulfill increasing certification requirements, but to broaden their professional and cultural knowledge. Rural California teacher Grace Canan Pogue attended one of her state's teachers colleges every third summer from the 1920s into the 1940s "in order to keep abreast of educational trends" (Pogue, 1957, p. 81); she undertook such a grueling schedule at San Jose in 1939 that she was admitted to the hospital. At the University of Tennessee in the 1900s and early 1910s, the Summer School of the South (SSS) offered courses with prominent education professors including Dewey, Hall, Paul Monroe, and Edward Thorndike, as well as addresses by nationally known scholars and public figures including Liberty Hyde Bailey and William Jennings Bryan. Lecture topics ranged from literary and historical subjects to popular science (Allison, 1998; Ogren, 2016). SSS director Philander Claxton (1941) reflected, "Country school teachers who had never been to high school . . . listened to lecturers whose voice carried across the continent" (p. 137). Teachers with marginalized identities also demonstrated through their summer studies that they too belonged at prestigious centers of learning. Southern Black teachers spent summers at Columbia University, and women teachers lived in the otherwise all-male residence halls in hallowed Harvard Yard. Such experiences broadened teachers' minds and enabled them to gain the intellectual self-confidence to make their own decisions in the classroom.

By the turn of the 20th century, school leaders also advocated that teachers join in the middle class's new enthusiasm for tourism as another means of professional development. Education journals published articles such as "Travel—A Higher Education," in which a professor reflected, "I know of nothing which so successfully makes good teachers into better ones" (Payne, 1925). As advertisements for tours and travel companies became ubiquitous in the journals, one invited readers to "Add to your cultural capital, to your enthusiasm and your teaching ability the first-hand contact with the great civilizations of Europe" (Intercollegiate Tours, 1921). A small number of teachers received a modicum of support from their school districts, and many economized so that they could travel to national parks in the American West and historic sites in the East and South, or spend the summer on a grand tour of Europe. As early as 1901, a principal in Chicago observed, "The teachers are the greatest traveling class now-a-days" (Watt, 1901), and in the 1920s and 1930s, 10 to 20% of teachers engaged in tourism each summer, with high school teachers being more and elementary teachers being less likely to travel (Gough, 2011).

For teachers, these summertime trips were a welcome break from the classroom but not from their larger responsibilities as educators. They returned from summer tours with new knowledge and occasionally brought souvenirs to augment their lessons. Regarding a trip to Southern California and Mexico in 1933, Pogue (1957) reported, "the glass bottom boat at Catalina furnished material for many stories when I returned to my pupils in September. The trip to Tia Juana and the souvenirs collected provided the basis for a social studies unit" (p. 82). And after touring Europe, history teacher Iola Quigley (1935) of Des Moines, Iowa, implored other teachers to do the same, explaining, "every day in your classroom some such memory will add its gleam to make real and vital the characters of history." Lila Fyan returned from a summer in Europe not only with "a more intimate feeling for literature and history, but also in warmer sympathy with different nationalities and races" ("Investing a Vacation," 1923), and a similar experience strengthened Ella Preston's (1934) conviction that she needed to provide her students, "potential citizens of the world," with "some idea of the cultures, past and present, of the lands beyond the sea." Not only did tourism widen teachers' worlds, but in finding their way across Europe or venturing to new parts of the United States, women teachers were able to assert an uncommon level of autonomy.

While directing teachers to study and travel, school officials continued to also call for them to rest during the summer. But the middle class began by the late 19th century to view not quietude but fresh air and physical activity as ideal means of revitalization, enabling some women teachers to "rest" by exploring national parks, "wheeling" on bicycles, and hiking up mountains (Ogren, 2018). While on summer break from teaching, Anna Mills (later Johnston) in 1878 was the first woman to summit Mount Whitney, and Fay Fuller in 1890 was the first woman to climb Mount Rainier. Johnston (1902) found that the mountain air seemed to "put new blood into" her veins. Summer activities that stretched gender norms through physical robustness would have increased women teachers' sense of agency during the other months of the year.

In their detailed instructions regarding summer activities, paternalistic administrators also warned that labor for pay was not restful and did not befit a professional educator; the Seattle school board in the 1910s even prohibited outside employment for teachers (Pieroth, 2004). Nevertheless, since the onset of the 9-month school year, teachers have commonly needed to augment their salaries in order to maintain a professional middle-class standard of living. "I find it absolutely necessary to go out as waitress or something of the sort in the summer," replied a woman elementary school teacher in New Haven, Connecticut, to a 1913 NEA salary survey (National Education Association, 1913, p. 233). As a teacher and homesteader in South Dakota in the 1910s, Bess Corey devoted her summers to working as a cook or a housekeeper in a nearby town in order to make ends meet as well as defying gender norms and asserting her independence through hard manual labor on her own land; after building a fence, she proudly wrote to her family, "The neighbors brag on it. It looks good and is solid" (Gerber, 1990, p. 356).

Some teachers added a dose of adventure to summer service work by cleaning rooms at Yellowstone and other national parks, or stoked their sense of independence through sales positions that involved travel. An ad recruiting teachers to work as salespeople for publisher F. E. Compton Company quoted English teacher Elizabeth James, who stated that her summer working for Compton had helped to draw her "out of my one-sided view of life . . . yet keep me in touch with my ideals of education" (Pleasure, 1921). Other teachers implemented progressive instructional techniques as playground directors, camp counselors, or seasonal park rangers. In the vacation schools that convened in urban public schools, teachers were able to focus on "cutting-edge" topics and approaches such as nature study, manual training, and field trips (Gold, 2002). After vacation schools gave way in the 1910s to summer courses in more traditional subjects, teachers had another option for earning extra money, if not also honing their own approach to professionalism.

Rules that barred women teachers from marrying finally disappeared by the mid-20th century, after which family obligations also shaped many teachers' summer pursuits as they continued to adapt school officials' directions regarding the summer to suit their own version of professionalism. Teachers used the summer to shape themselves not as the compliant workers administrators desired but as broad-minded, worldly, independent professionals. Although school districts did not grant them full authority to implement all that they learned during the summer, teachers' break from the routine of teaching prepared them to better serve students by making autonomous, well-informed decisions in the classroom.

Recently, a proliferation of tweets under the hashtag #NoSummersOff has documented schoolteachers' summer work for additional income, attendance at professional and academic programs, efforts to prepare curricula and classrooms for the coming year, and ineffectual attempts to overcome burnout, while media coverage of teachers' multifaceted efforts during the pandemic summers of 2020 and 2021 confirmed how essential the summer months are for teachers' work during the school year (Ogren, 2021). Persistence of the myth that teachers take the summer off from their work in the schools keeps parents, taxpayers, legislators, and policymakers from recognizing the crucial role of summer activities in shaping a professional teaching force and from rewarding teachers appropriately.

REFERENCES

Allison, C. B. (1983). Training Dixie's teachers: The University of Tennessee's summer normal institutes. *Journal of Thought, 18*(3), 27–36.

Allison, C. B. (1998). *Teachers for the South: Pedagogy and educationists in the University of Tennessee, 1844–1995*. Peter Lang.

Aurner, C. R. (1914). *History of education in Iowa, vol. 2*. State Historical Society of Iowa.

Claxton, P. P. (1941). Summer School of the South. *Teacher-Education Journal, 3*, 135–138.

Clifford, G. J. (2014). *Those good Gertrudes: A social history of women teachers in America*. Johns Hopkins University Press.

D'Amico Pawlewicz, D. (2020). *Blaming teachers: Professionalization policies and the failure of reform in American history*. Rutgers University Press.

Fairclough, A. (2007). *A class of their own: Black teachers in the segregated South*. Belknap Press of Harvard University Press.

Fey, T. (Writer), & Adams, A. (Director). (2021, January 21). The Sac (Season 1, Episode 4) [Television series episode]. In T. Fey, J. Richmond, R. Carlock, & D. Miner (Executive producers), *Mr. Mayor*. Little Stranger; Bevel Gears; 3 Arts Entertainment; Universal Television.

George Washington University (advertisement). (1925). *Journal of the National Education Association, 14*(5), A-135.

Gerber, P. L. (Ed.). (1990). *Bachelor Bess: The homesteading letters of Elizabeth Corey, 1909–1919*. University of Iowa Press.

Gold, K. M. (2002). *School's in: The history of summer education in American public schools*. Peter Lang.

Goodlad, J. I. (1990). *Teachers for our nation's schools*. Jossey-Bass.
Gorton, G. L. (1889). Remarks. *Transactions of the Michigan State Teachers Association . . . 1889*, 50.
Gough, R. (2011). What I did on my summer vacation: The significance of tourism for American teachers, 1919–1940. *Journal of Tourism History, 3*(3), 267–287.
Intercollegiate Tours (advertisement). (1921). *Midland Schools, 35*(6), 196.
Investing a vacation. (1923). *Journal of the National Education Association, 12*(6), 219.
James, W. (1899). *Talks to teachers*. Henry Holt and Company.
Johnston, A. M. (1902). A trip to Mt. Whitney in 1878. *Mt. Whitney Club Journal, 1*(1), 18.
Judd, C., et al. (1914). Educational news and notes. *Elementary School Teacher, 14*(9), 410.
Juddson v. Board of Educ. of the City of New York, 255 App. Div. 1024 (N.Y. App. Div. 1938).
Lortie, D. C. (1975). *Schoolteacher: A sociological study*. University of Chicago Press.
National Education Association. (1913). *Report of the committee on teachers' salaries and cost of living*. National Education Association.
News and notes. (1892). *Texas School Journal, 10*(9), 681.
Ogren, C. A. (2016). Out-of-class project: American teachers' summertime activities, 1880s–1930s. *History of Education Quarterly, 56*(1), 8–35.
Ogren, C. A. (2018). Revitalizing teachers' bodies: Prescriptions for rest and teachers' summer activities in the United States, 1880s–1930s. *Paedogogica Historica, 14*(1–2), 154–168.
Ogren, C. A. (2021, September 7). The pandemic has made it obvious: Schoolteachers don't really have summers "off." *The Washington Post*. Retrieved from https://www.washingtonpost.com/outlook/2021/09/07/pandemic-has-made-it-obvious-schoolteachers-dont-really-have-summers-off/
Payne, C. (1925). Travel—A higher education. *Midland Schools, 39*(8), 321.
Pieroth, D. H. (2004). *Seattle's women teachers of the interwar years: Shapers of a livable city*. University of Washington Press.
Pleasure and profit in the long vacation (advertisement). (1921). *Midland Schools, 35*(6), 202.
Podgursky, M. (2003). Fringe benefits. *Education Next 3*(3). Retrieved from https://www.educationnext.org/fringebenefits/
Pogue, G. C. (1957). *The swift seasons*. Cloister Press.
Preston, E. E. (1934). Fruits of a European tour. *Midland Schools, 48*(8), 242.
Proceedings. (1923). *The Bulletin: Official Organ of the N. A. T. C. S., 3*(4), 6.
Quigley, I. B. (1935). European travel for the teacher. *Midland Schools, 49*(7), 212.
Radke, A. (2000). "I am very aspiring": Muirl Dorrough and the Alliance Junior Normal School. *Nebraska History, 81*(1), 2–11.
Rankin, N. R. (1928). World understanding given prominence at Minneapolis meeting. *News Bulletin of the Department of Classroom Teachers of the National Education Association, 2*(1), 1.
Selvig, C. G. (1951). *A tale of two valleys*. Grover Jones Press.
Shackelford, O. M. (1911). *Seeking the best*. Burton Publishing Company.

Swider, G. (2018, December 12). [Letter to the editor]. *Los Angeles Times*. Retrieved from https://www.latimes.com/opinion/readersreact/la-ol-le-teachers-resources-funding-20181212-story.html

Tuskegee Institute (advertisement). (1929). *The Bulletin: Official Organ of the National Association of Teachers in Colored Schools, 9*(7), 28.

University of Denver (advertisement). (1936). *Journal of the National Education Association, 25*(3), A-48.

A village school ma'am. (1892). The institute or summer vacation, which? *Iowa Normal Monthly, 16*(2), 72.

Walters, R. (1926, July). On the summer-school campus. *Scribner's Magazine*, 60–66.

Watt, W. E. (1901). Teachers as travelers. *Intelligence, 21*(10), 371.

What shall we do with the long vacation? (1878). *Iowa Normal Monthly, 1*(12), 360–361.

CHAPTER 15

The Myth of Harmful Teacher Tenure

Diana D'Amico Pawlewicz

With a job for life, critics argue, tenure policies are sure to make teachers lazy or radicalized and schools difficult places to manage. One conservative foundation warned that tenure would protect inept teachers and make it "difficult to encourage excellence" (Burke, 2014). From New York to Minnesota to California, other groups turned to the courts, arguing that teacher tenure deprives students of "their fundamental right to a thorough and efficient education" (Rich, 2016). In his decision in *Vergara v. California*, the case that questioned the constitutionality of teacher tenure laws, Los Angeles County Superior Court judge Rolf Treu wrote, "grossly ineffective teachers substantially undermine the ability of a child to succeed in school" and "[shock] the conscience" (2016).

In the post-Trump years, depictions of teachers as dangerous to students only accelerated. Virginia governor Glenn Youngkin created an anonymous tip line so parents could report teachers who they felt violated their student's rights by teaching topics that caused discomfort. And in her first act as governor of Arkansas, Sarah Huckabee Sanders banned the teaching of critical race theory in the state's public schools to prevent teachers from "indoctrinat[ing] students" and "brainwashing our children with a left-wing political agenda" (Downey, 2023, n.p.).

Fears that tenure would either make schools difficult places to govern or expose students to teachers prone to sloth or ideological extremism are not new. In 1917, William G. Willcox, president of the New York City Board of Education, charged that public schools were "'burdened and clogged with many teachers who are unfit and unsatisfactory,' and whom it is practically impossible to remove because of their 'permanent tenure'" ("Asks for Removal of Unfit Teachers," 1917, p. 12).

But these fears of tenure, even as they are historical, are rooted in myths. Even as policies have varied over time and from district to district, tenure privileges have never granted teachers a job for life. Instead, tenure has offered teachers due process and established that supervisors must document cause for dismissal. Maybe even more importantly, tenure has never granted public school teachers academic freedom, much less the ability to say and do what they wish when standing at the board. Told and retold over time, the myth of teacher tenure has set the drumbeat for public school reform and stoked fears that the *real* problems plaguing the nation's schools are the teachers who staff them. This chapter explores the rise of tenure practices and the vulnerabilities teachers experienced even with the protection of a so-called job for life. Blaming teachers has been a defining characteristic of American education policy and reform, but fears of freewheeling teachers grinding the bureaucratic order of the public schools to a halt or indoctrinating innocent children were much like fears of the monster under the bed: a terrifying idea that never came to be (D'Amico Pawlewicz, 2022).

* * *

By the second half of the 1800s, municipally supported public school systems developed across the Eastern Seaboard and spread westward. Immigration, population shifts, and child labor laws all combined to rapidly increase the school-going population and the need for teachers. While school leaders and elected officials at the state and federal levels touted the importance of teachers not just for schools but for the future of the nation, teachers faced difficult working conditions. Class sizes in places like New York City soared to 50 pupils for every one teacher and before construction could keep pace with enrollment, schooling often took place in ad hoc arrangements including damp basements and dark hallways. Teachers described working in spaces that forced them to huddle with children "like sheep in a pen," to stand "in the closet, on the table—anywhere" ("The Salaries of Public School Teachers," 1867). And, despite the growing consensus around the importance of teachers, their salary was low from the start, with one report finding that teachers earned less than street sweepers and stablemen, even as their work required additional education and training ("The Week: Education and Teachers," 1897).

School leaders drew on well-worn Victorian gendered assumptions and beckoned women to the public schools, reasoning that as natural rule followers and nurturers they would be uniquely well suited to teach. Meanwhile, women flocked to the schools, recognizing the unprecedented opportunity for professional employment and independence. But without the right to vote and limited public authority, this female-dominated workforce was a largely powerless one. Strained working conditions and low salaries weren't the only challenges teachers faced. From district to district, each year teachers were forced to reapply for their positions. Hired, fired, and moved from school to school at the whims of school leaders, public school teachers' employment was tenuous (D'Amico Pawlewicz, 2020).

By the 1880s, teachers from New York, to Baltimore, to Los Angeles began to press for tenure rights. For these teachers—as their successors—the protection they sought had nothing to do with a job for life or the freedom to teach whatever they wished. Rather, as teachers in San Francisco explained, tenure would mean that teachers "cannot be removed at the pleasure of the appointing power [and] they can only be dismissed for violating the rules of the Board of Education, for incompetency, or for unprofessional or immoral conduct" ("Teachers Protected in Their Positions," 1890). At first, school leaders were adamantly opposed to the idea. One Baltimore school commissioner scoffed at a teachers' proposal calling teachers "foolish" ("No Tenure for Teachers," 1883). A superintendent from Massachusetts pointed out that the instability teachers felt wasn't accidental at all. Instead, in his estimation, the need to reapply for their positions was a "spur that helps keep [teachers] up with the times" ("Teachers' Tenure," 1885).

But by the close of the 19th century, school leaders across the country came to understand tenure in different terms. First, they recognized that the effort to rehire teachers each year was inefficient and came at a high administrative cost. More importantly, though, there was another problem preoccupying school leaders: Teacher turnover was high. School leaders not only spent time each year searching for teachers, but they invested funds and resources training them only to have them leave within a short period of time. In his report *City School Systems in the United States*, John Philbrick explained "the ordeal of annual election is coeval with the modern organization and development of our common school system." Not only would tenure rights for teachers come at a low cost for districts, but it could help create the "ideal teaching corps" (1885, pp. 110–112). By the early years of the 20th century, many cities had tenure protections in place, and states were beginning to adopt policies. Hardly a leader in this area, by the time tenure practices emerged in the United States, they were already firmly entrenched in Germany, Denmark, Switzerland, Netherlands, Finland, Norway, Sweden, Great Britain, and France (*Court Cases Affecting Teacher Tenure*, 1925).

Even with the protection of tenure, teachers continued to be dismissed when supervisors claimed ineffectiveness, immorality, or insubordination. Two key causes for dismissal that administrators variously categorized under these headings were when female teachers married or became pregnant. While school leaders in New York City forced the resignation of female teachers when they married by charging them with "neglect of duty," administrators in Indiana reasoned that there was no need for formal paperwork when a female teacher wed as she "married out of her position" ("Dismiss Women Teachers," 1911; "Epidemic of Marriage Robs Schools of Their Teachers," 1904). Even with tenure protection, many teachers remained vulnerable.

The case of Bridget Peixotto captured national headlines. Peixotto was a veteran teacher with 18 years of experience who ascended to the rank of teacher in charge of her school in the Bronx. On February 3, 1913, Peixotto filed for a medical leave of absence for an upper respiratory matter. A physician's certificate accompanied her application, and it was granted. However, school leaders soon learned that Peixotto had secretly married the year before, and when she took her leave, in addition to a sinus infection, she was also more than 7 months pregnant. School leaders rescinded her initial leave and dismissed Peixotto for neglect of duty. Even once the New York Supreme Court sided with Peixotto on the grounds that any policy that discouraged women to have children was bad for society, the New York City Board of Education upheld her dismissal on the grounds that she was deceptive. In 1915, the New York State Commissioner of Education reinstated Peixotto, and her case became a key factor in changing rules that barred married and pregnant woman from teaching in public schools. Tenure offered Peixotto and legions of other unnamed women no protection; rather, it was only due to their activism and persistence beyond the schools that led to equitable employment practices and job security (Carter, 2002; D'Amico Pawlewicz, 2020, pp. 63–64).

In 1915, under the leadership of John Dewey, the Association of University Professors adopted its "Declaration of Principles" and argued that tenure and academic freedom together were fundamental to professors' ability to "rightly render [their] distinctive and indispensable service to society" (The American Association of University Professors, 1915). Leaders in the newly formed American Federation of Teachers sought to use this framing to extend teachers' tenure rights into the realm of academic freedom. However, on this point school leaders across the United States remained unswayed and opposed. And public school teachers found themselves dismissed, even when they had tenure protection, for expressing views or taking part in activities that supervisors deemed dangerous.

Over the 20th century, the suggestion of any brand of social or political radicalism led to the investigation and dismissal of teachers in school districts around the country. In 1917, Samuel Schmalhausen was dismissed for failing to adequately correct a student who, in a writing prompt, chastised President Wilson for declaring war ("Board Will Hear Accused Teachers," 1917). Loyalty oaths became standard practice in the nation's school districts, and, tenure or not, suspicion often provided ample grounds for dismissal.

But by the 1930s, some educators began to wonder if the efforts to censure teachers were leading to unintended consequences. A survey from the National Education Association's committee on academic freedom found that the repressive climate of the schools was creating a fear that pushed teachers out of the profession ("Job Fear," 1939). A growing cohort of scholars argued that the consequences of teacher fear were far-reaching. First, as Robert Hutchins, president of the University of Chicago, observed, the climate severely impeded recruitment. "As long as teachers may be hired and fired for any reason at all," public school systems would always struggle to lure talented individuals to the schools from other opportunities ("Hutchins Assails Education System," 1936). As school districts began to confront waves of widespread teacher shortages following the Second

World War, Hutchins's warning was a serious one. But the climate of fear wouldn't just thwart recruitment and retention efforts, some educators alerted; it would also impact what and how teachers taught. According to one observer, "teachers themselves keep away from controversy or anything that might offend a member of the school board or the community or the self-appointed censors of the schools. The result is that students get a milk and water curriculum" ("Frightened Teachers," 1951).

The Education Policies Commission, a group of leading education leaders including General Dwight Eisenhower, then serving as president of Columbia University, cautioned that the climate of fear teachers faced would have consequences beyond the schools. After days of closed meetings at the Westchester Country Club in Rye, New York, the Commission issued a statement that warned citizens to "condemn the careless application of such words as 'Red' and 'Communist' to teachers and other persons who merely have views different from those of the accusers." The situation was undermining key aspects of American democracy, the commission alerted. According to the commission's statement, "anxieties that accompany a sense of danger must not be permitted to impair civil liberties" (Illson, 1949). But local leaders tended to dismiss those cautions. Within a few years, hundreds of teachers around the country found themselves under investigation as part of a campaign to purge communists from the schools (Hartman, 2011; Taylor, 2011). Tenure offered no protection for teachers like 27-year-old Brockman Schumacher, a veteran of World War II, who lost his job in the St. Louis public schools for subversion simply because he participated in a Peace Committee event ("Fire Teacher in St. Louis," 1951).

Doubts about teachers' loyalty to the country were not the only cause for dismissal. Tenure similarly offered no protection for the teachers accused of disloyalty to their respective school systems. Teacher James Worley was chair of his school's English department in Westchester, New York, where district leaders implemented a policy that required all teachers to submit lesson plans at least 2 weeks in advance. For the local board of education, the new requirement would force teachers to think ahead, allow administrators to check on student progress, and help with substitute plans. For Worley, the new requirement was just another example of administrative overreach, "a scab on a festering sore that hinders imaginative teaching." And he refused to submit his plans. He was found "guilty of insubordination" and fired. Responding to the outcry over his dismissal, the board released a statement explaining that even as Worley was widely regarded as "an able teacher," "a teacher must recognize and respect the balance of administrative authority and teacher freedom" (Folsom, 1959).

Worley was far from alone in facing situations like this one, but the circumstances were even more dire for the nation's teachers of color who often used their place in the schools to also press for racial justice. In 1938, Howard Pindell had been teaching for 5 years in the Anne Arundel County public schools and had earned tenure. Across Maryland, as in most other states at the time, Black teachers earned significantly less than their White peers. Pindell gained notoriety when he joined with other community members to press for salary justice, becoming the first teacher in the state to cooperate with legal action. Later, several other teachers joined Pindell in the fight, but they were early career teachers and had yet to earn tenure rights; in turn, school leaders fired them without cause. But dealing with Pindell was slightly more complicated. While reigning tenure practices meant that he could not be fired without cause, he could be transferred to another district; and that is exactly what school leaders did. When Pindell began his new position as a principal in the Frederick County schools, he soon learned that his tenure privileges were not transferable and he, too, was fired ("Teachers Who Sought Equal Wages, Fired," 1938). In Arkansas, where White teachers earned twice the salary of Black teachers, the superintendent of the North Little Rock school system sent a survey to teachers inquiring if they expected a pay increase. The majority of those who indicated that they would were fired—15 teachers of color lost their job in the summer of 1942 because they indicated they would not accept the status quo ("15 Arkansas Teachers Fired for Seeking Higher Pay," 1942). James Wise was a teacher and coach at the Gould Colored High School and brought forward a suit in federal court for salary equalization that would pay teachers according to qualification, not race. Wise filed his suit on January 9, 1954, and was fired 5 days later ("Teacher Sues for Equal Pay," 1954).

In the wake of the *Brown v. Board of Education* decision, Black teachers were fired and displaced by the thousands (Tillman, 2004). Some were fired when schools for children of color closed and others for their civil rights activities. In 1956, 17 South Carolina teachers—all rated as competent or higher—were fired when they refused to fill out a questionnaire detailing their affiliation with the NAACP and views on equality ("17 Teachers Charge South Carolina's Anti-NAACP Law Violates Constitution," 1956). A report by the National Education Association in 1965 found that "hundreds of Negro teachers are being fired, demoted, blacklisted, and barred from the classroom on racial grounds." Tenure or not, the report chronicled how administrators intimidated teachers of color by threatening to fire or demote them as a way to "inhibit their personal and professional activities" ("668 Negro Teachers Displaced or Demoted," 1965). That NEA report found that "the threat of job loss is so great in many places that an aura of fear permeates the teaching force" (Barkdoll, 1965).

* * *

From the second half of the 20th century and into the 21st, tenure protections have become widespread in school districts across the United States, owing in large degree to the growth of teachers' unions. If tenure doesn't grant teachers a job for life, why haven't more been fired? To begin with, even as policymakers and educators tout the importance of teacher quality on student outcomes, there is far less certainty about the characteristics that demarcate such an individual. Is it about student achievement as measured by standardized test scores? Researchers have long documented that a host of within and beyond school factors inform educational outcomes (Schneider, 2017). Maybe it's instead about rapport with students—but how can or should that be measured and evaluated? Perhaps more importantly, firing teachers assumes there are legions of better ones waiting in the wings. And that has rarely been the case (D'Amico Pawlewicz, 2021).

And what of the concerns that tenure will somehow make teachers inefficient and lazy? As public education has expanded, it has also intensified. While salaries have remained stubbornly low, teachers' responsibilities have grown. Not only are teachers evaluated more frequently than ever before, but the rise of standardized testing has meant more assessments, all while budget cuts mean that teachers are tasked with caring for more of students' in-school needs. Echoing the same concerns Hutchins expressed in the 1930s, in 1980, NEA president Willard H. McGuire characterized teacher burnout as a "major new malady . . . that threatens to reach epidemic proportions if it isn't checked soon" (Barnes, 1980). During the COVID-19 pandemic, elected officials and school leaders first turned to teachers to figure out how to bring instruction online and later turned to them to head back into the schools even as the virus continued to rage so that parents could return to work. One study found that teachers not only experienced an intensification of work but also experienced higher stress levels than even health-care workers (Kush et al., 2022).

If tenure rights haven't made teachers lazy, perhaps it has made them radical. To this supposition, like the prior, the answer is a resounding no. Today as in the past, teachers report being afraid and uncertain. What can they teach? If a parent or politician objects, will they be fired? Will their teaching license be revoked? As one teacher from New Hampshire reflected, "we don't want to risk our livelihoods when we're not sure what the rules are." The climate of fear that shapes teachers' work lives is far from myth. Florida education commissioner Richard Corcoran boasted of policing teachers. "I've censored or fired or terminated numerous teachers," he bragged to a reporter (Meckler & Natanson, 2022).

And in spite of all of this, the myth of teacher tenure persists. Why? The simple answer is that it—like all myths—serves a purpose. For some school leaders, visions of teacher power or shared governance smack of bureaucratic inefficiency and promise to topple the reigning organizational structure of the schools. Attempts to abolish tenure fit hand to glove with broader attempts to diminish teachers' individual and shared authority. For conservative critics and philanthropists who see the market and charter schools as a panacea, criticisms of tenure are part and parcel of broader criticisms of public schools and attempts to destabilize them. For others still, criticisms of tenure are ways to impede teachers who press for change and justice and to thwart social change and equity in favor of a status quo that grants primacy to Whiteness and masculinity.

The irony of this history and the myth of teacher tenure is that it brings into sharp focus the conclusion that more protections and freedoms for teachers—not less—are essential to the nation's public schools and American society, writ large. In expanding teachers' authority lies a path not yet taken in efforts to stem shortages and recruit and retain teachers. But perhaps even more importantly, as civil discourse erodes, the need for critical thinking, listening, and communication skills is more important than ever before (D'Amico Pawlewicz, 2023). Expanding teachers' tenure rights to include academic freedom might just be one of the most powerful ways to safeguard American democracy.

REFERENCES

15 Arkansas teachers fired for seeking higher pay. (1942, June 6). *Pittsburgh Courier*, 1.
17 teachers charge South Carolina's Anti-NAACP law violates constitution. (1956, November 23). *Atlanta Daily World*, 1.
668 Negro teachers displaced or demoted. (1965, December 22). *Atlanta Constitution*, 6.
The American Association of University Professors. (1915). *Declaration of principles*.
Asks for removal of unfit teachers. (1917, December 23). *The New York Times*, 12.
Barkdoll, R. (1965, December 22). NEA charges 452 Dixie Negro teachers fired. *Los Angeles Times*, 1.
Barnes, B. (1980, April 17). Teacher burnout: A major malady. *The Washington Post*, MD1.
Board will hear accused teachers. (1917, November 18). *The New York Times*, 4.
Burke, L. (2014, July 8). *Tenure creates the wrong incentives*. Heritage Foundation. Retrieved from https://www.heritage.org/education/commentary/tenure-creates-the-wrong-incentives
Carter, P. A. (2002). *"Everybody's paid but the teacher": The teaching profession and the women's movement*. Teachers College Press.
Court cases affecting teacher tenure (Research Bulletin). (1925). Research Division of the National Education Association of the United States.
D'Amico Pawlewicz, D. (2020). *Blaming teachers: Professionalization policies and the failure of reform in American history*. Rutgers University Press.
D'Amico Pawlewicz, D. (2021, November 18). Today's teacher shortages are part of a longer pattern. *The Washington Post*.
D'Amico Pawlewicz, D. (2022). Teacher blame as the grammar of public school reform. *History of Education Quarterly, 62*(3), 291–311.
D'Amico Pawlewicz, D. (2023, May 11). 4 factors that contributed to the record low history scores for US eighth graders. *The Conversation*.

Dismiss women teachers. (1911, December 28). *The New York Times*, 3.
Downey, C. (2023, January 11). Arkansas governor Huckabee Sanders signs CRT ban. *National Review*. Retrieved from https://www.nationalreview.com/news/arkansas-governor-sarah-huckabee-sanders-bans-critical-race-theory-in-k-12/
Epidemic of marriage robs schools of their teachers. (1904, December 4). *Chicago Daily Tribune*, G4.
Fire teacher in St. Louis. (1951, August 11). *Courier*, 6.
Folsom, M. (1959, November 24). Westchester teacher dismissed for refusing to file class plans. *The New York Times*, 1.
Frightened teachers. (1951, July 10). *The Washington Post*, 10.
Hartman, A. (2011). *Education and the Cold War: The battle for the American school* (Reprint ed.). Palgrave Macmillan.
Hutchins assails education system. (1936, November 16). *The New York Times*, 21.
Illson, M. (1949, October 9). Educators warn on loyalty oaths. *The New York Times*, 1.
Job fear called teaching curb. (1939, July 3). *Los Angeles Times*, A.
Kush, J. M., Badillo-Goicoechea, E., Musci, R. J., & Stuart, E. A. (2022). Teachers' mental health during the COVID-19 pandemic. *Educational Researcher*. Retrieved from https://doi.org/10.3102/0013189X221134281
Meckler, L., & Natanson, H. (2022, February 15). New critical race theory laws have teachers scared, confused and self-censoring. *Washington Post*.
No tenure for teachers. (1883, June 13). *The Sun*, 1.
Philbrick, J. D. (1885). *City school systems in the United States*. Government Printing Office. Retrieved from http://hdl.handle.net/2027/hvd.32044096985429
Rich, M. (2016, April 14). Job tenure for teachers again faces a challenge: Wealthy foundations back Minnesota lawsuit. *The New York Times*, A11.
The salaries of public school teachers. (1867, April 4). *The New York Times*, 4.
Schneider, J. (2017). *Beyond test scores: A better way to measure school quality*. Harvard University Press.
Taylor, C. (2011). *Reds at the blackboard: Communism, civil rights, and the New York City teachers union*. Columbia University Press.
Teacher sues for equal pay. (1954, January 30). *The Chicago Defender*, 3.
Teachers protected in their positions. (1890, January 11). *Los Angeles Daily Herald*.
Teachers' tenure. (1885, March 27). *Boston Daily Globe*, 5.
Teachers who sought equal wages, fired. (1938, July 2). *New York Amsterdam News*.
Tillman, L. C. (2004). (Un)Intended consequences?: The impact of the *Brown v. Board of Education* decision on the employment status of Black educators. *Education and Urban Society, 36*(3), 280–303.
Vergara v. California, 246 Cal.App.4th 619 (2016).
The week: Education and teachers. (1897, April 10). *The Outlook*, 966–967.

Part IV

MYTHS ABOUT INEVITABILITY

CHAPTER 16

The Du Bois–Washington Myth of Black Male Educational Thinkers

Dellyssa Edinboro

When thinking of Black individuals who were fundamental to debates about Black education at the turn of the 20th century, many immediately refer to Black male educators and reformers W. E. B. Du Bois (1868–1963) and Booker T. Washington (1858–1915). The common narrative is that these luminaries presented fundamentally differing viewpoints about the intersection between Black social progress and Black people's educational attainment: Du Bois on the side of elite liberal education (especially for future Black teachers) and Washington on the side of industrial education that accommodated the development of Jim Crow. Present-day discussions about Black education, as seen in books, news articles, and public commentary, continue to revisit and rely on Du Bois's and Washington's educational visions and, in doing so, frame both individuals as the central voices of Black educational thought (e.g., Closson, 2023; Gates, 2023).

By centering Du Bois's and Washington's educational visions and offering little to no mention of other individuals' contributions to educational debates, a myth emerged that the most relevant intellectual leaders in debates about Black education during this period were Black men. But this focus on Washington and Du Bois ignores several key women who were leaders in their own right in Black education circles, most notably Dr. Anna. J. Cooper (1858–1964), whose contributions existed outside the narrow framing of a dichotomy between industrial education and elite liberal education.

In her 1930 essay "On Education," Dr. Cooper stated that "the aim of education for the human soul is to train aright, to give power, and right direction to the intellect, the sensibilities, and the will" (Cooper, 1930b, p. 3). More generally, to Cooper, Black teachers had the capacity to interrupt the impact of social barriers in the classroom. By utilizing pedagogical approaches and methods that acknowledged broader social contexts and issues, Black teachers could cultivate Black students' educational progress (Cooper, 1930b). Also, by striving for accountability in their practice, gathering relevant information to assist students, fairly assessing students' development, and making connections between students, parents, and communities, Black teachers could help Black students yield their returns on their education, which, as Cooper stated, represented the "safest and richest investment possible to men" (Cooper, 1892a, p. 168; Evans, 2007). In her other essays, as well as speeches, newspaper articles, pamphlets, and books, Cooper's views about the aims of education belong properly in the African American intellectual history of Progressive Era debates about education's capacity to empower, challenge, and advance individuals (Johnson, 2000; May, 2007; Evans, 2007).

This chapter focuses on Cooper's educational visions and their context, which both predated and existed alongside the perspectives of Du Bois and Washington, offering a more complex mix that addressed women's education, the roles of teachers, and the broader purpose of education. Cooper's perspectives on education underscored her academic brilliance, investment in her community, and awareness of her unique standpoint as a Black woman (May, 2007, 2021; Sulé, 2013).

THE MILIEU FOR WASHINGTON, DU BOIS, AND COOPER

Cooper drew from her extensive academic and professional experiences, a process common among Black intellectuals—men and women—during the post-Reconstruction era, when the most prominent members of Black communities could include both formerly enslaved individuals born just before the Civil War (as Cooper was) and also those born into freedom. In that milieu, the individuals who gained visibility for their educational ideas absolutely included W. E. B. Du Bois and Booker T. Washington. While Du Bois gained recognition for emphasizing Black students' investment in their academic training, Washington received exposure for his efforts to maintain Black students' manual training.

Born in 1868 to a working-class family in Massachusetts, Du Bois completed his liberal arts training at institutions such as Fisk University in Tennessee and Friedrich Wilhelm University in Berlin, Germany. He was the first Black American to graduate with a PhD from Harvard University in 1895, cofounder of the National Association for the Advancement of Colored People (NAACP), and author of *The Souls of Black Folk* (1903). Such interactions with educational and social institutions also encouraged Du Bois's contemplations about education's bearing on Black communities (Alridge, 2018). According to Du Bois, for an elite group of Black Americans, known as the "Talented Tenth," engagement with a liberal arts education provided them with the intellectual awareness and leadership skills necessary to elevate Black communities (Du Bois, 1903a). Even though the Talented Tenth were socially and economically distanced from the masses of Black Americans, Du Bois asserted that this exceptional group of Black people best served the interest of everyone in their race (Alridge, 2018).

For many, Du Bois's alignment with classical or liberal arts education at the turn of the 20th century juxtaposed with Washington's alignment with industrial or manual training. Washington was born an enslaved person on a plantation in Franklin County, Virginia, in 1856. His determination led him to Hampton Normal and Agricultural Institute in Virginia, where he graduated in 1875, and he later studied at Wayland Seminary in Washington, D.C. (Anderson, 1988; Harland, 1970). In his autobiography *Up From Slavery* (1901) and "Atlanta Compromise" speech in 1865, Washington turned his life's narrative into an argument for the "Hampton-Tuskegee Idea," an extension of the Hampton model of education, which trained Black students for industrial and agricultural jobs in the South, even though it reconciled Black education with the social capitalist order of the South (Anderson, 1988).

Some myths about Du Bois and Washington are about the distance between their ideas. The two remained in cordial correspondence despite being portrayed as archnemeses; their leaning toward a particular type of education model did not result in them completely disregarding other models of education (Alridge, 2018). While we should not assume their views were the only ones that are relevant to the early 20th-century history of Black thought, Washington and Du Bois's transition from the margin to the center of discourses about educational history have allowed educators and scholars to confront misconceptions about their educational thought. As the next section shows, like her counterparts, Cooper also presented detailed analyses of critical educational issues during this period.

COOPER'S DEFENSE OF WOMEN'S EDUCATION

Dr. Anna. J. Cooper was born to Hannah Stanley Haywood, her enslaved mother, and Dr. Fabius J. Haywood, her mother's enslaver, in 1858 (May, 2007). After the Civil War, at the age of 9, Cooper enrolled at Saint Augustine's Normal School and Collegiate Institute in Raleigh, North Carolina, where she studied for 14 years and completed her studies in classical courses like Latin and Greek. (Like many normal schools, Saint Augustine's included primary and secondary programs as well as the teacher training program.) In 1884, she graduated in classics from Oberlin College, a racially integrated, coeducational institution in Ohio. She also earned a master's degree in mathematics from Oberlin in 1887. Almost 4 decades later, in 1925, Cooper earned a doctoral degree from the University of Sorbonne in Paris, France—the first Black woman to earn a doctorate at the Sorbonne and the fourth Black woman from America with a doctorate. Professionally, Cooper was a teacher, a principal, a public speaker, and the author of *A Voice from the South by a Black Woman of the South* (1892), which examined social conditions in America. She taught at Wilberforce University and at Preparatory High School for Colored Youth (M Street High School), both historically Black schools in Ohio and Washington, D.C., respectively, and at her alma mater Saint Augustine, and served as the principal at M Street High School (Evans 2007; Johnson, 2000; May, 2007). Her writings on education thus came with both deep academic and professional experiences.

Cooper's writings during the late 19th century emphasized the role of education in women's liberation and empowerment. In the colonial and antebellum eras, a select and mostly elite group of Black women cultivated their intellectual development at formal educational institutions such as Oberlin College (Evans, 2007). Their formal education led them to opportunities that aided their communities—most went on to become educators who recognized the ties between Black education and Black people's progress and, in doing so, espoused the ideology of "racial uplift" (Perkins, 1983). By the late 19th century, more formal educational opportunities opened for Black women, albeit with extensive variation because of geographic location, class, gendered expectations, sexist attitudes, racism, and institution type (Breaux, 2002; Evans, 2007). Despite these constraints Black women, like Cooper, persisted in their educational goals (Sulé, 2013).

In her early life, Cooper had encountered financial hardships, gender discrimination, and racial barriers. For instance, while she was at St. Augustine, the school's administrators advised her not to pursue courses in Greek and Latin because of her gender. Cooper resisted their advice and earned her high school diploma and formative teaching experience from St. Augustine (May, 2007). While studying at Oberlin in 1881, she also received advice not to pursue particular courses because of her gender. Again, Cooper overcame such barriers and enrolled in the school's "Gentleman's Course"—accessing the superior classical education solely offered to male students (Johnson, 2000). After these experiences, which reinforced to her the impact of education in women's lives, Cooper used her writings to position her educational thought on this matter.

Well before Du Bois presented his ideas on how a college education aided Black men's self-discovery and talents in "Of the Training of Black Men" in 1903, Cooper's 1890 essay "The Higher Education of Women" had offered her perspectives on education's impact on women. In this essay, Cooper insisted that women's access to a college education supported their growth, autonomy, and vision and should not be limited by perceptions of their social status (Cooper, 1890). Despite the benefits of women's higher education, Cooper realized that women encountered lack of institutional "support, stimulus, and encouragement" because of their status (Cooper, 1890, p. 86). She defended women's education by arguing that their access to education led to their "self-reliance and capacity for earning a livelihood ... [and] render[ed] [them] less dependent on marriage relation for physical support." Women's education also provided them with a sensation comparable to sexual love, added "tone and relish, movement and vim" to their lives, and resulted in them challenging and questioning dogmatic or sexist principles in academic discourses (Cooper, 1890, p. 82).

COOPER'S DEFENSE OF TEACHERS AS PROFESSIONALS

Cooper drew from her experiences and critical awareness of social conditions to craft her intellectual thought about the role of teachers. Although she confronted institutional barriers as a student at St. Augustine and Oberlin, Cooper met teachers who helped her when she was a young Black female student, aiding her navigation of issues of race, gender, and class in her schooling and helping her to strengthen her critical consciousness about education (Evans, 2007; Johnson, 2000). More specifically, her mentors offered her a framework of how to view and understand the role of teachers. By the late 19th century, Cooper bolstered such awareness by teaching at institutions such as St. Augustine, Oberlin College, Wilberforce College in Ohio, and M Street High School in Washington, D.C.

Like many other Black women, Cooper centered her professional life on being an educator. By the turn of the 20th century, teaching represented a profession where Black women's numbers either compared to or exceeded that of Black men. In 1890, the U.S. Census listed 7,864 Black female educators and 7,236 Black male educators; in 1900, 13,524 Black women and 7,734 Black men in education, respectively (Hine, 1997, p. 16). In part, Black women's inclusion in the teaching profession reflected their socialization about teaching being a respectable and noble profession through which women could meet their goal of uplifting Black communities. Black women across geographic locations encountered difficulties in the field—low pay, inadequate educational resources, segregation, overcrowding, and insufficient school funding (Hine, 1997). This group of educators fought against such barriers in the interest of Black students, and some went on to establish Black schools or to advocate for school reforms (McCluskey, 2014). Overall, Black female educators were foundational to Black education during this pivotal period.

Cooper emphasized teachers' capacity to foster social change through innovative classroom practices. She noted that racism and historical contexts adversely impacted Black students' pursuit of education's practical and intellectual objectives (Evans, 2007). While Cooper embraced the positive social impact of Black teachers, she also recognized institutional pressure, wherein teachers working in segregated schools consumed extensive, new, and changing pedagogical ideas and materials at summer schools and institutes. This short time frame limited their ability to "inwardly digest" materials and heightened their wariness toward uncertain educational standards (Cooper, 1930a, p. 234). As Cooper affirmed, these institutional expectations diminished "the naturalness on the part of students, initiative, and an easy give and take in discussing a thought or its application to life." Cooper challenged institutions that viewed teachers as "machines" who provided automated responses based on pedagogical standards promoted by White authors (Cooper, 1930a, p. 234). Instead, she argued for teachers' innovative thought in the classroom, which aided the responsiveness of their students.

Cooper was willing to risk institutional retaliation for standing up for teachers' innovative capacity and academic integrity. After serving as an educator at M Street High School, the largest public high school for Black Americans at the turn of the 20th century, Cooper was promoted to principal in 1901. In that position, she refused to use racist textbooks mandated by the school district. She also challenged White administrators' attempt to pivot the school from its liberal arts curriculum to the industrial and vocational educational model promoted by Booker. T. Washington. While Cooper did not believe in a rigid antagonism between liberal arts and industrial and vocational training, she insisted on students' foundation in liberal arts (May, 2007), after her years of experiences as a Black female educational professional and intellectual thinker who viewed teachers as "social and moral agents" (Johnson, 2000, p. 105). Washington, D.C., educational administrators eventually fired her from M Street High School in 1905 (May 2007).

COOPER'S NUANCE ON THE AIMS OF EDUCATION

Despite her reputation as supporter of a strong liberal arts education, Cooper maintained a pragmatic educational perspective, and she held that the best educational program included liberal arts and manual training (Johnson, 2000). On the one hand, as Cooper emphasized, a liberal arts education broadened students' cultural thought and critical thinking and provided them with pathways to advanced studies and into fields such as law or medicine. On the other hand, when offered through trade or technical schools, manual training provided Black students access to technical or service jobs. Cooper recognized manual training's lengthy and problematic legacy among Black people. During slavery, Black enslaved people's manual training resulted in them being involuntarily trained to meet the economic needs of their enslavers. This early form of training "suppress[ed] or ignore[d] the soul of Black people" and aimed to make them a "hand" for white enslavers. Later on, Black people's manual training prepared them solely for professions such as farming or domestic work (Cooper, 1930b, p. 252). Even with its historical context, Cooper concluded that training for technical or service jobs met the needs of Black Americans, similar to how liberal arts training at Black colleges such as Fisk University also met Black people's needs.

Her openness to manual training did not mean that Cooper agreed with the Hampton-Tuskegee model. She insisted that, separate from any educational specialization, students should complete a liberal art–based high school course. Further, she indicated that both paths of education should account for the moral, physical, and mental development of students so that they, in turn, assume beneficial positions in their communities. Cooper further noted that occupations linked to both areas "deserve[d] the treatment that [was] accorded [to] intelligent and efficient services" (Cooper, 1930b, p. 10). More broadly, she pointed out that no profession should diminish an individual's dignity or limit their ability to expand their intellectual awareness (Cooper, 1930b).

Cooper's vision about liberal arts and manual training did not neglect collectivity or sociohistorical factors. To Cooper, teachers, parents, and community members were each responsible for developing Black students' talent and knowledge. This assertion shifted the outcomes of Black students' progress from a sole reliance on teachers and educational administrators by asserting the impact of the involvement and participation of surrounding communities (Evans, 2007). Any community's efforts in education existed in the broader social and historical climate of the country. While Cooper believed that "the color of a man's face . . . has no more to do with his worthiness and companionableness than the color of his eyes or the shades of his eyes," she was well aware that America had a "race problem" (Cooper, 1892a, p. 163; Cooper, 1892b, p. 131). This irrational problem constrained the efforts of communities that aimed to support Black students. By considering and confronting how unjust racist systems influenced students' education, communities could help establish healthy and inclusive learning environments and curricula (Sulé, 2013).

In "What Are We Worth?" (1892), Cooper urged individuals to contemplate the outcome of education by reflecting on the following: "*What sort of men does it turn out? Does [the] system make boys and girls superficial and mechanical? Is it a producing of average percentages or a rounding out of manhood—a sound, thorough, and practical development—or a scramble for standing and marks?*" (Cooper, 1892a, p. 186). Her educational thought did not shy away from directly addressing these questions and, in doing so, formulated key perspectives on women's education, the roles of teachers, and the purpose of education and positioned her as one of the pivotal Black educational thinkers at the turn of the 20th century.

REFERENCES

Alridge, D. P. (2018). *The educational thought of W. E. B. Du Bois: An intellectual history*. Teachers College Press.

Anderson, J. D. (1988). *The education of Blacks in the South, 1860–1935*. University of North Carolina Press.

Breaux, R. M. (2002). "Maintaining a home for girls": The Iowa Federation of Colored Women's Clubs at the University of Iowa, 1919–1950. *Journal of African American History, 87*(2), 236–255.

Closson, T. (2023, March 22). Inside a Brooklyn school teaching the course that Florida banned. *The New York Times.* Retrieved from https://www.nytimes.com/2023/03/22/nyregion/ap-african-american-studies-brooklyn.html

Cooper, A. J. (1890). The higher education of women. In L. Charles & E. Bhan (Eds.), *The voice of Anna Julia Cooper: Including a voice from the South and other important essays, papers, and letters* (pp. 72–88). Rowman & Littlefield.

Cooper, A. J. (1892a). What are we worth? In L. Charles & E. Bhan (Eds.), *The voice of Anna Julia Cooper: Including a voice from the South and other important essays, papers, and letters* (pp. 72–88). Rowman & Littlefield.

Cooper, A. J. (1892b). Has America a race problem? If so, how can it best be solved? In L. Charles & E. Bhan (Eds.), *The voice of Anna Julia Cooper: Including a voice from the South and other important essays, papers, and letters* (pp. 72–88). Rowman & Littlefield.

Cooper, A. J. (1930a). The humor of teaching. In L. Charles & E. Bhan (Eds.), *The voice of Anna Julia Cooper: Including a voice from the South and other important essays, papers, and letters* (pp. 72–88). Rowman & Littlefield.

Cooper, A. J. (1930b). On education. In L. Charles & E. Bhan (Eds.), *The voice of Anna Julia Cooper: Including a voice from the South and other important essays, papers, and letters* (pp. 248–259). Rowman & Littlefield.

Du Bois, W. E. B. (1903a). The talented tenth. In E. F. Provenzo (Ed.), *Du Bois on education* (pp. 75–92). Rowman & Littlefield.

Du Bois, W. E. B. (1903b). Of the training of Black men. In E. F. Provenzo (Ed.), *Du Bois on education* (pp. 51–65). Rowman & Littlefield.

Evans, S. Y. (2007). *Black women in the ivory tower, 1850–1954: An intellectual history.* University Press of Florida.

Gates, H. L., Jr. (2023, February 17). Who's afraid of Black history? *The New York Times.* Retrieved from https://www.nytimes.com/2023/02/17/opinion/desantis-florida-african-american-studies-black-history.html

Harlan, L. R. (1970). Booker T. Washington in perspective. In R. W. Smock (Ed.), *Booker T. Washington in perspective: Essays of Louis R. Harlan* (pp. 3–22). University Press of Mississippi, 1988.

Hine, D. C. (Ed.). (1997). *Facts on File encyclopedia of Black women in America: Education.* Facts on File.

Johnson, K. (2000). *Uplifting the women and the race: The lives, educational philosophies and social activism of Anna Julia Cooper and Nannie Helen Burroughs.* Taylor & Francis.

May, V. M. (2007). *Anna Julia Cooper, visionary Black feminist: A critical introduction.* Taylor & Francis.

May, V. M. (2021). Anna Julia Cooper, archival absences, and Black women's "muffled" knowledge. *Tulsa Studies in Women's Literature, 40*(2), 241–272.

McCluskey, A. T. (2014). *A forgotten sisterhood: Pioneering Black women educators and activists in the Jim Crow South.* Rowman & Littlefield.

Perkins, L. M. (1983). The impact of the "cult of true womanhood" on the education of Black women. *Journal of Social Issues, 39*(3), 17–28.

Sulé, V. T. (2013). Intellectual activism: The praxis of Dr. Anna Julia Cooper as a blueprint for equity-based pedagogy. *Feminist Teacher, 23*(3), 211–229.

CHAPTER 17

The Myth of Gender Dominance in Higher Education

Linda Eisenmann

Most people recognize that the earliest American colleges were for men only. The new United States needed professionals like lawyers, ministers, physicians, and statesmen—none of whom would be women. In fact, the 20 colleges that existed in 1800 were all created by men for male students; only in the 1830s did small numbers of women begin to attend advanced education although initially in institutions that rarely met college standards. This longstanding male dominance led to a feeling that women have been routinely disadvantaged by higher education, and deeply need the many programs that try to bolster their overall attendance or their participation in specific fields like the sciences and mathematics. But in recent decades, as women have prospered, a new view has emerged that men are losing out in higher education. This concern over a "male crisis" in American colleges highlights the belief—a myth—that when one gender dominates collegiate populations, the other must surely be suffering discrimination.

Around 1980, women's collegiate enrollment overtook men's, and today, women predominate among college students, creating what one article calls "the highest recorded gender imbalance favoring women seen in U.S. college enrollment" (Leukhina & Smaldone, 2022). The National Center for Education Statistics shows that in 2020, women were 58% of all undergraduates, and further, that their graduation rate is about 7 percentage points higher than men's (NCES, 2022). At many institutions, women constitute almost two-thirds of all students, including at many Historically Black Colleges and Universities, where men represent only one in three undergraduates (Harris & Stephens, 2023). NCES further notes that men's college enrollment has been declining over recent years, especially so during the COVID pandemic; in fall 2020, only 41% of college students overall were men (Reeves & Smith, 2021). All of this has led to a spate of both popular and scholarly articles worrying about women's dominance and men's departure from college, framing it as a "male college crisis," asking why men are "giving up on college" and what colleges can do to attract more male students (Belkin, 2021; Harris & Stephens, 2023; Krupnick, 2023; Reeves & Smith, 2021).

How did the American college scene change so dramatically, going from completely excluding women to one where men are now seen as losing out in higher education? How did we forget the recognition that women generally rely on advanced educational credentials to counterbalance the job market's traditional favoritism toward men? How did we move from celebrating women's progress to a worry over educational backlash against men? This chapter will look at participation by women and men in higher education over time, looking for periods when gender influenced college attendance. We will see an uphill gain for women without a loss for men, at least until recently. In examining the myths around gender dominance, we will also see how women thought about their place in higher education. If we had to pick a tipping point, where both women and men started thinking differently about college, we should start with World War II, when women moved into spaces vacated by men, and then move into the postwar period, when the GI Bill and a huge rise in federal funding for higher education boosted college attendance by everyone. Although the postwar period didn't change enrollments permanently, it set up conditions that moved us toward the current situation.

THE IMPACT OF WORLD WAR II

When we think about American women during World War II and shortly thereafter, Rosie the Riveter often comes to mind as a symbol of women stepping up to do what was necessary to support the war effort and fill in for absent men. Rosie and her female colleagues didn't want to usurp men's roles; rather, they were needed to manage work that could no longer be done by men heading to the armed forces. So, sacrifice and serving the common good marked wartime women's efforts. And it was matched by a sense that after war's end, these same women stepped back, giving up the jobs they had taken on, graciously returning to home and family when the men came home. Their willingness to do so helped build families and pave the way for the new middle-class lifestyle that would bloom in 1950s America.

In colleges and universities, the same swap occurred as in the job market. During wartime, many colleges simply would have closed for lack of enrollment if women had not taken men's places in classrooms and campus leadership positions. Yet, when the war finished and male veterans returned home, the job market could absorb only some of them, leading a huge number of former soldiers to use the new GI Bill to attend college and gain new skills. But that surge created problems for the women students: Without enough space now for everyone on campus, women students stepped aside, either leaving college or simply not entering at all. Ultimately, the generous federal support of the GI Bill not only helped ease servicemen's return to civilian life, but also, the thinking suggests, permanently changed college-going in America into a much more democratic practice that now reached a wider variety of students.

COLLEGE ENROLLMENTS OVER TIME

But how did this shift in college-going lead to women's current predominance, especially if more men were finding their way into higher education? To get a fuller picture of how the war and postwar affected college choice, we can look at enrollment changes over time. Early on, college was seen as a place either for the wealthy or for extremely earnest students. In 1900, only 2.3% of the 18–24 age group (men and women) attended college, and the percentage grew to only 4.7% by 1920. Just before the start of WWII in 1940, only 14% of the 18–21 age group pursued higher education (NCES, 1993, p. 76).

Yet, even with these low numbers, colleges had become increasingly appealing to both American women and men by about the 1920s. The older view was giving way to a youth culture that brought in a wider variety of students—both male and female—who valued campus social life, cultural opportunities, and athletic contests (Horowitz, 1988). In fact, after decades of being told that college was neither important nor useful for them, women in 1920 represented nearly half (47%) of all college students (the percentage dropped to 43% in the 1930s Depression). At the start of WWII, there were 1.4 million American college students, and 41.6% were women (Eisenmann, 2006). A large portion of these women students were preparing for jobs in teaching or nursing, but both women and men had begun to view college as a stepping stone to professional jobs in growing industries like banking, advertising, and merchandising. Students now attended many kinds of colleges, from the ever-growing state colleges and universities to the smaller liberal arts colleges, teacher-training institutions, religious institutions, and single-sex colleges. The community colleges—then known as junior colleges—would not grow in prominence until the 1960s. So, women were making steady—if not always consistent—gains as college-goers over time.

The enrollment balance changed during WWII, however. As more and more men were called to military service, women students stayed in college, once again constituting half of the student population. Generally, college women did not leave school to join the workforce; those Rosie the Riveter wartime jobs were filled by women who were not in college, primarily unmarried women (4 times as many women workers were single than married in 1940). Only recently has research begun to focus on women's college-going during the war itself. As historian Charles Dorn (2018) explains, our customary view that women advanced only because the men were missing paints women students as just "passively benefiting from a scarcity of civilian men on campus" (p. 536). Instead, he suggests, women were active wartime students, looking for ways to support the national defense effort by studying scientific fields like chemistry, engineering, and mathematics; moving confidently into campus and statewide leadership roles (often defeating male candidates for these positions); and preparing themselves for the work world after college. In Dorn's study of the University of California at Berkeley—where women were 63% of all students in 1944—the number of women earning degrees in mathematics doubled during the war. In other words, women college students were building for their postwar futures, not envisioning a quick retreat to family and home.

THE VETERANS ARRIVE

The enrollment picture changed again at war's end, and it did so rapidly. In 1945, only 5.2% of the college population were returning veterans. But by 1946, veterans' use of the new GI Bill was in full swing. In both 1946 and 1947, veterans were 49% of all college enrollments (Eisenmann, 2006). Consider the impact of such a change: In just two years, across campuses of all types, half of the students were veterans studying under the GI Bill. Why was the GI Bill so appealing? In addition to low-interest housing loans and unemployment insurance, its educational benefits gave a full year of educational support to all veterans who had served at least 90 days, plus money for one day of schooling for each additional day of their service (up to 48 months). For the average veteran, this amounted to $500 for tuition, books, and fees, plus a monthly living stipend, and it might easily cover 4 full years of college. Male veterans used the GI Bill at higher rates than female veterans (about 41% to 35%). In fact, when women veterans were asked about claiming their benefit, they often said that the men had contributed more, generally seeing themselves in supporting roles.

Overall, the veterans pushed for entry into the best schools they could get into. Private colleges and universities and high-prestige schools attracted huge interest from veterans who could now pay for any school that accepted them. When seats filled in those institutions, veterans then chose teachers colleges, junior colleges, and small institutions—places where women had previously swelled enrollments. Nationally, a rather romantic view of these returning soldiers developed, with magazines and newspapers carrying stories and photos of veterans strolling across campus, surrounded by their young families and supportive wives. In most of these, if women were visible at all, it was as helpmates to men, rarely as career-minded or studious fellow classmates, even though women still constituted nearly 30% of the student body. Over time, and especially as college-going increased throughout the 1950s, 1960s, and 1970s, the GI Bill was credited with expanding collegiate opportunity to a wider group of Americans, changing their experiences and their fortunes.

Historians have recognized, however, that not all of the huge influx of veterans comprised students new to college. In fact, many of the veterans were actually returning to degree work that had been interrupted by the war. Studies suggest that about 20% of the collegiate veterans were men who would not have attended college without the GI Bill. So, yes, college-going expanded, but less than the monumental shift often attributed to the GI Bill and its veterans.

And what happened to the women students who had sustained campuses during the war and pursued degrees designed for new postwar roles? How did these changes affect the gender balance of higher education? When the veterans came in 1946 with the first GI Bill funds in hand, colleges rushed to accommodate them, often offering spaces that women had occupied. Hunter College, for instance, had been a public women's college focused on preparing teachers; it became coeducational to serve male veterans, shifting its focus away from its traditional base. With higher enrollment demand, many colleges created quotas to limit the numbers of both women and nonveterans in their student bodies. Schools that had eagerly taken women students just 5 years earlier were now rejecting them in favor of the steady supply of well-funded veterans. The University of Michigan, for example, reduced its enrollment of 1st-year women by a third and kept that quota for 8 years; UC Berkeley reduced its percentage of women from the wartime high of 63% to only one-third of all its students (Dorn, 2008; Eisenmann, 2006).

THE IMPACT ON COLLEGIATE WOMEN

A traditional—and rather convenient—aspect of the myth about gender balance suggests that women graciously and willingly stepped aside from both the job market and the college campus to accommodate men's preferences. If this were so, then men's gains would not necessarily cause women's losses, as the myth foretells. But this view deeply underestimates the extent to which women were intentionally sidelined after the war. It is true that the youngest women in the wartime job market left work shortly afterward, presumably to start families. But women over the age of 30 actually increased their job market participation; women whose families were already started or grown showed a participation increase of more than 10 percentage points from 1940 to 1950 (Eisenmann, 2006). Yet, unfortunately for women's long-term prospects, employers generally viewed them as short-term, substitute workers who would leave employment as family needs arose or as men needed those jobs. So, investments in women as long-term, serious professional workers rarely happened. "Womanpower" might have been appealing during the war, but it was seldom invoked afterward as a way to build the postwar workforce.

Further, as the creation of collegiate quotas shows, women did not willingly step aside from campuses, disciplines, and roles they had built during the war. Because of choices made by both the veterans and the universities, women found themselves at smaller institutions geared toward traditionally female careers. Making matters worse for the long term, however, the biggest growth in higher education—in terms of size, research support, and prestige—began to occur at the very types of schools that now were least committed to women students. In effect, then, men's gains did mean losses for women students.

The 1950s brought enormous financial investment from the federal government. Even after the WWII veterans finished college, both the government and industry began to pour money into research institutions like the universities of Michigan and California and private schools like MIT and Stanford, hoping to capitalize on defense developments from the war and the new needs of a postwar environment. To show how quickly this financing helped higher education, at the end of the war, only eight universities were larger than 20,000 students. But 20 years later, in 1967, 55 schools exceeded that size, many of them public universities. As these schools grew, so did the variety of funding to support them. Higher education's overall spending increased tenfold from 1950 ($2.2 billion) to 1970 ($21 billion) (Eisenmann, 2006).

Women, however, were not well-positioned at these wealthy, research-oriented universities; in fact, these were the very schools that had created quotas in favor of veterans and men. Overall, less than one-third of all women students attended large universities by 1962, which served men so well. Women's largest percentages by far were at teachers colleges and liberal arts schools. The overall drop in women's participation was especially keen at the graduate school level. During and just after the war, women had maintained a strong place in graduate programs, earning nearly one-half of all master's degrees. Although their participation as PhD students had never been especially strong, it had reached about 20% during the war. However, as those students finished, fewer women moved into graduate work, finding little encouragement for their advanced training in research-oriented settings. Women's proportion of master's students dropped from 50% in 1946, to 32% in 1948, and under 30% by 1951. Throughout the growth period of higher education to 1965, women remained merely a third of master's degrees earned and only 10% of doctoral degrees (Eisenmann, 2006).

Even though these numbers show women as about one-third of undergraduate and master's students in the 1950s and early 1960s, few campus leaders gave them proportionate attention. Just as women workers were treated as substitute, nonserious employees, so too were women students treated as ancillary. That is, campus policies, practices, and procedures were seldom created with women's needs in mind; women were important to bolster enrollments, yes, but they were treated as incidental in terms of their curriculum, their funding, and their research opportunities. The focus was on men who would more readily find training and job opportunities in the postwar world. Interestingly, there was no concern about a "female crisis" in higher education as men's enrollment grew at the most prestigious and wealthy schools.

LONG-TERM IMPLICATIONS

The lower profile of women at big, research-oriented universities had long-term effects on their success as students and as professors, leading to later periods of affirmative action on their behalf. The biggest growth in higher education throughout the 1950s and 1960s came at the large institutions, especially because they were seen as hugely important to the nation's scientific and technological advancement. But because women were least present there, they missed out on the well-funded preparation of scientists and other researchers that occurred throughout this period. Likewise, with fewer women pursuing graduate degrees, there were scant numbers of women available to become the professors and leading researchers in these various fields. When the 1970s women's movement began to push women to consider "non-traditional" careers in law, medicine, and business, it was reacting to several decades of people asserting that these were roles best filled by men. And when 1990s scholars began to question the low participation of women in science, they were recognizing the impact of a trend that started with the post–WWII era.

POSTSCRIPT

It took women 35 years to regain the level of educational participation they experienced during World War II, when they supposedly stepped aside to support men. Only in 1980 did women once again become a full half of all college students, as they had been in 1944 (and earlier, in 1920) (Solomon, 1985). Eventually, encouragement for women to pursue a variety of fields, as well as graduate work, allowed them to succeed in areas previously closed to them. For instance, more than half of current law students and medical students are women, and at the undergraduate level, about 60% of all students identify as women. On the federal level, funding from the Higher Education Act and Pell grants has financially supported women's college efforts, and Title IX has helped their ability to study safely and equitably; the women's movement has supported their advancement into new areas (Rose, 2018).

And yet this progress, so hard-won over time, is now producing the backlash around "the male college crisis." The popular press and even higher education organizations take the view that women's predominance in higher education must somehow discriminate against, or at least discourage, men from participating (Belkin, 2021; Harris & Stephens, 2023; Krupnick, 2023; Reeves & Smith, 2021). Some men express worry that college is unnecessary to their future and "might be a scam," whereas women have always relied on educational credentials to help with the job market—an important explanation for women's ongoing commitment to completing college (Belkin, 2021; Krupnick, 2023).

So, rather than celebrating women's progress—which was the focus in the 1990s and early 2000s—critics now see a crisis around male student participation. Rather like the post–WWII era, women are being seen as the "add-ons" who support higher education, rather than as the central players. While few would actively argue against women choosing college, a feeling (myth?) remains that the enterprise is most complete and successful when it serves men best.

REFERENCES

Belkin, D. (2021, September 6). A generation of American men give up on college: "I just feel lost." *The Wall Street Journal*. Retrieved from https://www.wsj.com/articles/college-university-fall-higher-education-men-women-enrollment-admissions-back-to-school-11630948233

Dorn, C. (2008). "A woman's world": The University of California, Berkeley, during the Second World War. *History of Education Quarterly, 48*, 534–564.

Eisenmann, L. (2006). *Higher education for women in postwar America, 1945–1965*. Johns Hopkins University Press.

Harris, N., & Stephens, S. (2023, April 22). At many HBCUs, just 1 in 3 students are men. Here's why that matters. *The Washington Post*. Retrieved from https://www.washingtonpost.com/education/2023/04/22/hbcus-black-men-enrollment/

Horowitz, H. H. (1988). *Campus life: Undergraduate cultures from the end of the eighteenth century to the present*. University of Chicago Press.

Krupnick, M. (2023, May 8). The latest group to get special attention from college admissions offices: Men. *The Hechinger Report*. Retrieved from https://hechingerreport.org/the-latest-group-to-get-special-attention-from-college-admissions-offices-men/

Leukhina, O., & Smaldone, A. (2022, March 15). Why do women outnumber men in college enrollment? *Federal Reserve Bank of St. Louis*. Retrieved from https://www.stlouisfed.org/on-the-economy/2022/mar/why-women-outnumber-men-college-enrollment

National Center for Education Statistics (NCES). (1993). *120 years of American education: A statistical portrait*. Retrieved from https://nces.ed.gov/pubs93/93442.pdf

National Center for Education Statistics. (2022). Integrated Postsecondary Education Data System (IPEDS), Winter 2020–21, Graduation Rates component. See *Digest of Education Statistics 2021*, table 326.10. Retrieved from https://nces.ed.gov/fastfacts/display.asp?id=98

Reeves, R., & Smith, E. (2021, October 8). The male college crisis is not just in enrollment but completion. *Brookings Institute*. Retrieved from https://www.brookings.edu/blog/up-front/2021/10/08/the-male-college-crisis-is-not-just-in-enrollment-but-completion/

Rose, D. (2018). *Citizens by degree: Higher education policy and the changing gender dynamics of American citizenship*. Oxford University Press.

Solomon, B. M. (1985). *In the company of educated women: A history of women and higher education in America*. Yale University Press.

CHAPTER 18

The Myth of the Asian American Model Minority, American Individualism, and Meritocracy

Sharon S. Lee and Yoon K. Pak

At the time of writing this chapter, Asian Americans have been making headlines. On October 31, 2022, the Supreme Court heard the cases *Students for Fair Admissions (SFFA) v. Harvard* and *Students for Fair Admissions v. University of North Carolina (UNC)*. SFFA argued that universities' consideration of race in admissions was unconstitutional. In particular, conservative strategist Ed Blum, founder of SFFA, recruited Asian Americans for these cases, claiming that affirmative action set a de facto quota limiting Asian American admissions (Lee, 2021). Framed as a model minority that had achieved stellar academic success, Asian Americans represented a compelling victim of race-conscious admissions policies.

This narrative is part of an enduring falsehood about Asian Americans, what scholars and activists call the model minority myth. Since the 1960s, strategists, educators, and journalists have embraced this myth that lauds Asian Americans as exemplars of a racial minority quietly overcoming racism and poverty through hard work and sacrifice, bolstered by the "right" cultural values of self-reliance, obedience, and reverence for education. The model minority myth proposes that Asian cultural dispositions involve putting one's head down and not making trouble or demanding government handouts. Asian American success, "evidenced" by aggregate average statistics, has allowed them to assimilate and move beyond race, as SFFA argues. As racial minorities, they are poster children who "prove" that racism is over.

Despite this praise, Asian Americans are also making headlines for other reasons. The COVID-19 pandemic has ushered in a pandemic of racial hatred, blaming Asians for the deadly virus due to its origins in China. In 2020, the organization Stop AAPI Hate reported nearly 3,800 incidents of anti-Asian hate in all 50 states, a large and alarming increase from the year before, with incidents including verbal harassment, physical assault, civil rights violations, and online harassment (Jeung et al., 2020). The March 2021 shooting deaths of eight victims at Asian-owned spas in Atlanta further demonstrated the rise in anti-Asian violence specifically targeted to women.

On the surface, these two images seem to conflict: How can Asian Americans be both lauded and reviled? How can they be praised as model minorities who have overcome racism yet also bear the brunt of such racialized hatred and violence? The reality is that the model minority image is indeed a myth—despite its alluring appeal of color-blindness and promise of individual meritocracy, it ignores historical and present-day structural barriers that have kept people of color from being fully embraced in U.S. society and the ways Asian Americans in particular are racialized as foreigners and never truly American. This chapter will detangle these messages by first outlining the origins of the model minority myth in a larger context of U.S. race relations. It will then debunk the myth, exposing its flawed foundations on cultural difference and identifying continued structural barriers and discrimination that Asian Americans face, as well as the many harms of the myth. It will lastly highlight the important ways Asian Americans have been actively involved protesting racial injustice, refusing to be part of a model minority narrative that paints them as passive and that pits communities of color against each other. By exposing the ways Asian Americans are props that bolster the myth of American individualism, we hope readers can see how Asian Americans are not model minorities that are inherently or culturally primed for success nor stand as proof that racism is over.

ASIAN AMERICAN HISTORY AND THE ORIGINS OF THE MODEL MINORITY MYTH

The view of Asians as unassimilable has been a part of the U.S. imagination from the earliest settlements of Filipino sailors in Louisiana in the 1750s. They were seen as "Orientals" who were racially inferior to Caucasians, resulting in local and national legislation banning immigrants from China, Japan, Korea, India, and the Philippines from owning land, testifying in court, or marrying outside of their race during the 19th and 20th centuries (Lee, 2015). White laborers lynched and drove Asian immigrants out of towns along the West Coast, as they were seen as cheap competitors. Anti-Asian racism restricted Asian immigrants from gaining citizenship as the Supreme Court ruled in *Ozawa v. United States* (1922) and *United States v. Bhagat Singh Thind* (1923) that only Caucasian and White persons could naturalize. Ultimately, xenophobia blocked Asian immigration to the United States starting with the 1882 Chinese Exclusion Act through the World War II era.

Asian Americans were always identified with their "home" countries in Asia, so during times of national crisis, they were demonized as disloyal and suspect. One of the most egregious examples of this foreigner racialization is the World War II incarceration of 120,000 Japanese Americans (two-thirds of whom were U.S. citizens) after the bombing of Pearl Harbor, despite no evidence of their espionage or disloyalty.

The depiction of Asian Americans as disloyal, unassimilable aliens sharply shifted during World War II. As the United States fought a war for democracy while maintaining segregated military ranks, new political pressures emerged for racial integration and equity in the postwar Civil Rights Movement. It was during this time when popular press articles emphasized domestic harmony and U.S. exceptionalism by featuring Chinese and Japanese Americans as model minorities, groups that had assimilated and overcome racism without complaint through individual hard work. In 1966, William Petersen of *The New York Times* and a sociologist from UC Berkeley highlighted Japanese American success post-incarceration due to a purported respect for authority, tenacity, and self-reliance. Similarly, a 1996 *U.S. News and World Report* article touted Chinese Americans as rising up from discrimination through self-respect and hard work. Ultimately, "At a time when it is being proposed that hundreds of billions be spent to uplift Negroes and other minorities, the nation's 300,000 Chinese-Americans are moving ahead on their own—with no help from anyone else" ("Success Story," 1966, p. 6). As African American civil rights activists pushed for institutional reforms toward racial equity, both liberals and conservatives held up the Asian model minority as evidence of assimilation, individualism, and success beyond race and the promise of democracy.

The alluring model minority myth continued during the 1980s, aligning with the neoconservative era under Ronald Reagan that included rollback of enforcement of civil rights legislation and cuts in funding for social programs for the poor. A 1987 *Time* magazine cover story touted Asian American whiz kids and reinforced the model minority message that anything was achievable through education and hard work, asserting that Asian Americans "have already shown that U.S. education can still produce excellence. The largely successful Asian-American experience is a challenging counterpoint to the charges that U.S. schools are now producing less-educated mainstream students and failing to help underclass blacks and Hispanics" (Brand, 1987, p. 51). Thus, nothing was wrong with the system.

The image of Asian American success fueled arguments against race-conscious admissions policies during the 1980s and 1990s, and which SFFA continues today. During the 1980s, despite the growth in Asian American applications to prestigious universities, their admission rates had flattened, leading to investigations to assess if quotas were being imposed to limit Asian American numbers. While the initial focus was on the ways universities gave White students (more often legacy admits, donors, and recruited athletes) a structural advantage to admission, conservative pundits began to embrace Asian Americans as "victims" of race-conscious admissions that gave consideration to underrepresented and "unqualified" students of color

(Takagi, 1992). Sociologist Dana Takagi (1992) notes that bringing Asian Americans into the debate was a way to argue that an anti-affirmative action position was not racist but rather promoted individual fairness, and that Asian Americans as a non-White group were actually harmed by affirmative action. The Asian American model minority image supported arguments for admission based on individual meritocracy and became a powerful rhetorical tool to justify a system rooted in the White status quo, ignoring historical and structural racial discrimination.

A historical analysis of the Asian American model minority myth reveals the ways that the trope of individual success, meritocracy, self-reliance, and quiet assimilation emerged in a specific context when civil rights activists were pushing for systemic change to address racial inequity. The model minority myth bolsters the individual meritocracy narrative and the myth of racial equality in the United States and serves a political purpose of ending race-conscious policies and services and maintaining the normalcy of Whiteness.

DEBUNKING THE MYTH

Asians Americans Are Diverse

One of the biggest problems with the model minority myth is that, as with any myth, it broadly overgeneralizes a population. Asian Americans (and Pacific Islanders who are also often lumped into an Asian Pacific American category) are vastly diverse along ethnicity (of which there are at least 40), socioeconomic status, religion, culture, and immigration/refugee trajectory to the United States. The trope of Asian American academic success is dominated by stories of East and South Asian immigrant populations that obscure the totality of experiences of underserved groups such as Southeast Asian and Pacific Islander populations, where household income and college completion rates remain low (Teranishi, 2010). There are also significant socioeconomic variations within an ethnic group: In 2010, Chinese Americans had a higher average personal income than the general population, and yet 14% of that population lived in poverty (Lee, 2015). By embracing a myth of Asian American success, many Asian American subgroups' needs are erased.

The Limits of Model Minority Praise:
Asian Americans Are Forever Foreigners

It is clear that to claim that *all* Asian Americans are academically and financially successful is profoundly inaccurate, so we must emphasize the diversity of this population. Yet at the same time, Asian Americans encounter shared racialization not only as model minorities but as foreigners, with examples being the 1982 murder of Chinese American Vincent Chin (blamed by unemployed White auto workers in Detroit for presumably being Japanese); the rise of anti-Muslim and anti-Sikh violence in the wake of September 11; and present-day anti-Asian hate during the COVID-19 pandemic (Lee, 2015).

While many may say that the model minority myth is a compliment, it is important to understand that it is a false adoration; in fact, it is premised on Asian foreignness. The myth is grounded in the presumption that Asian Americans distinctly value education and sacrifice due to their cultural otherness. As the model minority myth is based on foreigner racialization, the model minority can be both lauded for industry and intelligence and deemed unfairly competitive, sneaky, nerdy, and clannish (Lee, 2006). History shows that model minority praise easily flips into resentment against Asian Americans who are seen as foreigners, threats, and never truly "American."

Structural Avenues for Success and Limitations

In the aggregate, Asian Americans appear to have "made it," achieving high household incomes and educational levels. However, disaggregated data show greater variation that stems from structural and historical barriers as well as intricate histories of various Asian ethnic populations in the context of U.S. imperialism, global warfare, and displacement. Research has revealed that it is not about culture, or Confucian values, but rather the conditions of immigration policy post-1965 that gave way to a preference for a more educated and professional population to enter the United States Lee (2014) outlines how about a third of post-1965 immigrants from Asia were professionals; for groups such as those from India, a majority represented physicians, engineers, and scientists. This provided ways for certain groups such as those in the medical, science, and engineering fields to gain entry.

While the 1965 immigration legislation gave preference to professionals, having a professional degree did not ensure success. In fact, many Asians experienced downward mobility due to language and employment barriers that did not recognize degrees earned in Asia. For example, in 1973, only one-third of Korean nurses had state licenses, and 600 Korean physicians could not practice medicine in Southern California (Lee, 2014). Vietnamese, Chinese, Korean, South Asians, and Filipino immigrants engaged in self-entrepreneurship at high rates, shut out of fields due to state licensing barriers. Such experiences resulted in emphasizing educational attainment among some immigrant parents, as a strategy for upward mobility given limited ways to achieve the supposed American dream. Whereas other White European immigrant groups had multiple means to attain employment, especially union jobs with benefits, Asians were essentially foreclosed from the beginning.

For Asian subgroups who have attained high rates of education and income, glass ceilings persist for raises and job promotion, revealing the limitations of how high this model minority can achieve (Chou & Feagin, 2008). For instance, a 2018 report found that Asian Americans' median household income in Chicago was nearly $15,000 less than Whites; that Asian Americans experience a return on education that was one-third less than Whites; and Asian Americans with a college degree were 25% less likely than Whites to work in management (Scarborough et al., 2018). Research also shows that while Asian American representation in higher education enrollment is high, they are vastly underrepresented at the highest levels of university presidents (Ono, 2013).

The model minority myth is a fallacy. It harms Asian American students by culturally essentializing and erasing their complex experiences and identities; ignoring those who continue to struggle and lack resources; placing undue pressure to succeed; and ignoring the ways anti-Asian hate and foreigner racialization persist. It ignores legislation and structures that have both facilitated and blocked success for this diverse community, claiming that the right attitude and culture are all that are needed to succeed (Ng et al., 2007).

NOT YOUR MODEL MINORITY: ASIAN AMERICAN ACTIVISM

One last facet of the model minority myth lies in its depiction of Asian Americans as successful not only due to hard work and values but also because they do not complain. Their success comes from keeping quiet and enduring injustice. Yet this too is untrue. There is a long history of activism by Asian and Asian American communities for educational equity and civil rights. For example, shortly after the passage of the 1882 Chinese Exclusion Act, the landmark *Tape v. Hurley* (1885) school segregation case in San Francisco brought attention to Chinese exclusion in the (White) public schools. Joseph and Mary Tape sued the San Francisco Board of Education and the principal of Spring Valley Primary School, Jennie Hurley, for barring their eldest daughter, Mamie Tape, from attending the White public school. The Superior Court Judge ruled in favor of the Tapes in 1885, but the passage of the California State Assembly's Bill 268 in the same year allowed for the establishment of separate schools for children of "Mongolian or Chinese" descent, thus setting a foundation to legalize "separate but equal" under *Plessy v. Ferguson* (1896). The Tape case was one of several important school segregation cases where Asian immigrant parents, who were legally excluded from attaining naturalized citizenship in the United States prior to 1952, used the power of the courts to argue for civil rights for their U.S.-born children. Similarly, *Aoki v. Deane* (1907) in San Francisco and *Gong Lum v. Rice* (1927) in Rosedale, Mississippi, were historic legal battles that questioned the basis of racial exclusion of Asian American children in the White public schools (Loewen, 1971; Wollenberg, 1976).

In the 1960s and 1970s, Asian American college students and community leaders participated in interracial coalitions during the Civil Rights Movement. The Third World Liberation Front at San Francisco State College in 1968 was established to confront U.S. colonialism during the Vietnam war, question structural racial and class inequalities, and foment changes in higher education to include ethnic studies and a culturally relevant curriculum (Umemoto, 1989).

In the present day, Asian American activists have been vocal in raising awareness of growing anti-Asian violence in the wake of COVID-19. Organizations such as Stop AAPI Hate formed in March 2020 in response to the escalation of anti-Asian hate to report incidents of violence, harassment, and discrimination. Organizations like Asian Americans Advancing Justice have hosted bystander trainings, and community organizations in Los Angeles led self-defense classes for Asian elders (Zhou, 2022). Ignorance about the long history of Asians in the United States also propelled activists and educators to push for the passage of curriculum changes to require Asian American history in K–12 public education. Illinois was the first such state to pass this legislation in July 2021, with New Jersey to follow shortly thereafter (Committee of 100, n.d.).

In these important ways, Asian American activists have rejected the empty promise of a color-blind meritocracy. They challenge the injustice and racial discrimination they face, knowing that regardless of how hard they work, they are not assured racial equity. Asian American communities have also allied with other communities of color to reject the model minority myth of individual meritocracy. As mentioned earlier, as politicians and the media embraced Asian Americans as model minorities during the Civil Rights Movement, and in doing so, shunned African American and Latinx communities for lacking the "correct" cultural values and family structures and for relying on the welfare state. These arguments persist today, such as in Ruby Payne's framework of poverty that blames poverty on the failure of Black and Brown communities to adopt the "right" cultural values of morality and hard work rather than on larger structural barriers, lack of resources, segregation, and tracking (Gorski, 2006; Ng & Rury, 2006).

The model minority myth works to pit communities against each other—in its embrace of one group, it denigrates another and fuels resentment and bolsters a racial pecking order. However, Asian American communities have worked with other communities in cross-racial collaboration for racial equity. For example, in 1965, Larry Itliong organized Filipino American grape workers in Delano, California, and worked with Cesar Chavez and Mexican American farmworkers in a series of strikes that led to pay raises, health-care benefits, and safety protections. Additionally, Asian American activists in the 1960s such as Grace Lee Boggs in Detroit and Yuri

Kochiyama in New York City fought for civil rights, women's rights, and Black power. And several Asian American organizations have supported Black Lives Matter protests, providing multilingual resources to facilitate intergenerational conversations about anti-Black racism (Jones, 2021). And while Asian American plaintiffs in the SFFA Supreme Court cases argued against affirmative action, the majority of Asian American organizations rejected the notion that they were model minorities injured by race-conscious admissions that favored Blacks and Latinx students. The National Asian Pacific American Bar Association, Asian Americans Advancing Justice, and the Asian American Legal Defense and Education Fund filed amicus briefs in support of race-conscious admissions and diversity for all students of color. The Asian American Legal Defense and Education Fund argues that "SFFA attempts to use Asian Americans and the model-minority myth as a way to deny opportunities to other underrepresented minorities, which harms all minorities and benefits only white applicants" (Erskine et al., 2022, para. 27). It is through these important activist movements that Asian Americans defy the stereotype of passivity and raise their voices to challenge the structural inequity that persists for all people of color.

The Asian American model minority myth is a fallacy and one of the biggest ideas everyone gets wrong about the history of American education. Yet its perpetual allure lies in the way it supports the larger American narrative of individual meritocracy and the American Dream—a narrative that is employed in an ahistorical manner and by involving a historical amnesia that forgets the ways that immigration, housing, education, banking, voting, and similar legislation (all of which were impacted by racism and racial ideologies) have shaped and blocked opportunities given to different communities in the United States.

The value of education and immigrant sacrifice is not a cultural, innate value that Asians have a monopoly on and that other groups lack. It is also not something that guarantees Asian American success—as Asian Americans continue to be racialized as foreigners, they continue to experience discrimination and barriers to their full acceptance as Americans, an acceptance premised on the privileges of Whiteness. The myth implies that hard work and quiet assimilation will ensure success; however, decades of Asian American activism shows that this community has engaged in political resistance to advance their rights and in alliance with other communities of color.

In this historic time of the COVID pandemic, rising awareness of police brutality through the Black Lives Matter movement, and pressures to silence diverse histories through the Don't Say Gay Bill and anti-critical race theory, a critical understanding of history is paramount in order to debunk false myths. As the model minority myth needs to be dismantled, so do the myths of individual meritocracy and the American dream. Historical and structural barriers have shaped the opportunities afforded to and denied to racialized non-White communities in the United States. It is only by understanding this history that we can reject the myth and begin to see a diverse population such as Asian Americans in their full complexity and humanity.

REFERENCES

Aoki v. Deane, Cal 4754 (1907). Retrieved from https://archive.org/details/hejapaneseschool00burk/page/6/mode/2up

Brand, D. (1987, August 31). The new whiz kids. *Time Magazine, 130*, 42–51.

Chou, R. S., & Feagin, J. R. (2008). *The myth of the model minority: Asian Americans facing racism*. Paradigm Publishers.

Committee of 100. (n.d.). AAPI and ethnic studies requirements for K-12 students in America's public schools. Retrieved from https://www.committee100.org/our-work/k-12-asian-american-and-pacific-islander-and-ethnic-studies-in-the-united-states/

Erskine, E., Gou, A., & Snyder, E. (2022, October 29). A guide to the amicus briefs in the affirmative-action cases. *SCOTUSblog*. Retrieved from https://www.scotusblog.com/2022/10/a-guide-to-the-amicus-briefs-in-the-affirmative-action-cases/

Gong Lum v. Rice, 275 U.S. 78, 48 S. Ct. 91 (1927). Retrieved from https://casetext.com/case/gong-lum-v-rice

Gorski, P. (2006). Savage unrealities: Classism and racism abound in Ruby Payne's framework. *Rethinking Schools, 21*(2), 16–19.

Jeung, R., Yellow Horse, A., Popovic, T., & Lim, R. (March 2020). *Stop AAPI Hate National Report*. Retrieved from https://stopaapihate.org/wp-content/uploads/2021/05/Stop-AAPI-Hate-Report-National-210316.pdf

Jones, V. (2021, March 20). Black-Asian solidarity has a long and storied history in America. *CNN Opinion*. Retrieved from https://www.cnn.com/2021/03/19/opinions/black-asian-american-solidarity-jones

Lee, E. (2015). *The making of Asian America: A history*. Simon and Schuster.

Lee, J. (2021). Asian Americans, affirmative action, and the rise in anti-Asian hate. *Daedalus: The Journal of the American Academy of Arts & Sciences, 150*(2), 180–198.

Lee, S. (2014). *A new history of Asian America*. Routledge.

Lee, S. S. (2006). Over-represented and de-minoritized: The racialization of Asian Americans in higher education. *InterActions: UCLA Journal of Education and Information Studies, 2*(2). Retrieved from https://escholarship.org/uc/item/4r7161b2

Loewen, J. W. (1971). *The Mississippi Chinese: Between Black and White*. Harvard University Press.

Ng, J., Lee, S. S., & Pak, Y. K. (2007). Contesting the model minority and perpetual foreigner stereotypes: A critical review of literature on Asian Americans in education. *Review of Research in Education, 31*(1), 95–130.

Ng, J., & Rury, J. (2006, July 18). Poverty and education: A critical analysis of the Ruby Payne phenomenon. *Teachers College Record, 18*(50), 370–396.

Ono, S. J. (2013, October 28). Why so few Asians are college presidents. *Chronicle of Higher Education*. Retrieved from https://www.chronicle.com/article/why-so-few-asians-are-college-presidents/?cid=gen_sign_in

Ozawa v. United States, 260 U.S. 178 (1922). Retrieved from https://supreme.justia.com/cases/federal/us/260/178/

Peterson, W. (1966, January 9). Success story, Japanese American style. *The New York Times Magazine*, 20–21, 33, 36, 38, 40–41, 43.

Plessy v. Ferguson, 163 U.S. 537 (1896).

Scarborough, W., Lewis, A. E., & Arenas, I. (2018). A tale of diversity, disparity, and discrimination: The state of racial justice for Asian American Chicagoans. University of Illinois Chicago Institute for Research on Race and Public Policy. Retrieved from https://uofi.app.box.com/s/4b7q34e3sp9r25l7v8pw2wbgon70yz9q

"Success story of one minority group in the U.S." (1966, December 26). *U.S. News & World Report*. In A. Tachiki, E. Wong, & F. Odo (Eds.), (1971). *Roots: An Asian American reader*. UCLA Asian American Studies Center.

Takagi, D. Y. (1992). *The retreat from race: Asian-American admissions and racial politics*. Rutgers University Press.

Tape v. Hurley, 66 Cal. 473, 6 (Cal. 1885). Retrieved from https://casetext.com/case/tape-v-hurley

Teranishi, R. (2010). *Asians in the ivory tower: Dilemmas of racial inequality in American higher education*. Teachers College Press.

Umemoto, K. (1989). "On strike!" San Francisco State College strike, 1968–69: The role of Asian American students. *Amerasia Journal*, *15*(1), 3–41.

United States v. Bhagat Singh Thind, 261 U.S. 204 (1923). Retrieved from https://supreme.justia.com/cases/federal/us/261/204/

Wollenberg, C. (1976). *All deliberate speed: Segregation and exclusion in California schools, 1855–1975*. University of California Press.

Zhou, L. (2022, March 15). The stop Asian hate movement is at a crossroads. *Vox*. Retrieved from https://www.vox.com/22820364/stop-asian-hate-movement-atlanta-shootings

Part V

MYTH-ING VOICES AND QUESTIONS

CHAPTER 19

The Myth of De Facto Segregation

Ansley T. Erickson and Andrew R. Highsmith

Whether through racial zoning, federal mortgage insurance and public housing programs, school district gerrymandering, or assorted other means, policymakers in every section of the United States and across the 20th century helped to draw the color line in education and beyond (Rothstein, 2017). Yet one key phrase, or idea, has helped public officials avoid responsibility for their actions: *de facto segregation* (Lassiter, 2010). As the Black author and activist James Baldwin tellingly quipped in 1965, "De facto segregation means that Negroes are segregated, but nobody did it" (Delmont, 2016, p. 6). The deceptively simple concept of de facto segregation paints segregated schools as the result not of government action but of constitutionally permissible decisions made by private individuals in the residential housing market.

Within the confines of the law, de facto segregation is equal parts myth and evasion. The term signals racial segregation "in fact," as contrasted with *de jure segregation*, meaning segregation "in law." A work of fantasy masquerading as history, the term de facto has shaped decades of court rulings and has served as a legal roadblock to school desegregation—more persistent and influential in many ways than the White supremacists who once blocked schoolhouse doors in defiance of the Supreme Court's 1954 *Brown v. Board of Education* ruling (Boddie, 2021; Lassiter, 2010).

Outside of the courts, in public discourse, the term has a history of varied and conflicting uses. Such debates and misunderstandings have persisted into the present. Indeed, de facto segregation is among the most protean, contested, and confusing concepts in the history of American education (Glass, 2018). And yet it remains commonplace for social studies teachers around the country to introduce students to the history of segregation by deploying the categories of de facto and de jure segregation (Rothstein, 2013).

Our brief history of de facto segregation seeks to bring clarity to an idea that has long muddied the waters of educational debate. We start by summarizing the history of segregation, particularly in housing and education, that de facto segregation claims to describe. Then we trace the term's use over time, through its varied invocations for multiple motives. Considering its contested and confounding history, we suggest discarding the use of de facto segregation as a descriptor of the color line and replacing it with concepts that more precisely reflect the dense web of laws, public policies, and private practices that have historically maintained racial segregation. At best a conceptual muddle, at worst a corrosive myth, de facto segregation should be put out to pasture.

SEGREGATING THE UNITED STATES

Evaluating the concept of de facto segregation requires first understanding the history of racial segregation in the United States. The U.S. color line ossified in the late 19th and early 20th centuries. As the reform impulse of the post–Civil War Reconstruction era gave way in the late 1870s and beyond to a resurgent tide of White supremacy, African Americans faced increasing levels of racist violence, disenfranchisement, economic exploitation, and racial segregation. Although African Americans nationwide experienced the emerging Jim Crow order, conditions were particularly oppressive in the South, home to the bulk of the country's Black population (Hunter, 1997; Litwack, 1998). On farms and plantations, coercive systems of sharecropping and tenancy kept many African Americans impoverished (Daniel, 1985; Kelley, 1990). Black children, if they attended school at all, did so in separate and unequal facilities (Anderson, 1988). And in the larger public sphere, Black citizens encountered a maze of racist laws, policies, and traditions, all buttressed by White violence (Berrey, 2015).

African Americans' frustration over conditions in the rural South helped to cause the Great Migration, one of the most significant resettlements in American history. Occurring in two phases spanning roughly from 1910 to 1930 and 1940 through the 1970s, the Great Migration radically transformed the nation's racial, political, economic, and cultural landscapes. Prior to the migration, approximately 90% of Black Americans lived in the South, predominantly in rural communities. By the 1970s, 8 in 10 African Americans called the city home, and nearly half of the Black population dwelled outside the South (Gregory, 2005; Trotter, 1991; Wilkerson, 2010).

While many rural Black Southerners benefited by moving to urban areas, most cities were segregated and unequal. Throughout the first relocation wave, segregation in urban areas was widespread (Drake & Cayton, 1945; Haynes, 1912; Trotter, 1991). Across the urban South, laws and policies dictated at least some degree of segregation in most public and private spaces (Hunter, 1997; Woodward, 1966). Outside the region, segregationist policies and practices varied by location and venue (Nicolaides, 2002; Sugrue, 2008; Theoharis & Woodard, 2003). Whites in all parts of the country regularly employed violence to further segregation and inequality (Hirsch, 1983; Johnson, 2020; Tyson, 1999).

Schools and neighborhoods were among the principal venues in which urban Whites enforced segregation. They did so by employing a range of tactics and mechanisms—some privately orchestrated, others via law and policy, and still others through hybrid means (Highsmith, 2015; Jenkins, 2017). Many White homeowners refused to sell or rent properties to African Americans. For their part, White lenders, builders, and realtors typically turned away Black and other minoritized customers. Rampant residential discrimination led to overcrowding and segregation in Black enclaves—neighborhoods such as Harlem in New York City, Houston's Fourth Ward, or Detroit's Black Bottom (Boyle, 2004; Erickson & Morrell, 2019; Pruitt, 2013). If Black home seekers circumvented such restrictions, then Whites routinely orchestrated buy-back schemes, engaged in panic selling, or resorted to violence. In Chicago, for instance, Whites in the 1910s and 1920s ignited scores of bombs to expel African Americans from desegregated neighborhoods (Chicago Commission on Race Relations, 1922, pp. 122–129).

Urban Whites also utilized legal and policy tools to divide cities by race. In the 1910s, lawmakers in Baltimore and elsewhere enacted racial zoning ordinances requiring segregated housing (Glotzer, 2020, pp. 83–114). Although the Supreme Court eventually overturned such laws with its 1917 ruling in *Buchanan v. Warley*, urban policymakers across the country continued to enforce racial zoning codes long after the decision (Rothstein, 2017, pp. 39–58).

Racially restrictive housing covenants also strengthened the color line. These were private but still legally enforceable agreements that blocked African Americans and others from purchasing, leasing, or occupying residential properties. Racial deed restrictions exploded in popularity as the Great Migration gathered momentum. Ultimately, members of the U.S. Supreme Court prohibited the enforcement of such covenants with their 1948 *Shelley v. Kraemer* ruling, but that decision arrived long after urban neighborhoods had become rigidly segregated (Gonda, 2015).

Redlining, or the denial of services such as home loans or mortgage insurance based on racial and geographic considerations, was yet another segregationist tool. Although lenders had long discriminated against non-White borrowers, the practice expanded after the 1934 establishment of the Federal Housing Administration (FHA), an agency that offered mortgage insurance to lenders (Hillier, 2003). By protecting lenders from default, the FHA's mortgage insurance program, along with similar initiatives directed by the Veterans Administration, triggered a nationwide boom in home construction and sales. Nevertheless, federal officials generally refused to insure mortgages for borrowers of color and, moreover, designated racially integrated communities as "hazardous" lending areas, often using red shading to delineate such neighborhoods on maps. Segregated White suburbs, by contrast, were eligible to receive the FHA's highest ratings. The result of federal redlining was an increasingly segregated metropolitan landscape (Freund, 2007; Jackson, 1985).

Urban renewal, highway construction, and public housing programs implemented before and after World War II further buttressed the color line. Across the United States, proponents of these and other government programs promised to replace urban "slums" with affordable housing and tax-boosting developments such as medical centers and factories. Instead, urban redevelopment projects displaced hundreds of thousands of disproportionately poor and minoritized people from their homes and neighborhoods. Unable to afford adequate replacement housing, many families moved to segregated public housing (Fullilove, 2004; Highsmith, 2015, pp. 175–199; Hirsch, 1983).

Systemic housing discrimination contributed substantially to school segregation. When urban education officials designed student attendance boundaries or planned new facilities, they often sought to promote "neighborhood schools"—buildings ideally situated within walking distance of every child's residence. Theoretically, then, neighborhood schools could be "de facto segregated" solely due to housing patterns (Delmont, 2016; Dewey, 1902; Perry, 1929). In most cases, however, school segregation emerged from both housing and education policies (Erickson & Highsmith, 2018).

Across the pre-*Brown* South, statutes and state constitutions generally required pupil segregation, but such mandates could also be found outside the region. In Indiana, for example, state law condoned school segregation until 1949. Nearby in Illinois, education officials in several of the state's districts forbade Black children from attending local high schools until well into the post–World War II era. And in Cincinnati, through the early 1950s, education authorities designated several all-Black facilities as "Separate Schools," thereby excluding them from the city's geographic attendance zones. Although laws in many northern and western states formally banned such forms of pupil segregation, Jim Crow schools were not exclusive to the South (Douglas, 2005, pp. 5, 149–153).

Nonetheless, urban school administrators in the North and West—and, eventually, the South—typically achieved pupil segregation through subtler administrative means. In many instances, local boards of education gerrymandered attendance districts. When Black or Brown families relocated to all-White school zones, administrators often redrew attendance boundaries. Such was the case in New Rochelle, New York, where gerrymandering practices implemented through the early 1960s forced White and Black children living next door to one another to attend separate schools. Officials in New Rochelle and other districts nationwide also oversaw racially biased student transfer policies to maintain segregation (Douglas, 2005, pp. 146–148, 269–272; Erickson, 2016; Garcia, 2018; Glass, 2018; Highsmith, 2015, pp. 54–77; Sugrue, 2008, pp. 163–199).

The dramatic growth in urban Black populations resulting from the Great Migration presented repeated opportunities to achieve integration, but many school officials continued to enforce segregation throughout the postwar era. In their attempts to relieve pupil overcrowding without disrupting the color line, administrators routinely turned basements, cafeterias, and trailers into classrooms. In the 1960s, for instance, the superintendent of the Chicago Public Schools, Benjamin C. Willis, oversaw the purchase of nearly 200 mobile school units for use in predominantly Black schools. Dubbed "Willis Wagons" by critics, the temporary classrooms eased pupil overcrowding while maintaining segregation (Seligman, 2005, p. 132; Todd-Breland, 2018, pp. 26–27). Administrators in the countywide school district serving Nashville, Tennessee, and its suburbs did something similar in the 1960s and 1970s, but on a wider metropolitan scale (Erickson, 2012, pp. 250–251).

Urban school districts also relied on logistically complex transportation initiatives to ensure segregation. During the 1950s and 1960s, boards of education in Milwaukee, St. Louis, and Cleveland responded to school overcrowding by implementing a system called "intact busing," which consisted of transporting entire classes of students to buildings with more space (Dougherty, 2005, pp. 94–98; Delmont, 2016, p. 91; Weathersby & Weathersby, 2019). Black students traveled on buses to new schools and, once there, remained together (or "intact") for the entire day (Dougherty, 2005, pp. 94–98). Oxnard, California, featured a similar kind of school-within-a-school segregation, with separate Mexican and White classes (Garcia, 2018, pp. 55–78).

Schemes such as these abounded in the campaign to maintain housing and school segregation in the 20th century. At times, segregationist mechanisms were akin to blunt instruments—tools that were openly separatist in nature. More often, though, segregationists worked discreetly. They quietly filed racially restrictive covenants at local government offices, created and circulated mortgage insurance guidelines away from the public's attention, devised irregularly shaped attendance boundaries for "neighborhood schools," or granted transfers to distressed White students. Regardless of the means used, it took hard work to maintain the color line in the face of rising metropolitan diversification. Ordinary Whites participated actively in such efforts, of course, but they did not and could not accomplish their aims without government assistance.

NARRATING SEGREGATION AS "DE FACTO"

If racial segregation has a history, one shaped by identifiable human actions and sustained by various political and economic agendas, then so too does the language of de facto segregation. Tracing that history makes it possible to understand what the term has meant, who used it, and why. It can also inform decisions today about whether to carry the term into the present or leave it in the past.

The conceptual distinction between de jure (in law) and de facto (in fact) has origins centuries deep in English common law (Glass, 2018). But a 1920 document from the National Association for the Advancement of Colored People (NAACP) is a good place to start tracing its use related to U.S. racial segregation (1920). A graphic on the last page of the NAACP's 1919 annual report calls out a contradiction. The 13th, 14th, and 15th Amendments to the Constitution—the Reconstruction amendments, ratified at the closing of the Civil War—formally abolished slavery, established birthright citizenship, and extended the right to vote to all men. These landmark amendments promised rights and "equal protection" to all citizens regardless of race. This was the law—"de jure." But "de facto," as the pages of the NAACP report tallied, hundreds of Black people lost their lives to lynching just in 1920 alone. Meanwhile, southern states thoroughly disenfranchised Black voters. The amendments were de jure protections of rights, but the de facto reality diverged, often brutally. This contradiction was "one reason," as the graphic put it, for the NAACP to exist. The NAACP's leaders were not explaining why voter suppression and lynching were happening, or how. Their core audience knew already. The organization was instead using the de facto label to call attention to a contradiction: The purported law of the land was broken every day in the Jim Crow South.

NAACP members and other civil rights workers repeatedly returned to the de facto label to challenge different kinds of contradictions over the next decades of school desegregation work (e.g., Glass, 2018; Highsmith, 2015; Lassiter, 2010; NAACP, 1958). They used it to point out segregation in the North or West when popular discourse seemed to focus only on the South. They also invoked it to highlight segregation that endured despite court-ordered desegregation plans. They chose the label on occasions when those in their advocacy networks knew full well segregation's origins and consequences, and yet lacked the resources to do the intricate work of identifying each link in the long chain of policies and administrative decisions that constructed segregated schools. De facto was a strategic and rhetorical tool for these activists, a way to name a contradiction and demand action (Glass, 2018).

But others, from President Richard Nixon to White mothers organizing against desegregation, adopted the term for the opposite purpose (Delmont, 2016; Nixon, 1970). They wanted to obscure rather than illuminate, to cast segregation's roots and mechanisms into shadow and allow its persistence.

Decades before *Brown*, when segregation in the North was not yet widely acknowledged—or was minimized as "voluntary"—the de facto label made talk of segregation possible. In 1935, Black intellectual Alain Locke spoke of "de facto segregation" in neighborhoods like Harlem as a "social practice" that he hoped would not "crystallize" into law as it had in the South (1935, p. 407). Locke seemed to understand school segregation to be the product of housing patterns only. He was also more willing to excuse state-sponsored segregation than many of his peers (1936). What Locke either did not know or did not choose to address, however, was how state power enforced residential segregation through means like restrictive covenants. He also made no mention of how local education policy—here, New York City's use of zoning to segregate its schools—revealed how Jim Crow was already well "crystallized" in New York City and other northern locales (Ment, 1975; Sugrue, 2008).

Just a few years later, White liberal journalist Gould Beech wrote in the national magazine *Survey Graphic* to indict the state of education for Black students nationally (1939, p. 615). Like Locke, he identified de facto segregation as resulting from housing policies, but he also recognized that some northern school boards and administrators made segregation official policy. When journalists from New York's *Amsterdam News* wrote about Beech's article, they said he conveyed the "subtle manner in which the same result," segregation in the North and South, "is achieved" ("School News," 1939).

The NAACP's Legal Defense Fund (LDF)—national desegregation advocates—made much use of the term de facto segregation in the 1950s and early 1960s. They adopted the phrase to call out northern segregation even where the era's popular rhetoric of southern racism and northern racial innocence denied its existence (Glass, 2018). The NAACP's "Operation North," led by Robert Carter and June Shagaloff, targeted northern examples of discriminatory action in school policy (like zoning or transfer policies). But they also set their sights on ending segregation whose exact policy origins were difficult to trace (Glass, 2018, p. 1207). The label thus helped open the way for attacks on segregation absent the clear target that southern Jim Crow statutes offered. Yet, foreshadowing trouble to come, their use of de facto helped foster the ahistorical idea of segregation without cause.

Writers such as Beech and Locke, and advocates like the NAACP LDF lawyers, wanted to attack all manner of segregation as a problem, and they found de facto one way to do so. But for others, including some open segregationists, the term helped deny segregation, or prevent action on it. Like Alain Locke and Gould Beech, White southern newspaperman Harry Ashmore, in 1954, linked de facto segregation to housing patterns. But he erased any sign of human action or state power: "It is inevitable that residential segregation should produce segregation in education. This properly can be described as a natural process" (1954, pp. 28, 67). Historian C. Vann Woodward moved even further from segregation's policy roots. In a 1966 edition of his widely read *The Strange Career of Jim Crow,* he explained de facto segregation existed in the North "without any legal support at all," stemming from "the prejudice of individuals, not the act of the state or local government" (1966, pp. 212–213). In the hands of White defenders of segregation, the term was a rhetorical "shield," as Michael Glass (2018) puts it. In 1965, one Alice Bosky, a member of a Chicago parents' organization, said "De facto segregation is a happenstance caused by living patterns and not a deliberate attempt to segregate or isolate Negro children." Therefore, her city and her community were not "morally bound" to do anything about it (Glass, 2018, p. 1199). President Richard Nixon (1970) carried the same shield in the Oval Office, claiming, "There is a fundamental distinction between so-called '*de jure*' and '*de facto*' segregation. *De jure* segregation arises by law or by the deliberate act of school officials and is unconstitutional; *de facto* segregation results from residential housing patterns and does not violate the Constitution."

For northern school administrators operating segregated school systems, talk of de facto segregation was very convenient (Glass, 2018). It absolved school officials of responsibility for their own segregationist policies. Like New York's superintendent William Jansen did in the 1950s, they hid behind claims that school segregation was "natural" and "accidental" (Glass, 2018, p. 1200). And it allowed these administrators to observe, but not to recognize any culpability for, segregation in housing. Perhaps the contradiction that de facto segregation helped these officials resolve was between their self-image as northern racial liberals and the segregated educational landscape that they supervised.

Alongside its troubled use in public discourse, the language of de facto segregation also moved through the courts, first in the North. Late 1950s and early 1960s cases in New York City and New Rochelle, New York, challenged school segregation, and judges refused to take the school district's claims of de facto segregation as sufficient excuse for segregation (*In the matter of Skipwith*, 1958; *Taylor*, 1961). Judges did not reject the term but called for action on segregation under any label. Still, after northern activists took additional school segregation cases to court, a jurisprudence of de facto segregation began to develop. Some judges—like the federal judge overseeing the Gary, Indiana, *Bell* (1963) case—codified de facto segregation as a defense for persistent northern school segregation. If a school district's segregation was de facto, it did not require legal intervention.

Yet when de facto segregation as a term began to appear in southern courtrooms, its multiplicity of conflicting meanings reemerged. In Charlotte, North Carolina, for example, substantial segregation remained in 1968 despite more than a decade of court-ordered desegregation. The school district's attorneys claimed de facto segregation as the reason (*Swann*, 1969). In sharp contrast to the *Bell* ruling, Charlotte's Judge James McMillan thoroughly rejected the term, reciting a litany of venues and methods of segregation, before concluding: "there [was] so much state action embedded in and shaping" residential and school segregation in Charlotte that the result was not "innocent or '*de facto*'" (*Swann*, 1969). McMillan rejected the notion that Charlotte's segregation was de facto and ordered busing for desegregation. Other judges, however, demonstrating yet another understanding of the term, labeled segregation in their districts de facto while also ordering busing for desegregation (Erickson, 2016). And meanwhile, yet others ordered no intervention when segregation was judged de facto.

Still, the idea of segregation without cause would continue to appear in subsequent judicial opinions over the next three decades. Notably, members of the Supreme Court called segregation's origins "unknown and perhaps unknowable" in the 1974 *Milliken v. Bradley* decision, a case involving segregated school districts in metropolitan Detroit.

Analyzing the 1950s and early 1960s, historian Michael Glass (2018) wisely characterizes the term de facto segregation as both a "sword"—a tool of civil rights advocates—and a "shield"—a deflector for recalcitrant school districts and outright segregationists. Earlier, in the 1930s, and later, in the 1970s, and across the United States rather than only in the North, we see a persistently conflictual use of the term. For some, it was a method of naming a contradiction between what was happening in fact (massive segregation and inequality bearing down most severely on Black students in the United States) and what was promised in law (the political equality of the Reconstruction amendments) and in rhetoric (a North that claimed racial innocence).

CONCLUSION

In 1920, the NAACP turned to the concept of de facto to identify a deep and powerful contradiction between legal promises of equality and the bitter reality of the Jim Crow order. More than a hundred years later, contradictions remain between what the law says about equality in education and what Black and Latinx children encounter in their schools. While we should recognize that contradiction and understand that some of our historical predecessors thought naming "de facto segregation" would help them do so, we should still abandon the term. Instead, we suggest terms such as "state-sponsored segregation" that highlight the broad range of laws and government policies that have encouraged and enforced U.S. racial segregation (Rothstein, 2017; for a more detailed taxonomy, see Highsmith, 2015, pp. 7–10).

Unlike earlier generations of advocates, who struggled to identify each piece in the segregationist puzzle, we now have the benefit of decades of scholarship built on archival records. This work gives us a more detailed understanding of state-sponsored segregation that crossed regions, traversed boundaries between public and private, and constructed housing and schooling together. With this knowledge, we can recognize the complex motives that led to the use of the term historically.

But we should distinguish that historical language from an accurate representation of the past. Historically, there has been no de facto segregation in the United States. Instead, an extensive and densely woven web of policy, administrative decision, law, private action, and state enforcement built the segregated metropolis, including its schools and housing. Considering this history, speaking of de facto segregation is misleading and historically inaccurate. So is teaching students to think of a past sorted neatly and often dichotomously into accounts of de jure and de facto segregation, as far too many texts still do (Rothstein, 2013).

Using de facto segregation to describe current-day segregation is similarly misleading. While there are no laws demanding explicit racial segregation in U.S. schools today, there are ample policies that foster segregation through assignment, zoning, admissions, tracking, and more. And these contemporary actions sit atop a landscape shaped enduringly by state-sponsored segregation in the past. Educators, advocates, policymakers, and anyone who seeks to understand segregation clearly must first reject the myth of de facto segregation.

REFERENCES

Anderson, J. D. (1988). *The education of Blacks in the South, 1860–1935*. University of North Carolina Press.

Ashmore, H. S. (1954). *The Negro and the schools*. University of North Carolina Press.

Beech, G. (1939, October). Schools for a minority. *Survey Graphic, 28*(10), 615–618.

Bell v. School City of Gary, Indiana, 213 F. Supp. 819 (1963).

Berrey, S. A. (2015). *The Jim Crow routine: Everyday performances of race, civil rights, and segregation in Mississippi*. University of North Carolina Press.

Boddie, E. C. (2021). The muddled distinction between de jure and de facto segregation. In K. L. Bowman (Ed.), *The Oxford handbook of U.S. education law* (pp. 253–273). Oxford University Press. Retrieved from https://doi.org/10.1093/oxfordhb/9780190697402.013.17

Boyle, K. (2004). *Arc of justice: A saga of race, civil rights, and murder in the Jazz Age*. Henry Holt.

Chicago Commission on Race Relations. (1922). *The Negro in Chicago: A study of race relations and a race riot*. University of Chicago Press.

Daniel, P. (1985). *Breaking the land: The transformation of cotton, tobacco, and rice cultures since 1880*. University of Illinois Press.

Delmont, M. F. (2016). *Why busing failed: Race, media, and the national resistance to school desegregation*. University of California Press.

Dewey, J. (1902). The school as social center. In J. A. Boydston (Ed.). (1976). *John Dewey: The middle works, 1899–1924* (pp. 81–93). Southern Illinois University Press.

Dougherty, J. (2005). *More than one struggle: The evolution of Black school reform in Milwaukee*. University of North Carolina Press.

Douglas, D. M. (2005). *Jim Crow moves north: The battle over northern school segregation, 1865–1954*. Cambridge University Press.

Drake, S. C., & Cayton, H. R. (1945). *Black metropolis: A study of Negro life in a northern city*. Harcourt, Brace.

Erickson, A. T. (2012). Building inequality: The spatial organization of schooling in Nashville, Tennessee, after *Brown*. *Journal of Urban History, 38*(2), 247–270. Retrieved from https://doi.org/10.1177/0096144211427115

Erickson, A. T. (2016). *Making the unequal metropolis: School desegregation and its limits*. University of Chicago Press.

Erickson, A. T., & Highsmith, A. R. (2018). The neighborhood unit: Schools, segregation, and the shaping of the modern metropolitan landscape. *Teachers College Record, 120*(3), 1–36. Retrieved from https://doi.org/10.1177/016146811812000308

Erickson, A. T., & Morrell, E. (Eds.). (2019). *Educating Harlem: A century of schooling and resistance in a Black community*. Columbia University Press.

Freund, D. M. P. (2007). *Colored property: State policy and White racial politics in suburban America*. University of Chicago Press.

Fullilove, M. T. (2004). *Root shock: How tearing up city neighborhoods hurts America, and what we can do about it*. One World/Ballantine Books.

Garcia, D. G. (2018). *Strategies of segregation: Race, residence, and the struggle for educational equality*. University of California Press.

Glass, M. R. (2018). From sword to shield to myth: Facing the facts of *de facto* school segregation. *Journal of Urban History, 44*(6), 1197–1226. Retrieved from https://doi.org/10.1177/0096144216675473

Glotzer, P. (2020). *How the suburbs were segregated: Developers and the business of exclusionary housing, 1890–1960*. Columbia University Press.

Gonda, J. D. (2015). *Unjust deeds: The restrictive covenant cases and the making of the Civil Rights Movement*. University of North Carolina Press.

Gregory, J. N. (2005). *The southern diaspora: How the Great Migrations of Black and White Southerners transformed America*. University of North Carolina Press.

Haynes, G. E. (1912). *The Negro at work in New York City: A study in economic progress*. Columbia University.

Highsmith, A. R. (2015). *Demolition means progress: Flint, Michigan, and the fate of the American metropolis*. University of Chicago Press.

Hillier, A. E. (2003). Redlining and the Home Owners' Loan Corporation. *Journal of Urban History, 29*(4), 394–420. Retrieved from https://doi.org/10.1177/0096144203029004002

Hirsch, A. R. (1983). *Making the second ghetto: Race and housing in Chicago, 1940–1960*. Cambridge University Press.

Hunter, T. W. (1997). *To 'joy my freedom: Southern Black women's lives and labors after the Civil War*. Harvard University Press.

In the Matter of Charlene Skipwith, 14 Misc. 2d 325 and 180 N.Y.S.2d 852 (1958).

Jackson, K. T. (1985). *Crabgrass frontier: The suburbanization of America*. Oxford University Press.

Jenkins, D. (2017, December 21). Who segregated America? Public Books. Retrieved from https://www.publicbooks.org/who-segregated-america/

Johnson, W. (2020). *The broken heart of America: St. Louis and the violent history of the United States*. Basic Books.

Kelley, R. D. G. (1990). *Hammer and hoe: Alabama communists during the Great Depression*. University of North Carolina Press.

Lassiter, M. D. (2010). De jure/de facto segregation: The long shadow of a national myth. In M. D. Lassiter & J. Crespino (Eds.), *The myth of southern exceptionalism* (pp. 25–48). Oxford University Press.

Litwack, L. F. (1998). *Trouble in mind: Black Southerners in the age of Jim Crow*. Knopf.

Locke, A. (1935). The dilemma of segregation. *Journal of Negro Education, 4*(3), 406–411. Retrieved from https://doi.org/10.2307/2291875

Locke, A. (1936, August). Harlem: Dark weather-vane. *Survey Graphic, 25*(8), 457–462.

Ment, D. (1975). Racial segregation in the public schools of New England and New York, 1840–1940 [Unpublished doctoral dissertation]. Columbia University.

Milliken v. Bradley, 418 U.S. 717 (1974).

National Association for the Advancement of Colored People. (1920). *Tenth annual report of the National Association for the Advancement of Colored People for the year 1919: A summary of work and an accounting.*

National Association for the Advancement of Colored People. (1958, February). De facto segregation in the Chicago Public Schools. *Crisis, 65*(2), 87–93, 126–127.

Nicolaides, B. M. (2002). *My blue heaven: Life and politics in the working-class suburbs of Los Angeles, 1920–1965*. University of Chicago Press.

Nixon, R. (1970). Statement about desegregation of elementary and secondary schools. *American Presidency Project*. Retrieved from https://www.presidency.ucsb.edu/node/241065

Perry, C. A. (1929). The neighborhood unit: A scheme of arrangement for the family life community. In *Regional plan of New York and its environs* (Vol. 7). Regional Plan Association.

Pruitt, B. (2013). *The other Great Migration: The movement of rural African Americans to Houston, 1900–1941*. Texas A&M University Press.

Rothstein, R. (2013). Our house divided: What US schools don't teach about US-style apartheid. *Zinn Education Project*. Retrieved from https://www.zinnedproject.org/featured-activity/our-house-divided-what-u-s-schools-dont-teach-about-u-s-style-apartheid/

Rothstein, R. (2017). *The color of law: A forgotten history of how our government segregated America*. Liveright.

School news. (1939, October 21). *New York Amsterdam News*, 4.

Seligman, A. I. (2005). *Block by block: Neighborhoods and public policy on Chicago's West Side*. University of Chicago Press.

Sugrue, T. J. (2008). *Sweet land of liberty: The forgotten struggle for civil rights in the North*. Random House.

Swann v. Charlotte-Mecklenburg Board of Education, 306 F. Supp. 1299 (1969).

Taylor v. Board of Education of New Rochelle, 195 F. Supp. 231 (1961).

Theoharis, J., & Woodard, K. (Eds.). (2003). *Freedom North: Black freedom struggles outside the South*. Palgrave Macmillan.

Todd-Breland, E. (2018). *A political education: Black politics and education reform in Chicago since the 1960s*. University of North Carolina Press.

Trotter, J. W. (Ed.). (1991). *The Great Migration in historical perspective: New dimensions of race, class, and gender*. Indiana University Press.

Tyson, T. B. (1999). *Radio free Dixie: Robert F. Williams and the roots of Black Power*. University of North Carolina Press.

Weathersby, C., & Weathersby, Y. (2019). The "intact busing" program in 1960s St. Louis Public Schools District. *Journal of Urban History, 45*(5), 908–924. Retrieved from https://doi.org/10.1177/0096144218778019

Wilkerson, I. (2010). *The warmth of other suns: The epic story of America's Great Migration*. Random House.

Woodward, C. V. (1966). *The strange career of Jim Crow* (2nd rev. ed.). Oxford University Press.

CHAPTER 20

The Myth That Technology Will Modernize Teaching

Victoria Cain

"Not since Johannes Gutenberg invented movable type has the air of the educational world been as charged as it is today with intimations of change," declared *The New York Times* (Bendiner, 1953). A bold new technology, the paper explained, now offered instantaneous access to the latest information presented by the world's best teachers and was sure to pull moribund classrooms into the future. The year? 1953. The technology? A 21" black-and-white television receiver on a rolling cart.

Ed-tech predictions of the past often elicit bemused grins, making us wonder how people could ever have thought a rabbit-eared television, a dial-up modem, or some other outdated tool would transform education. Yet when the next new tool arrives, most of us are intrigued by its possibilities. Perhaps tablets and smartboards will help struggling students learn more, better, faster (Dash, 2004; Takahashi, 2011). Perhaps personalized learning platforms will eliminate outmoded teaching or bored kids (Herold, 2017; Thompson, 2011). Perhaps thoughtful classroom use of ChatGPT will democratize access to tutoring and prepare students for citizenship in a brave new world of generative AI (Roose, 2023; Singer, 2023). Whatever the new tool is, we hope that this technology, this time, will bring schools into line with the needs and desires of our current moment.

Over the course of the last 100 years, technology occasionally upended traditional modes of teaching and learning. Far more often, however, it preserved the status quo or restored more conservative pedagogical methods. Still, the myth that new technologies will revolutionize education persists; after all, for more than a century, champions of educational technology (ed-tech) have pushed this seductively indefinite narrative our way, and it's hard to oppose the possibility of progress.

* * *

As soon as common schools were first established in the United States, people grasped at schemes to modernize them through technology. But "modernizing" education was a Rorschach test of an ambition: ambiguous enough to mean whatever reformers wanted it to mean. As a result, for more than 2 centuries, entrepreneurs and reformers declared that new technologies would provide solutions to whatever was the educational crisis of the moment. New tools would quickly raise the quality of teaching and learning for all kinds of students, they promised, and would do so in ways that were scalable, entertaining, and cost-effective (Ames, 2019; Cain, 2021; Reich, 2020; Watters, 2021).

In the early 20th century, such assertions grew louder and more persistent. Technology enthusiasts suggested that technologies would translate into more progressive classroom pedagogy, encouraging student engagement with the world outside the school. Technology would connect cloistered classrooms to the economic, political, and technological trends, maintained such reformers, and allow teachers to "revolt from the authoritarian, rote, thoughtless drill, textbook-worshipping methods" (Dale, 1944). In the 1930s, for instance, education professor Edgar Dale and others embraced the use of film, believing the medium would prompt meaningful classroom dialogue about the era's social problems. By watching and analyzing films together, wrote Dale, teachers and students could begin to deliberate empathetically and collectively about issues ranging from "the abolition of war, to a new point of view regarding crime and punishment, to the more satisfactory distribution of wealth, to a deeper insight into the problems of a democratic government, to an understanding of the Negro problem" (Dale, 1933). Other reformers argued technology would help schools transcend the limits of time, space, and local labor markets. Stereographs, film projectors and radios would "bring the world to the classroom . . . [making] universally available the services of the finest teachers [and] the inspiration of the greatest leaders," as Ohio School of the Air founder Benjamin Darrow put it (Darrow, 1932).

However compelling these pronouncements, few school districts could afford to spend money on much beyond teachers' salaries and basic needs, so classroom technology had to wait. But this changed after World War II, thanks to the wide dispersion of military training technologies into schools and a growing consensus that such classroom tools were essential weapons in modernizing the nation's educational arsenal (Saettler, 2004). Postwar technocrats declared that educational technology would bring the same modern efficiencies to schools as they had to the U.S. Navy and General Motors, transforming schools of uncertain quality into cost-effective systems whose educational outputs could be measured, standardized, and scaled (Cain, 2021). The more liberal-minded among them quietly suggested that a clean new form of democratic opportunity would accompany this outcome: consistently high-quality education for all American children, regardless of the color of their skin, the location of their home, or the poverty of their district (Cain, 2021).

Compelled by this vision, foundations began to pour money into projects pushing educational technology into U.S. schools. Districts, too, directed more funding to educational technology, and production and publishing companies quickly responded, churning out films that offered earnest instruction on subjects ranging from democracy to DNA to dating (Alexander, 2014; Orgeron et al., 2012). When Congress passed the National Defense Education Act in 1958, which funneled more than $1 billion to schools and included a special provision for educational technology purchasing, larger media and technology companies also entered the ed-tech market: Westinghouse, for instance, supported experiments with closed-circuit television, while textbook publishers, like D. C. Heath and the American Book Company, began to produce films and filmstrips for classrooms (Dow, 1991; Saettler, 2004).

In the late 1960s and 1970s, schools began to explore the possibilities of commercial media to reach an increasingly disaffected generation. Classrooms' "insular, isolationist, esoteric irrelevance" held no meaning to students coming of age during the social convulsions of the Vietnam War and Civil Rights Movement, FCC Educational Broadcasting Branch chief Robert Hilliard warned in 1970. Educators should reconsider prime-time television's possibilities, he wrote, seeing it "as a base for reaching, turning on and tuning in our youth" (Hilliard, 1970). By the early 1980s, teachers were regularly leaning on *TV Guide*, new niche cable television shows, and VCRs to expand the content available to their classrooms and improvise on established lesson plans (Cain, 2021).

Computer-assisted instruction, time-shared computing terminals, and PCs also entered schools in the last third of the century. Tech enthusiasts asserted that computers would at last provide a responsive and bespoke education to each student rather than the old-fashioned one-size-fits-all classroom, preparing them for an era of global competition and cooperation. "The resources needed for an increasingly individualized educational system are at the doorstep of public education and are already knocking for entry," University of Oregon education analyst John Lindelow announced (Lindelow, 1983). The hype became increasingly giddy: "you've heard it before, but this time it's true," declared *Wired* magazine. "Technology can reform our schools" (Leslie, 1993). By 1985, PCs had found their way into 94.2% of U.S. public schools ("Micro Use Is Up 75%, School Survey Shows," 1985). From there, investment in technology grew exponentially. In 1999 alone, schools spent an estimated $6.9 billion on computers, servers, routers, wiring, Internet access, and software (Kleiman, 2000).

By the beginning of the 21st century, educational technology had become a powerful industry, one intent on pushing the notion that new tools were the best way to make education better. Journalists and educational reformers reinforced this vision by amplifying complaints about one-size-fits-all pedagogical approaches. As Clive Thompson put it in a 2011 issue of *Wired*, classroom group learning "never really works: Advanced kids get bored and tune out, lagging ones get lost and tune out, and pretty soon half the class isn't paying attention" (Thompson, 2011). But cheap mobile screens, useful, usable online content, and responsive online platforms, suggested Thompson and other champions of personalization, made it possible to tailor each student's education to fit their own needs, strengths, and preferences.

The technologies changed over the century, but the promises stayed the same: New machines would make education modern, pulling old-fashioned teaching practices into the future and ensuring that all students—regardless of race, class, or ability—had access to the best, most up-to-date forms of education.

* * *

So where did these ideas come from? Corporations, governments, and media outlets routinely coupled educational technology and cutting-edge pedagogy, reinforcing the association between machines and modernity whenever they could. The idea that machines would revolutionize education was good for their bottom line, after all. Companies sold more hardware, media sold advertising space and hopeful headlines, and governments could easily point to subsidies for new technology as proof of their commitment to modernizing education.

In the 1990s, for instance, savvy tech executives quickly seized on the Internet as a route to industry growth. Advertisements played on familiar predictions about ways that technology would improve education: Internet-connected PCs would promote individualized and progressive pedagogy, free students from limits of location, and connect them to a network of far-flung experts, libraries, and museums. Microsoft founder Bill Gates sketched out a networked future where students would "create their own learning path . . . go wherever they want, with the control and flexibility to exercise their curiosity and discover the world," and Microsoft would happily supply the software and industry alliances to realize this vision (Gates, 1996).

Boosters like Bill Gates often cast their technology as a remedy to the educational status quo, hinting that location-based, teacher-led, age-graded classrooms were backward and boring while ed-tech was flexible and futuristic. Fearing unions' wrath and teachers' outrage, boosters of educational technology rarely said this explicitly. But they frequently compared education that incorporated new technologies with education that didn't, quietly emphasizing the deficiencies of the latter. Later proponents of ed-tech were balder in their criticism, publicly proclaiming, as MIT computer scientist and LOGO developer Seymour Papert did, that new tools would "free education of much of what is now painful, systematic, teacher-driven learning" (Hereford, 1982).

Profound disrespect for classroom teachers, much amplified by sexism, gave the myth additional tailwind (Cain, 2021; Goldstein, 2015; Pawlewicz, 2020). Reformers touting educational technology dismissed the abilities of teachers and what they described as the "educational establishment." In the 1950s, for example, officials at the Ford Foundation's Fund for the Advancement of Education likened teachers who objected to large-group instructional television viewing to medieval clergy resisting Copernican science. Teachers who saw mass viewing as a "sinister mechanistic threat" demonstrated the limits of their imagination, one Fund official sniffed (Eurich, 1969). In internal memos, Cold War multimedia curriculum developers maintained that new media technologies should be used to "teacher-proof" classrooms and curricula, because teachers were often "the least able people who had the greatest interest in security" (Dow, 1991).

* * *

But assertions that machines would make classrooms modern were usually hyperbolic. In some instances, certainly, new tools did lead to pedagogical innovation. Multimedia curricula introduced during the Cold War, such as Jerome Bruner's "Man: A Course of Study" (MACOS) or the diverse courses generated by the Physical Science Study Committee, stand as evidence (Rudolph, 2002). Yet such transformations were hardly guaranteed. More often, the technologies that survived in classrooms preserved traditional modes of teaching.

Efforts to keep expenses low often resulted in deeply conservative approaches to teaching and learning. Corporations preferred to repurpose existing technologies for classrooms rather than investing in new products pitched by education-oriented inventors: Sidney Pressey's struggle to find a company that would market his "Automatic Teacher" in the 1920s, IBM's slow-walk of Reynold Johnson's test-scoring "Markograph" in the 1930s, and Rheem Manufacturing's failures to produce a classroom-ready version of B. F. Skinner's famous teaching machines in the 1950s offer instructive examples (Watters, 2021). Shoestring budgets also forced nonprofit producers of educational technologies to lean on less-than-revolutionary pedagogy. Instructional television is a good example (Cain, 2021; Goldfarb, 2002; Reich, 2020). Its producers rarely used the medium's full capacities to teach; instead, amateur presenters, risk-averse performances, and terrible production values became the norm. "Had there been more money," later reflected Pittsburgh station WQED's chief of instructional television Rhea Sikes, "I am sure there would have been fewer 'talking faces'" (Sikes, 1982). Rather than transforming pedagogy, cost-conscious ed-tech usually translated into preserving its most traditional forms.

Even when the tools themselves promoted innovative pedagogy, the expense of training teachers to use them often killed their prospects. The multimedia MACOS curricula, for instance, was celebrated for its pioneering use of film in the late 1960s and early 1970s and heralded as a transformation in social studies education. But it cost nearly eight times more than other social studies curricula, and it required an additional 40 hours of teacher training to make effective use of the course. Many schools balked as a result, and sales of the curriculum foundered after a few years (Dow, 1991; Milam, 2019).

K–12 software purchases in the 1980s and 1990s are another case in point. To work in the much-heralded programming environment of LOGO, for instance, youngsters needed guidance from teachers who knew the program well enough to provide thoughtful instruction and challenges. But the "amount of in-service education required to bring the typical elementary school teacher up to speed in a LOGO environment exceeds both the typical school district's resources and the typical teacher's time," wrote David Moursund, editor in chief of *Computing Teacher* magazine (Moursund, 1985). As a result, rather than embrace an expensive, time-intensive version of an open-ended technology that required highly trained teachers to guide students toward high-level logic, schools often defaulted to software like Davidson & Associates' Math Blaster, which transformed flash card math drills into arcade-like video games (Cain, 2021).

Reformers' promises that screens and other forms of educational media would make education more equitable also proved empty. Champions of ed-tech often suggested that technology would serve as a great equalizer, allowing underserved students to take courses their schools couldn't offer, providing engaging, personalized learning experiences to students floundering in overcrowded classrooms. Instead, technology tended to amplify existing disparities. Poorer districts struggled to purchase and maintain technologies, while wealthier, Whiter areas readily acquired new tools. In the late 1950s, for instance, schools in the wealthy suburbs ringing New York City averaged one television for every 10 teachers, whereas most city schools possessed one for every 25 teachers, and most of those didn't work (Cain, 2021, p. 61). Corporate donations of hardware helped, but under-resourced schools couldn't afford the peripherals, upgrades, and teacher support necessary to make machines work for students in creative ways; nor could a student with a few minutes per week on a school computer compete with a kid with unlimited access to multiple machines at home and school. The result, National Science Foundation (NSF) computer specialist Andrew Molnar observed in 1982, was "a society of computer literates and illiterates—the haves and have nots of the new age" (Cain, 2021, p. 151).

As Larry Cuban has observed, technologies also failed to modernize education because they didn't meet established student and teacher needs—and so weren't heavily used in classrooms (Cuban, 1986). For much of the 20th century, educational technologies were too expensive, fragile, or complicated to easily integrate into daily practice. Film reels wore out. Television receivers picked up snowstorms of static. Computers rapidly became obsolete. Ed-tech rarely fit smoothly into schools' existing physical infrastructure, schedules, and curricula, and it often required expansive bureaucracy to procure, manage, and maintain. Consequently, those new tools that made it into classrooms rarely revolutionized pedagogical practice; indeed, after a few months, many were relegated to supply closets.

And yet the idea that a single tool might have the capacity to solve a major social problem or even just suggest to parents and taxpayers that schools were embracing the future retained extraordinary allure—even when there was no substantiation that technologies accomplished the intended goal. As Maryland principal Thomas Warren explained to a reporter in 1989, "we believe it improves the quality of education and increases excitement. But I can't give you any proof of that" (Shao, 1989). District officials like Warren were often willing to purchase a symbol of their commitment to future possibilities, as policymakers, parents, and administrators often demanded tangible proof of schools' commitment to modern education, but were less interested in how such machines were used; the very presence of technology often seemed to them evidence enough that classrooms were providing a modern education.

Classroom teachers, on the other hand, pushed back against the myth of educational technology as a clear agent of modern pedagogy. Intimately familiar with both the limitations of any given tool and the extraordinary expectations these tools raised, educators often played the role of Cassandra when discussing ed-tech. "No responsible educator should mislead the tax conscious public into believing that educational TV will provide better education for less money and with fewer teachers," scolded the editors of *Social Education* in 1957 ("Educational Television," 1957). Educators were also quick to argue that the emphasis on ed-tech's efficiencies often led to regressive pedagogical tactics. Rather than promoting flexible curricula and teaching methods that would "meet the individual needs of boys and girls on their own levels of intellectual and emotional maturity," he warned, educational technology was more likely to return classrooms "to the Little Red Schoolhouse philosophy of education," protested University of North Carolina audiovisual education chief Kenneth McIntyre in 1957 (McIntyre, 1957).

The fantasy that modern education could be purchased in the form of technology proved remarkably durable. It was recycled again and again by entrepreneurs looking for profit and by educational reformers eager to remake classrooms according to their own visions of teaching and learning. And, of course, it was desperately embraced by parents and citizens hoping to make a better path for their children. We shouldn't believe this myth, but we shouldn't judge those who did—who do—too harshly. After all, who hasn't hoped for a machine that makes magic? We should, though, think harder about what we mean by "modern education." What future do we hope to pursue exactly? Only with more clarity about what constitutes modern will we be able to develop and identify the right kinds of tools—and teaching—for that job.

REFERENCES

Alexander, G. (2014). *Films you saw in school: A critical review of 1,153 classroom educational films (1958–1985) in 74 subject categories*. McFarland.

Ames, M. G. (2019). *The charisma machine: The life, death, and legacy of One Laptop per Child*. MIT Press.

Bendiner, R. (1953, March 8). If T.V. moved into the classroom. *The New York Times Magazine*, SM9.

Cain, V. (2021). *Schools and screens: A watchful history*. MIT Press.

Cuban, L. (1986). *Teachers and machines: The classroom use of technology since 1920*. Teachers College Press.

Dale, E. (1933). *How to appreciate motion pictures*. Macmillan.

Dale, E. (1944). The real film problem. *The News Letter*, 10.

Darrow, B. H. (1932). *Radio: The assistant teacher*. R. G. Adams.

Dash, E. (2004, December 8). School blackboards are turning white and interactive. *The New York Times*, 9.

Dow, P. B. (1991). *Schoolhouse politics: Lessons from the Sputnik era*. Harvard University Press.

Educational television. (1957). *Social Education, 21*(4), 149.

Eurich, A. C. (1969). *Reforming American education: The innovative approach to improving our schools and colleges*. Harper & Row.

Gates, B. (1996). The connected learning community: Using technology for education. *T H E Journal, 23*(8), 10.

Goldfarb, B. (2002). *Visual pedagogy: Media cultures in and beyond the classroom*. Duke University Press.

Goldstein, D. (2015). *The teacher wars: A history of America's most embattled profession*. Anchor Books.

Hereford, N.-J. (1982, March). Computers are objects to think with: An interview with Seymour Papert. *Instructor, 91*(7), 86–87, 89.

Herold, B. (2017, March 28). Curriculum "playlists": A take on personalized learning. *Education Week, 36*(26), 19–23. Retrieved from https://www.edweek.org/ew/articles/2017/03/29/curriculum-playlists-a-take-on-personalized-learning.html

Hilliard, R. L. (1970, August 3). How're you going to keep them down on the farm after they've seen TV? *American Management Association's Sixth Annual Conference on Education and Training*, New York, NY. Retrieved from https://archive.org/stream/ERIC_ED064918

Kleiman, G. M. (2000). Myths and realities about technology in K-12 schools. In D. T. Gordon (Ed.), *The digital classroom: How technology is changing the way we teach and learn*. Harvard Education Letter.

Leslie, J. (1993, May 1). Kids connecting. *Wired*. Retrieved from https://www.wired.com/1993/05/kids-connecting/

Lindelow, J. (1983). *The emerging science of individualized instruction: A survey of findings on learning styles, brain research, and learning time with implications for administrative action*. Clearinghouse on Educational Management.

McIntyre, K. M. (1957). Robot in the classroom? *High School Journal, 40*(6), 231–236.

Micro use is up 75%, school survey shows. (1985, December). *School Library Journal, 32*(4), 12.

Milam, E. L. (2019). *Creatures of Cain: The hunt for human nature in Cold War America*. Princeton University Press.

Moursund, D. (1985). LOGO revisited. *Computing Teacher, 13*(6), 4–5.

Orgeron, D., Orgeron, M., & Streible, D. (Eds.). (2012). *Learning with the lights off: Educational film in the United States*. Oxford University Press.

Pawlewicz, D. D. A. (2020). *Blaming teachers: Professionalization policies and the failure of reform in American history*. Rutgers University Press.

Reich, J. (2020). *Failure to disrupt: Why technology alone can't transform education*. Harvard University Press.

Roose, K. (2023, January 12). Don't ban ChatGPT in schools. Teach with it. *The New York Times*, 1. Retrieved from https://www.nytimes.com/2023/01/12/technology/chatgpt-schools-teachers.html

Rudolph, J. (2002). *Scientists in the classroom: The Cold War reconstruction of American science education*. Palgrave Macmillan.

Saettler, P. (2004). *The evolution of American educational technology*. Information Age Publishing.

Shao, M., et al. (1989, July 17). Computers in school: A loser? Or a lost opportunity. *Business Week*, 108–110.

Sikes, R. (1982). Public television's roots oral history project [Interview]. Wisconsin Historical Society, Division of Library, Archives, and Museum Collections.

Singer, N. (2023, June 8). New A.I. chatbot tutors could upend student learning. *The New York Times*.

Takahashi, P. (2011, October 18). Vegas schools hope iPad program will boost test scores. *Education Week*. Retrieved from https://www.edweek.org/teaching-learning/vegas-schools-hope-ipad-program-will-boost-test-scores/2011/10

Thompson, C. (2011, July 15). How Khan academy is changing the rules of education. *Wired*. Retrieved from https://www.wired.com/2011/07/ff_khan/

Watters, A. (2021). *Teaching machines*. MIT Press.

CHAPTER 21

The Myth That School Spending Doesn't Affect Student Outcomes

Matthew Gardner Kelly

School funding is radically unequal in many states. Some public schools receive a great deal of money. Others receive very little. The districts that receive the most are disproportionately wealthy and White (e.g., Kelly, 2020). A disparate share of students attending underfunded districts are from low-income families, with children of color from low-income families shortchanged the most (e.g., EdBuild, 2019; Weathers & Sosina, 2022).

These disparities in education funding have far-reaching consequences. Yet for decades, a powerful myth about school funding and its effects has distracted from the significance of these disparities and the importance of correcting them. The myth is that school funding disparities are inconsequential for student outcomes, and it is perpetuated in various ways. Sometimes it is through the blunt assertion that "money does not matter." In other instances, it is through the claim that education spending has been increasing more than test scores in recent years. Sometimes purveyors of this myth present themselves as thoughtful commentators making a plea for nuance. What matters most is how money is spent, they claim, while glossing over the fact that no school can decide how to spend money it does not have. Across its various iterations, purveyors of this myth all come to the same place—they recast disparities as inconsequential, and they do so through a series of falsehoods and distortions.

This chapter begins by tracing the history of research on disparities in education funding, debunking the myth that money does not matter for what schools can accomplish. It then traces how the misleading claim that funding is inconsequential for student outcomes has been used to support alternative education reforms purportedly capable of improving schools without addressing the unfair way they are funded. With remarkable consistency, reformers in both the past and the present have proposed changes to teacher quality, the curriculum, and the role of markets in education as alternatives to increased funding. As important as reforms in some of these areas might be within certain contexts, these reform proposals have long obscured the centrality of funding disparities to educational inequality.

* * *

Research on education funding and student outcomes demonstrates that funding disparities have consequences because how much a school spends impacts what its students can achieve. The most recent and rigorous studies show that education spending has a substantial positive impact on student outcomes. Consider the findings of studies since 2010. Researchers have found a significant causal relationship between increased education spending and a host of positive student outcomes. Increased spending increases high school graduation rates (Abott et al., 2020; Candelaria & Shores, 2019; Jackson et al., 2016; Johnson, 2015; Kreisman & Steinberg, 2019; Miller, 2018). It decreases high school dropout rates (Cascio et al., 2013; Lee & Polachek, 2018). Education spending increases improve college enrollment rates (Baron, 2021; Hyman, 2017) and total years of education completed (Jackson et al., 2016). Spending improves the life trajectories of students even further into adulthood, increasing intergenerational mobility (Biasi, 2023) and future wages (Jackson et al., 2016; Johnson, 2015) while decreasing the probability a student will experience poverty as an adult (Jackson et al., 2016; Johnson, 2015). Improved spending is also associated with, of course, improved scores on tests (Abott et al., 2020; Brunner et al., 2020; Cellini et al., 2010; Conlin & Thompson, 2017; Gigliotti & Sorensen, 2018; Hong & Zimmer, 2016; Jackson et al., 2021; Kogan et al., 2017; Kreisman & Steinberg, 2019; Lafortune et al., 2018; Lafortune et al., 2022; Martorell et al., 2016; Neilson & Zimmerman, 2014; Rauscher, 2020; Roy, 2011).

The findings of these studies are hardly surprising. Moreover, they are hardly new. Researchers have long known what students and teachers in underfunded schools understand best through their lived experience—spending matters for outcomes and disparities have consequences. Yet researchers have had to continuously reprove the simple fact that not giving students the resources they need will impact what they experience at school. During the 1990s and 2000s, an economist at the conservative Hoover Institute, Eric Hanushek, purported to show that funding is not clearly connected to student outcomes, often testifying in civil rights cases that this was the case (e.g., Hanushek, 1997). However, the methodology used in these papers was flawed and widely criticized, (e.g., Baker, 2018, pp. 33–36). One group of researchers even reanalyzed the data used by Hanushek to support his claim. They found the opposite was true—the same data marshalled by Hanushek to question the association between spending and outcomes showed that increased spending did indeed improve student performance (Hedges et al., 1994). Hanushek has since admitted funding positively impacts outcomes (Barnum, 2023).

Hanushek first studied school funding in a seminar with James Coleman, a sociologist who authored a report, *Equality of Educational Opportunity* (1966), that is sometimes cast as the originator of a broader debate over whether money matters for student outcomes. The report seemed to show that spending and student outcomes were not strongly correlated, though its methods and conclusions about funding were deeply flawed. Moreover, when he authored his report, Coleman ignored—and many commentators at the time seemed to forget—a large body of work on the "cost–quality" relationship from the 1930s, 1940s, and 1950s. Decades of existing research on the cost–quality relationship already showed, unsurprisingly, that money does indeed matter for student outcomes (e.g., Bowyer, 1933; Mort, 1952; Woollatt, 1949). During these years, researchers favored methods that would permit them to compare highly similar schools in close proximity to one another. This helped them avoid apples and oranges comparisons. Powell (1933), for example, used an "equivalent-group method" and compared funding and outcomes for highly similar rural schools. Within those schools, he assessed achievement in several academic categories: reading accuracy, spelling, reading comprehension, language usage, geography, elementary science, and arithmetic. He also considered an indicator long since neglected from thinking about outcomes today: "general school happiness." Powell found, like many of the studies before and after his, a clear relationship between funding and outcomes. "Expenditures and returns do rise or fall together," he explained (Powell, 1933). Before the 1930s, a range of systematic studies also demonstrated the impact of funding on outcomes. These studies usually followed the academic standards of the day. In the 1920s, these studies focused more on quantification and the language of scientism. Taken together, they all illustrated the connection between spending and outcomes.

Research showing the impact of funding on outcomes has been produced and reproduced each generation because misleading claims about school funding have long dominated discussions about education reform in the United States. Neither Hanushek nor Coleman were the originators of the myth that money does not impact outcomes. In reality, commentators have perpetuated the myth that funding disparities are inconsequential since the inception of American public schools, prompting such a large body of work on education funding by researchers. Arthur Moehlman (1927) called the purveyors of this myth "critics," and he opened his school finance textbook in the 1920s with the observation that "critics, like disease, are ever with us" (p. 1).

* * *

Examining the history of the claims these critics have made about funding and outcomes over time can help us understand their signature feature—they are used to advance a reform program purportedly capable of fixing schools without providing equitable or adequate funding. In both the past and the present, arguments that funding and outcomes are disconnected have been used to advance other proposals—for supposedly innovative policies—that should be tried while funding disparities are ignored. These proposals are rarely new and almost always involve some call for teacher accountability, changes to the curriculum, or the empowerment of markets. The history of those reforms and their tendency to distract the public from meaningful school funding changes suggests they are little more than old, spoiled wine in new bottles.

Proposals for teacher accountability, instead of fair funding, have been among the most commonly proposed alternatives to confronting funding disparities and their impact. Even before publicly supported schools took hold nationally, critics cited evidence of supposedly high spending and poor outcomes to shape the conversation about the role state government should and should not play in educating youth. Some states were already providing modest state funding to locally operated schools by the 1820s and 1830s, the decades where most historians locate the origins of public schools as we understand them today. This early funding usually came from permanent state school funds that functioned like an institutional endowment today where interest from how the fund was invested would be used to support education. Across these states, advocates of common school reform noted a series of problems with existing schools that centered around the quality of teachers in states that already provided some funding, most notably Connecticut.

The claim by several common school reformers that lawmakers had already tried to increase school spending and that it did not work shaped conversations from the start about what was wrong with schools and how to fix them by fixing teachers. Since the problems antebellum school reformers perceived in common schools were found in states with and without a state school fund, the early critics claimed giving schools more resources would be foolish and wasteful. Reformers like Boston's William Woodridge even used the *American Annals of Education* to spread the claim that Connecticut's state school fund had made its schools worse, as evidenced by its teachers. The journal editorialized that Connecticut's fund had "encouraged the employment of inferior teachers and the neglect of duty in organizing and superintending the schools" ("Common Schools in New York," 1834, p. 107). The claim was repeated by a network of reformers in different states who read with interest publications like the *American Annals of Education* and thought about how they should organize their own state funding systems. When the Massachusetts legislature declined to create a state school fund in 1826, they based their decision on the claim that such a fund would distract from reforms addressing terrible teachers. "No school fund could greatly improve our schools," a state legislative committee tasked with examining funding explained, "while the instructors are so lamentably deficient" (quoted in Barnard, 1853, p. 157). Instead of dollars, they said, Massachusetts needed "a fund of competent knowledge in the instructors" (quoted in Barnard, 1853, p. 157). New York reformers argued against providing "too large a sum of public money" based on how it had purportedly been wasted in Connecticut while instead calling for improvements in instructor training to address "the prevailing incompetency of teachers" (Dix, 1834, p. 13). At the first session of the Illinois legislature (1835), lawmakers there claimed Connecticut's schools "have languished, and are now in a much worse condition than the schools in Massachusetts, where there never *was* a school fund" (Journal of the Senate, p. 425).

Critiques of teachers have been repeated for decades, and calls for changes to teacher training, supervision, and pay have long been offered as an explicit alternative to dealing with insufficient and inequitable approaches to funding. After the Civil War, Massachusetts educator Amory Mayo (1877) worried about waste in educational finance and felt "incompetent teachers" were to blame. Resolving to "pay money only on condition of first-rate work" would promote efficiency, Mayo insisted (p. 139). Similar proposals for this approach to pay were repeated in the early 20th century and again in the 1950s by critics like Roger Freeman, who blamed teacher unions and uniform pay scales for the educational troubles he perceived. Of course, for underfunded districts the biggest obstacle to attracting and retaining the best teachers is finding a way to pay them with money that does not exist.

Conversations about curriculum, too, have often been presented as an alternative to discussions of funding and resource disparities. At the turn of the 20th century, critics of increased funding insisted the schools spent too much and produced too little. A wasteful and poorly designed approach to what was taught in schools, they insisted, was to blame. *Ladies Home Journal*, for example, ran a series of disingenuous articles purporting to investigate "the returns" produced by the public school system in 1912. In these articles, the magazine purported to show how costs were growing and student outcomes were stagnant because of a wasteful curriculum. The elementary school curriculum was "stupid in method," one of the first articles insisted. It "costs over four hundred and three million dollars a year," the author explained, but it was "wrongly educating, mal-educating or absolutely harming nearly eighteen million children every year." The reason was supposedly uniform curriculum that wasted money by attempting an "impossible feat": giving every child the chance to learn the same thing, "irrespective of physical strength, mentality, inheritance, home environment, or whether the children are to become lawyers or blacksmiths" (Lynch, 1912, p. 4). The high school curriculum was supposedly no better. It was a total waste, another author claimed in the series. It offered too much instruction in subjects that were too irrelevant and too academic. The "algebraic formulas without application" that students were learning were supposedly a waste (McAndrew, 1912, p. 6).

Henry Pritchett (1922), founding president of the Carnegie Foundation for the Advancement of Teaching, called for the revival of a traditional high school curriculum while making a similar argument about spending, outcomes, and waste. Lamenting how the "sound virtues" of a classical high school curriculum focused on Greek and Latin were increasingly rare, he cited the growth of educational expenditures after World War I—an era of increasing enrollments and rampant inflation—to question whether public education was still "justifying itself in the results which it brings forth" (p. 173). He contended it did not. Nothing had "done more to increase the cost of public education" than "the so-called 'enrichment' of the curriculum," Pritchett insisted (p. 178). For Pritchett, like similar funding critics at the time, the problem of supposedly growing costs and stagnant outcomes that could be solved via the curriculum was rooted in who was being educated. It was ultimately the decision to admit those "great numbers of pupils whose intellectual endowment is ill-suited for formal study" that he found troubling and responsible for growing costs associated with a new curriculum (p. 178). In short, critics like Pritchett claimed money was being wasted by educating all children.

After World War II, it was more of the same as influential commentators continued their refusal to acknowledge the reality of inequitable funding by focusing on the need for curricular reform. With a dramatic increase in the number of births during the baby boom, school enrollments and costs increased. The continued growth of high school attendance produced increases in spending as well. Critics again questioned the connection between that spending and desirable outcomes, and they again pointed to purported issues with the curriculum to make their case. Some used spending in areas like vocational education and technology courses to argue money was being wasted and spending need not increase. Others focused on debunking research demonstrating how expenditures could increase outcomes. Antigovernment economist Roger A. Freeman insisted all education spending was "pork barrel" and called for like-minded researchers to "offset" the academic literature on the consequences of funding disparities. Freeman actually praised the sophistication of the work he sought to "offset" but still considered it "propaganda" since he found its conclusions disagreeable (quoted in MacLean, 2017, p. 68). Freeman went on to spend the remainder of his career, until his retirement from the Hoover Institution in 1975, questioning the importance of funding disparities and casting doubt on the idea that spending impacted educational outcomes.

Even advocacy for market-based reform—supposedly the newest of the substitutes for fair funding—is an old and tired idea. When California reformer Zachariah Montgomery (1881) presented his alternative to fairer spending in California after the Civil War in thinly veiled calls for state funding of Catholic schools, he focused on the need to replace the influence of the state with the power of markets. "The whole business of educating and training the young shall, like other professions, be open to private enterprise and free competition," he wrote (p. 146).

The repetitiveness of these supposedly novel ideas about reform is hardly surprising. As educational historians have repeatedly shown, the story of American school reform is largely a history of faulty assumptions and familiar ideas being repeated. This is an important reminder as detractors of funding fairness continue to make their overblown claims that some purportedly innovative reform is in order.

* * *

Standing in the present, it is easy to see how misleading claims about costs and outcomes were in the educational past. The consistency of those misleading claims about funding and outcomes over time can help us spot how the same precarious logic shapes similar assertions today. It is also important to examine how this logic operates and what it does to children in practice, too. Consider a recent example of the claim from a news article published following the release of comparative data from the Organisation for Economic Co-operation and Development (OECD) in 2018. The title told the story: "The US Spends More on Education Than Other Countries. Why Is It Falling Behind?" the headline asked. The assertion that the United States is falling behind uses data that is less clear and more controversial than the article suggests. The real trouble with the headline, though, comes from the broad assertion that the United States spends more on education than other countries. A little more context can put that claim into perspective. The figure supporting the assertion about spending is $16,268 per pupil, a mean figure from 2014. In reality, however, there are large racial and economic gaps in school funding. Using a single average becomes more than a little misleading. In Reading School District in Pennsylvania, for example, spending was $6,189 lower than the figure from the article in question during that year. Ninety-three percent of the students attending schools in Reading were children of color. Over 90% of Reading's student population was designated low income by the state, too. New Hope Solebury School District, meanwhile, spent a little more than twice as much as Reading, about $4,000 more than the average from the article. Only 12% of the students attending schools in New Hope Solebury were students of color. Less than 5% of New Hope Solebury's student population was designated low income.[1]

Revising the headline of the article with this in mind, it would be best to reframe the question like this: "The U.S. spends a great deal on public

---

1. Data based on current expenditures per average daily member reported in Pennsylvania Department of Education Annual Financial Report Files.

schools educating *White children from affluent families*, but substantially less on *schools that educate children from low-income families, especially when a majority of a school's students are children of color.*"

The final question from the headline—"Why is it falling behind?"—then answers itself.

REFERENCES

Abott, C., Kogan, V., Lavertu, S., & Peskowitz, Z. (2020). School district operational spending and student outcomes: Evidence from tax elections in seven states. *Journal of Public Economics, 183*(C), 104–142.

Baker, B. (2018). *Educational inequality and school finance: Why money matters for America's students.* Harvard Education Press.

Barnard, H. (1853). *Report of the Board of Education 1852–53.* Alfred E. Barr State Printer.

Barnum, M. (2023, May 16). An economist spent decades saying money wouldn't help schools. Now his research suggests otherwise. *Chalkbeat.* Retrieved from https://www.chalkbeat.org/2023/5/16/23724474/school-funding-research-studies-hanushek-does-money-matter

Baron, J. (2021). School spending and student outcomes: Evidence from revenue limit elections in Wisconsin. *American Economic Journal: Economic Policy, 14*(1), 1–39.

Biasi, B. (2023). School finance equalization increases intergenerational mobility. *Journal of Labor Economics, 41*(1), 1–38.

Bowyer, V. (1933). Does a reduction of school costs help taxpayers? *Phi Delta Kappan, 15*(6), 170–172.

Brunner, E., Hyman, J., & Ju, A. (2020). School finance reforms, teachers' unions, and the allocation of school resources. *Review of Economics and Statistics, 102*(3), 473–489

Candelaria, C. A., & Shores, K. A. (2019). Court-ordered finance reforms in the adequacy era: Heterogeneous causal effects and sensitivity. *Education Finance and Policy, 14*(1), 31–60.

Cascio, E. U., Gordon, N., & Reber, S. (2013). Local responses to federal grants: Evidence from the introduction of Title I in the South. *American Economic Journal: Economic Policy, 5*(3), 126–159.

Cellini, S. R., Ferreira, F., & Rothstein, J. (2010). The value of school facility investments: Evidence from a dynamic regression discontinuity design. *Quarterly Journal of Economics, 125*(1), 215–261.

Coleman, J. S., Campbell, E. Q., Hobson, C. J., McPartland, J., Mood, A. M., Weinfeld, A. D., York, R. L. (1966). *Equality of educational opportunity.* Washington, DC: U.S. Government Printing Office.

"Common schools in New York." (1834). *American Annals of Education,* 107.

Conlin, M., & Thompson, P. N. (2017). Impacts of new school facility construction: An analysis of a state-financed capital subsidy program in Ohio. *Economics of Education Review, 59,* 13–28.

Dix, J. (1834). *Annual Report of the Superintendent of Common School (New York).* Croswell, Printer to the State.

EdBuild. (2019). Nonwhite school districts get $23 billion less than White districts despite serving the same number of students. Retrieved from https://edbuild.org/content/23-billion

Gigliotti, P., & Sorensen, L. C. (2018). Educational resources and student achievement: Evidence from the Save Harmless provision in New York State. *Economics of Education Review, 66*, 167–182.

Hanushek, E. A. (1997). Assessing the effects of school resources on student performance: An update. *Educational Evaluation and Policy Analysis, 19*(2), 141–164.

Hedges, L. V., Laine, R. D., & Greenwald, R. (1994). Does money matter? A meta-analysis of studies of the effects of differential inputs on student outcomes. *Educational Researcher, 23*(3), 5–14.

Hong, K., & Zimmer, R. (2016). Does investing in school capital infrastructure improve student achievement? *Economics of Education Review, 53*, 143–158.

Hyman, J. (2017). Does money matter in the long run? Effects of school spending on educational attainment. *American Economic Journal: Economic Policy, 9*(4), 256–280.

Illinois General Assembly. (1835). *Journal of the Senate of the General Assembly of the State of Illinois Volume I.* J. Y. Sawyer, State Printer

Jackson, C. K., Johnson, R. C., & Persico, C. (2016). The effects of school spending on educational and economic outcomes: Evidence from school finance reforms. *Quarterly Journal of Economics, 131*(1), 157–218.

Jackson, C. K., Wigger, C., & Xiong, H. (2021). Do School Spending Cuts Matter? Evidence from the Great Recession. *American Economic Journal: Economic Policy, 13*(2), 304–335. Retrieved from https://doi.org/10.1257/pol.20180674

Johnson, R. C. (2015). Follow the money: School spending from Title I to adult earnings. *RSF: The Russell Sage Foundation Journal of the Social Sciences, 1*(3), 50–76.

Kelly, M. G. (2020). The curious case of the missing tail: Trends among the top 1% of school districts in the United States, 2000–2015. *Educational Researcher, 49*(5), 312–320.

Kogan, V., Lavertu, S., & Peskowitz, Z. (2017). Direct democracy and administrative disruption. *Journal of Public Administration Research and Theory, 27*(3), 381–399.

Kreisman, D., & Steinberg, M. P. (2019). The effect of increased funding on student achievement: Evidence from Texas's small district adjustment. *Journal of Public Economics, 176*, 118–141.

Lafortune, J., Rothstein, J., & Schanzenbach, D. W. (2018). School finance reform and the distribution of student achievement. *American Economic Journal: Applied Economics, 10*(2), 1–26.

Lafortune, J., & Schönholzer, D. (2022). The Impact of School Facility Investments on Students and Homeowners: Evidence from Los Angeles. *American Economic Journal: Applied Economics, 14*(3), 254–289. Retrieved from https://doi.org/10.1257/app.20200467

Lee, K.-G., & Polachek, S. W. (2018). Do school budgets matter? The effect of budget referenda on student dropout rates. *Education Economics, 26*(2), 129–144.

Lynch, E. F. (1912). Is the public school a failure? *Ladies' Home Journal, 29*(8), 3435.

MacLean, N. (2017). *Democracy in chains: The deep history of the radical right's stealth plan for America*. Viking.
Martorell, P., Stange, K., & McFarlin, I. (2016). Investing in schools: Capital spending, facility conditions, and student achievement. *Journal of Public Economics, 140*, 13–29.
Mayo, A. D. (1877). Economy in schools. *New England Journal of Education, 5*(12), 139.
McAndrew, W. (1912). The danger of running a fool factory. *The Ladies' Home Journal, 29*(9), 6.
Miller, C. L. (2018). The effect of education spending on student achievement: Evidence from property values and school finance rules. Working Paper. Retrieved from https://www.corbinmiller.website/paper/jmp/jmp.pdf
Moehlman, A. B. (1927). *Public school finance*. Rand McNally.
Montgomery, Z. (1881). The Chico enterprise. *The Family's Defender, 1*(4), 145–151.
Mort, P. R. (1952). Cost-quality relationship in education. In R. L. Johns & E. L. Morphet (Eds.), *Problems and issues in public school finance* (pp. 9–63). Teachers College Press.
Neilson, C. A., & Zimmerman, S. D. (2014). The effect of school construction on test scores, school enrollment, and home prices. *Journal of Public Economics, 120*, 18–31.
Powell, O. E. (1933). *Educational returns at varying expenditure levels*. Teachers College Press.
Pritchett, H. S. (1922). The rising cost of education. *American Law School Review, 5*(1), 171–190.
Rauscher, E. (2020). Delayed benefits: Effects of California school district bond elections on achievement by socioeconomic status. *Sociology of Education, 93*(2), 110–131.
Roy, J. (2011). Impact of school finance reform on resource equalization and academic performance: Evidence from Michigan. *Education Finance and Policy, 6*(2), 137–167.
Weathers, E. S., & Sosina, V. E. (2022). Separate remains unequal: Contemporary segregation and racial disparities in school district revenue. *American Educational Research Journal, 59*(5), 905–938.
Woollatt, L. H. (1949). *The cost-quality relationship on the growing edge*. Teachers College Press.

CHAPTER 22

The Myth That Preschool Education Is a Panacea

Barbara Beatty

Promising preschool education as a panacea has been a theme in the history of education for centuries. The core promise is that all preschool education is good for all children and will foster large social reforms. A huge terrain, preschool education encompasses a multitude of different programs. I am defining it broadly as early childhood care and education for 3-, 4-, and 5-year-olds, not younger children (Beatty, 1995).

I will argue that big promises about the effects of educating little children have sometimes diverted attention from the significance of program quality and from the systemic societal problems preschool education has been said to help to solve. At the same time, promoting preschool education as a panacea has perhaps proven useful in campaigns to provide more education and services to young children and their families. To examine these tensions in a balanced way, I will provide some historical examples, beginning and ending with my own experiences as a kindergarten teacher in the Boston Public Schools more than 50 years ago.

When I started teaching prekindergarten for 4-year-olds in 1968 during a teacher shortage, I had limited training. Assigned to a janitor's former storeroom, I had to use my own money to buy supplies. I got little supervision or professional development. I witnessed racism. With double sessions of 20 children in the morning and 20 in the afternoon, I did not have an aide. It was hard.

In 1971, I became the teacher of Boston's first all-day kindergarten for 4- and 5-year-olds who otherwise were not attending school. With funding from Title I of the federal Elementary and Secondary Education Act of 1965, the program in which I taught was a response to the 1970 report *The Way We Go to School in Boston: Exclusion of Children in Boston*. The report documented that Black and "Culturally Different"—primarily Spanish-speaking children—made up the largest proportion of out-of-school children. Many "Physically Different Children" and "Mentally and Behaviorally Different Children" were also excluded (Task Force on Children Out of School, 1970).

With an aide, I recruited out-of-school children from a local housing project and surrounding neighborhood. I spoke Spanish, which helped.

With a full-day program, budget, and 18 in the class, we were able to provide many of the educational and social services the report on excluded children recommended. We bought materials and designed our curriculum. We gave the children breakfast and hot lunch. I made home visits and talked about lead paint screening, physical checkups, and other health issues. Although our classroom was in a trailer, parents could visit and cook culturally diverse food without having to get through the locked metal door of the big elementary school with which we were associated. Some of the children had mental and behavioral health problems for which I could not get support, however, which made meeting their needs and those of other children difficult.

Preschool education generally has been prone to promises, in part because it remains untried universally. I have chosen some older and modern examples of big promises, about reducing racism and poverty and promoting assimilation, themes that have run through the history of preschool education. I will not discuss promises about child development, play, creativity, happiness, independence, cooperation, and other individual goods often coupled with and presented as necessary to achieve large social goals.

Some promises about preschool education, such as increasing the number of kindergartens across the country and incorporating them into the public schools, mostly came true, others did not. Some unrealized promises became myths about the future. Throughout a long history of waiting for support, and many disappointments, advocates continued to express hope, which sometimes seemed unrealistic. But big promises may have helped keep the preschool movement alive, at the risk of overpromising what preschools could do for society as a whole (Beatty, 1995; Cuban, 1992; Grubb & Lazerson, 1982, 2004; Karch, 2013; Kirp, 2007; Rose, 2010).

PRESCHOOL EDUCATION WILL REDUCE RACISM

In her 1835 *Memoir of the Life of James Jackson,* Susan Paul, a Black abolitionist teacher at a segregated Boston public primary school, hoped that her published account of Jackson's high achievement and good behavior would dispel racist stereotypes of African Americans' inferior intelligence and immorality. Jackson, who had been admitted to her class at the age of 3, learned in "a very short time," Paul said, "all his letters, and began to read in syllables." Criticizing white prejudice, Paul emphasized his "high intelligence" and that he was a *"very* good boy," even if some might "dislike him because he was coloured" (Paul, 1835, pp. 70, 71, 72).

Paul's book, the first biography of an African American published in the United States, and the work of her father, Reverend Thomas Paul, and many others, helped lead to the 1849 Massachusetts Supreme Judicial Court case of *Roberts v. City of Boston.* The case centered on Sarah Roberts, who was forced to walk past White primary schools in Boston to attend a segregated school. Although Sarah's suit was not successful, it highlighted the importance of desegregating public schools in Massachusetts, and the state legislature ultimately outlawed segregation in 1855. Racism remained in the schools, however, and for some Black children in classrooms with White children and White teachers, it may have been worse (Baumgartner, 2019; Brown, 2000; Kendrick and Kendrick, 2004; Moss, 2009).

In 1878, after the Civil War, kindergarten promoter Elizabeth Peabody wrote that she hoped that "American mothers" would now "come together *at last* to *understand* one another instead of meeting . . . to prey on each other." Implying that kindergartens were a way to unite mothers and reunite the country, she said mothers needed to understand that "the first word of our nationality was, *is,* and *ever shall be,* 'all men are *created* free and equal.'" In 1901, however, Josephine Silone Yates of the National Association of Colored Women, found that Black and White mothers had not come together to support kindergartens in the Jim Crow South, where she found *no* public kindergartens for Black children (Peabody, 1878, p. 7; Yates, 1905, p. 308).

More recently, as Katherine M. Zinsser shows, preschool education has not reduced racist views about many young Black boys. They suffer from the highest rates of expulsion from preschool education in the United States (Zinsser, 2022).

PRESCHOOL EDUCATION WILL ASSIMILATE MIGRANT AND CULTURALLY DIVERSE CHILDREN AND FAMILIES

Assimilating migrant and culturally diverse children and families was a common rationale for public kindergartens at the beginning of the 20th century. As children's book author Kate Douglas Wiggin, director of a charity kindergarten in San Francisco, promised in the early 1900s, kindergartens would "help in the absorption and amalgamation of our foreign element" and enhance "citizen-virtues" (quoted in Locke, 1909–1911, p. 3). Bessie Locke, who founded the National Kindergarten Association (NKA) in 1909, promised kindergartens "for all the nation's children." In 1913, the NKA and its state and local members succeeded in getting a bill enabling public kindergartens passed by the California legislature, as they did in a number of other states, but not all school districts approved funding (Beatty, 2000, 2007; Locke, 1909–1911, p. 1).

Some attempts to enroll migrant children met with resistance. When Caroline Pratt founded a play-based nursery school in New York City in 1913, one of the first in the United States, she especially wanted to attract children from migrant and working-class families. As she later wrote, when she would not promise to push "the three R's on the children" to prepare them for school, many migrant parents withdrew or refused to send their children (Pratt, 1948, p. 40).

The nation's children still do not have universal access to kindergarten or preschool education. The National Center for Education Statistics (NCES) documented that in 2020, some six states did not require local school districts to offer public kindergartens, although some of these states are changing their requirements. Studies show that rates of preschool attendance vary considerably based on migration status, language, and cultural diversity. Latino and Latino migrant children attend at lower levels (Lopez & Grindal, 2020, pp. 1–3; NCES, n.d., State Education Practices, Table 1.3).

PRESCHOOL EDUCATION WILL REDUCE POVERTY

The promise of Head Start, founded in 1965 as part of President Lyndon B. Johnson's Great Society programs, was that it would reduce poverty by preparing very low-income children for school, hiring low-income mothers, and offering comprehensive social services. Although some policy analysts have estimated that poverty declined some 3.7% between 1965 and 1972, due in part to programs such as Head Start, the poverty rate soon went back up, for a variety of reasons (Haveman et al., 2015, pp. 593–638).

Head Start enhanced educational opportunities for low-income children, but learning gaps remained. Some initial studies found that cognitive and academic achievement gains tended to fade in the upper grades. Supposed preschool outcomes could be used for negative purposes. In a controversial 1969 article in the *Harvard Educational Review*, educational psychologist Arthur Jensen used data from Head Start and other preschool programs to claim that inherited racial differences in intelligence prevented the success of education programs for disadvantaged children (Beatty, 2012; Jensen, 1969; Vinovskis, 2005).

Comprehensive social services linked to Head Start increased, but Head Start remained dependent on federal budgeting, not an entitlement. Income requirements and long waiting lists limited access. Head Start, never a unified program, had quality issues that may have hampered its success, as did the need for more funding, though that grew (Mongeau, 2016; Rose, 2010; Zigler & Styfco, 2010).

MODERN PROMISES THAT PRESCHOOL EDUCATION WILL PROVIDE LASTING, COST-BENEFICIAL SOCIETAL OUTCOMES

Some modern experimental studies of model preschool programs document lasting, positive, cost-beneficial societal outcomes. From 1962 to 1967, the Perry Preschool Project in Ypsilanti, Michigan, provided preschool education to half of a randomized group of 123 very low-income, African American children; researchers have followed these children into adulthood. Among other benefits, adults in the treatment group had fewer teenage pregnancies, were more likely to graduate high school, more likely to hold jobs and have higher earnings, more likely to own homes and cars, and committed fewer crimes. Perry researchers argue that by the time participants were 40, the program had saved society $16.14 for every dollar invested (Heckman, 2022; Schweinhart, 2018, pp. 1–21).

Researchers at the Carolina Abecedarian Project at the Frank Porter Graham Center for Child Development at the University of North Carolina at Chapel Hill have been following a randomized group of mostly low-income African American children born between 1972 and 1977. According to longitudinal studies, children in the treatment group maintained statistically significant higher intelligence and academic test scores, were more likely to attend 4-year colleges, and less likely to become teenage parents and report symptoms of depression and other health problems. Abecedarian researchers argue that 30 years later, a dollar invested saved society $2.50, due to higher salaries and less use of government and health care services (Campbell et al., 2014; Carolina Abecedarian Project Follow-up Studies, 2014).

Randomized studies of children from low-income families who attended kindergarten and preschool programs begun in 2008 in the Boston Public Schools also show positive outcomes that may translate into societal savings. Some other model programs do, as well (Bardige et al., 2018; Weiland & Yoshikawa, 2013).

Modern promises showing societal benefits from preschool education come from *high-quality programs*, with small class sizes, well-trained and well-paid teachers, classroom aides, carefully planned and implemented curricula, parent engagement, ongoing assessment, support services, and other optimal features that enable program goals. While impressive, such data may understate lack of comparability among preschool programs generally and the difficulty of maximizing quality. Although high quality can be hard to define and expensive, it is necessary to attain and sustain long-term, positive gains, which may be cost-beneficial for society. Preschool educators emphasize the need for high quality, especially for children from low-income families, many of whom attend low-quality programs (Bowman et al., 2001; Gordon & Farran, 2022, pp. 374–378; Horm et al., 2022).

Lack of support for preschool promises often comes from concerns about federal control and costs. Some parents see children aged four and under as part of the private family, not subject to top-down government mandates. When President Richard M. Nixon vetoed the Comprehensive Child Development Act in 1971, seen by some historians as the greatest disappointment in universalizing preschool education, he used the rationale that it was un-American. It would "commit the vast moral authority of the National Government to the side of communal approaches to child rearing over against the family-centered approach," his veto stated. The veto was also about the cost of instituting federally sponsored universal preschool education, still a dream today (Nixon, 1971, p. 5; also see Beatty, 1995).

CONCLUSION

As public preschools increase at the state and local level, we may be at an inflection point. We need to understand the enormous variation in the huge patchwork of preschool and child care programs, as well as the competition among public and private preschools and other education and social services. During the Great Depression, for instance, when the National Kindergarten Association and the National Education Association (NEA) fought unsuccessfully to gain federal support, the NEA excluded the NKA from the debate as they competed for funding. Preschool education continues to vie with other programs for funding for support (Beatty, 2007, p. 204).

Often part of ideology about social justice, big preschool promises can be seen as efforts to increase equality, an elusive goal, along with getting funding for new programs and research. At the same time, big promises may make it easier to promote positive outcomes without attending sufficiently to program quality. Achieving quality at the practical level of individual programs is difficult. Input from teachers, principals, parents, activists, researchers, politicians, and other stakeholders is important. So are understanding and supporting racial, cultural, and linguistic diversity and special needs, and rejecting deficit models that blame disadvantaged young children and their families (Beatty, 2012; Nelson, 2005).

The lack of universal preschool education can be used as an implicit excuse for unrealized goals and negative outcomes in education as a whole. Shortcomings in education generally can be attributed in part to the lack of a solid foundation for young children when they enter school, making it harder to see and link specific ways to improve education at all levels (Takanishi, 2016). As some historians point out, however, education reforms often proceed in cycles, from initial exaggerated hopes to disillusionment. Expectations evolve, change is incremental, as "tinkering," as David Tyack and Larry Cuban call it, goes on (Tyack & Cuban, 1995).

Big promises also may overshadow the large structural issues and systemic problems preschool education is being promoted to ameliorate. As some policy analysts argue, using preschool education to educationalize social reform can obscure the political commitment needed to address inequalities. And attendance or not at a high-quality preschool can lead to inequities (Grubb & Lazerson, 2004).

I knew my one little preschool program was helping, but not enough. The children and their families were facing desperate circumstances outside of my classroom. Racism, poverty, lack of health care, incarceration, housing and food insecurity, substance abuse, and other problems were everywhere. The neighborhood was unsafe. My aide and I worked as hard as we could, but knew we were barely making a dent in the needs of out-of-school preschoolers in Boston, much less in the large social problems we saw all around us. After teaching kindergarten in the Boston Public Schools, I was motivated to try harder and joined the campaign for high-quality, universal preschool education.

Educating little children is not a panacea for big social problems, but it may help. The longer I have studied preschool education, the more I have seen the importance of quality. Hopefully, perspective on the history of preschool promises can help us provide high-quality preschools for all young children.

REFERENCES

Bardige, B., Baker, M., & Mardell, B. (2018). *Children at the Center: Transforming early childhood education in the Boston public schools.* Harvard Education Press.

Baumgartner, K. (2019). *In pursuit of knowledge: Black women and educational activism in antebellum America.* New York University Press.

Beatty, B. (1995). *Preschool education in America: The culture of young children from the colonial era to the present.* Yale University Press.

Beatty, B. (2000). The letter killeth: Americanization and multiculturalism in kindergartens in the United States, 1856–1920. In R. Wollons (Ed.), *Kindergartens and cultures: The global diffusion of an idea* (pp. 42–58). Yale University Press.

Beatty, B. (2007). Politics are quite perplexing: Bessie Locke and the National Kindergarten Association. In A. M. Knupfer & C. Woyshner (Eds.), *The educational work of women's organizations, 1890–1960* (pp. 195–214). Palgrave Macmillan.

Beatty, B. (2012). The debate over the young disadvantaged child: Preschool intervention, developmental psychology, and compensatory education in the 1960s and early 1970s. *Teachers College Record, 114,* 1–36.

Brown, L. (2000). Introduction. In L. Brown (Ed.), *Memoir of James Jackson* (pp. 1–63). Harvard University Press.

Bowman, B. T., Donovan, M. S., & Burns, M. S. (2001). *Eager to learn: Educating our preschoolers.* Washington, DC: National Academy Press.

Campbell, F., et al. (2014). High-quality early education and child care bring healthy benefits 30 years later. *Science, 343*(6178), 1478–1495.

Carolina Abecedarian Project follow-up studies (2014). Frank Porter Graham Child Development Institute. Chapel Hill: University of North Carolina. Retrieved from https://abc.fpg.unc.edu/follow-up-studies/

Cuban, L. (1992). Why some reforms last: The case of the kindergarten. *American Journal of Education, 100*(2), 166–194.

Gordon, R. A., & Farran, D. (2022). Introduction to ECRQ special issue measuring quality in early care and education: Past, present, and future. *Early Childhood Research Quarterly, 60,* 374–378.

Grubb, W. N., & Lazerson, M. (1982). *Broken promises: How Americans fail their children.* Basic Books.

Grubb, W. N., & Lazerson, M. (2004). *The education gospel: The economic power of schooling.* Harvard University Press.

Haveman, R., Blank, R., Moffitt, R., Smeeding, T., & Wallace, G. (2015). The War on Poverty: Measurement, trends, and policy, *Journal of Policy Analysis and Management, 34*(3), 593–638.

Heckman, J. J. (2022). *The Heckman equation.* Retrieved from https://heckmanequation.org/the-heckman-equation/

Horm, D. M., Jeon, S., Clavijo, M. V., & Acton, M. (2022). Kindergarten through grade 3 outcomes associated with participation in high-quality early care and education: A RCT follow-up study. *Education Sciences, 12*(12). Retrieved from https://doi.org/10.3390/educsci12120908

Jensen, A. (1969). How much can we boost IQ and scholastic achievement? *Harvard Educational Review, 39*(1), 1–123.

Karch, A. (2013). *Early Start: Preschool politics in the United States.* Ann Arbor: University of Michigan Press.

Kendrick, P., & Kendrick, S. (2004). *Sarah's long walk: The free Blacks and how the struggle for equality changed America.* Beacon Press.

Kirp, D. L. (2007). *The sandbox investment: The preschool movement and kids-first politics.* Harvard University Press.

Locke, B. (1909–1911). *Annual Report 1909–1911, National Kindergarten Association.* Washington, DC: National Kindergarten Association.

Lopez, M., & Grindal, T. (2020). Early care and education among Latinos: Access, utilization, and outcomes. *Early Childhood Research Quarterly, 52,* 1–3.

Mongeau, L. (2016). Is Head Start a failure? The federal government has invested billions. What more could we do? *The Hechinger Report.* Retrieved from https://hechingerreport.org/is-head-start-a-failure/

Moss, H. J. (2009). *Schooling citizens: The struggle for African American education.* Chicago: University of Chicago Press.

National Center for Education Statistics (NCES). (n.d.). *Types of state and district requirements for kindergarten entrance and attendance, by state: 2020.* Retrieved from https://nces.ed.gov/programs/statereform/tab1_3-2020.asp

Nelson, A. (2005). *The elusive ideal: Equal educational opportunity and the federal role in Boston's public schools.* Chicago: University of Chicago Press.

Nixon, R. M. (1971, December 9). Veto message: Economic Opportunity Amendment of 1971. U.S. Senate Document No. 92–48.

Paul, S. (1835). *Memoir of James Jackson, the attentive and obedient scholar who died in Boston, October 31, 1833.* Boston: James Loring.

Peabody, E. (1878). American Preface, in *Froebel's mother-play and nursery songs by Friedrich Froebel,* trans. Josephine Jarvis. Boston: Lee and Shepard.

Pratt, C. (1948). *I learn from children: An adventure in progressive education.* New York: Simon & Schuster.

Rose, E. R. (2010). *The promise of preschool: From Head Start to universal pre-kindergarten.* Oxford University Press.

Schweinhart, L. J. (2018). *The High/Scope Perry Preschool Study through age 40: Summary, conclusions, and frequently asked questions.* High/Scope Educational Research Foundation. Retrieved from https://highscope.org/wp-content/uploads/2018/11/perry-preschool-summary-40.pdf

Takanishi, R. (2016). *First things first! Creating the new American primary school.* New York: Teachers College Press.

Task Force on Children Out of School in Boston (1970). *The way we go to school: The exclusion of children in Boston.* Retrieved from https://eric.ed.gov/?id=ED046140

Tyack, D. B., & Cuban, L. (1995). *Tinkering toward utopia: A century of public school reform.* Harvard University Press.

Vinovskis, M. A. (2005). *The birth of Head Start.* Chicago: University of Chicago Press.

Weiland, C., & Yoshikawa, H. (2013). Impacts of a prekindergarten program on children's mathematics, language, literacy, executive function, and emotional skills. *Child Development, 84*(6), 2112–2130.

Wiggin, K. D. (1909–1911). *Annual report 1909–1911.* National Kindergarten Association. Gutman Library, Harvard Graduate School of Education.

Yates, J. S. (1905). Kindergartens and mother' clubs. *Colored American Magazine, 8*, 308.

Zigler, E. F., & Styfco, S. (2010). *The hidden history of Head Start.* Oxford University Press.

Zinsser, K. M. (2022). *No longer welcome: The epidemic of expulsion from early childhood education.* Oxford University Press.

CHAPTER 23

The Myth of Patriotic Education as a Unifying Force

Cody Dodge Ewert

The *San Francisco Bulletin* did not mince words on October 23, 1915, when it ran the headline "The Patriotic Teaching of History—A Crime." The author, Jerome B. Landfield, a former history professor at the University of California in Berkeley, excoriated the contemporary movement spearheaded by the Grand Army of the Republic (GAR), a leading veteran's group, to inject patriotism into American classrooms. To Landfield, the kind of instruction the GAR wanted children to receive was not true patriotism. Instead, the group aimed to have "the facts of history colored and distorted so as to make the school child an incurable jingo." "This is a strong statement," Landfield acknowledged, adding, "I hesitate to make it lest I be taken for a pacifist—and I despise pacifists" (Landfield, 1915, p. 9). War had broken out in Europe just a year prior, and Landfield saw the brand of patriotism championed by the GAR as calculated to make the nation's schoolchildren eager to join the fray. To thinkers like Landfield, patriotism and militarism simply did not mix.

Of course, the idea of teaching patriotism did not originate with the GAR, nor were they the only advocates of the concept. Indeed, many of the nation's leading educators, politicians, and thinkers endorsed a movement that aimed to present schools as hubs of American sentiment around the turn of the 20th century. They did so, however, for markedly different reasons. Some groups, like the GAR, wanted schools to produce flag-waving citizens prepared to fight for their country should the need arise. Others aimed simply to cast schools themselves in a positive light, to highlight the key role public education could play in moving the nation into the 20th century. In other words, while a broad cross section of people championed patriotic education, few agreed on what it should actually entail. Still others found the concept itself too divisive and limited to be of use; one harsh assessment of patriotic education printed in the *Nation* dismissed most versions of it as merely "idiotic flag fetishism" (Mather, 1900, p. 440).

The notion that schools can heal social and political divisions by teaching patriotism is a pervasive myth. In the 2020s, over a century after World

War I drew to a close, several states began considering legislation aimed at keeping "divisive concepts"—especially those pertaining to questions of race, namely the teaching of critical race theory, and gender—out of the classroom. Instead, they suggested, the nation's schools should offer a positive and unifying vision of the United States and its history. The advocates of such measures, typically political conservatives, championed flag-waving reappraisals of American history such as the Trump administration's 1776 Report (President's Advisory 1776 Commission, 2021) or Texas's Lone Star-centric 1836 Project (LaGrone & Phillips, 2022). While such projects framed more critical examinations of the nation's past as baldly unpatriotic, defenders of teaching materials such as the "1619 Project," which posited slavery as a driving force in American history, argued the contrary (Smith, 2019). In short, around the time when so-called "divisive concepts" bills began proliferating, Americans remained as divided as ever over what it meant to be patriotic.

Such divisions are not simply the product of a time of intense polarization. Indeed, public schools have long been sites where questions of what it meant to be an American have been contested. Around the turn of the 20th century when patriotism and citizenship became major educational buzzwords, educators, politicians, and parents openly debated the meaning of such terms. Most everyone, it seemed, could agree that turning students into patriots and upstanding citizens was a noble goal, but they differed greatly on the specifics. Two subjects in particular—war, especially debates over military training, and politics, namely the question of socialism—split self-proclaimed patriots hoping to transform the nation's classrooms. The debates over these issues, furthermore, would have a lasting impact on the day-to-day workings of American public schools.

In his 1885 book *Our Country*, staunch nationalist Josiah Strong called for Americans to look to their schools to safeguard against what he cast as the imminent threats of socialism and anarchism. Immigrants, Strong claimed, were pouring into the country and bringing un-American ideas with them. "Most of the Internationals, the anarchic socialists, in this country," Strong wrote, "are Germans, whose numbers are constantly being recruited by immigration" (Strong, 1885, p. 92). His solution: "Christianize the Immigrant . . . and he will be easily Americanized." The nation's public schools—which in Strong's mind were de facto Protestant institutions—would instill respect for the flag, the cross, and free enterprise. Yet not all Americans agreed that patriotism and Christianity were incompatible with socialism. Take, for instance, Francis Bellamy, the ardent Christian socialist long credited with writing the "Pledge of Allegiance." Injecting patriotism into the schools, in Bellamy's mind, would help erase divisions of class and ethnicity. As he put it in an 1892 edition of the *Journal of Education*, "The state fosters the school; it is the school's business to make for the state a substantial bottom of citizenship. . . . All the centuries have been praising the patriotic soldier, the patriotic statesman; the 20th century must be above all the age of the patriotic school-master" (Bellamy, 1892, p. 107).

Bellamy stirred enthusiasm for patriotic education through his work with the popular Boston-based magazine *The Youth's Companion* and his heavy involvement in promoting a national school celebration to coincide with Columbus Day of 1892. While his views on economics did not factor into his efforts to promote this issue, neither were they a guarded secret (Ellis, 2005, pp. 28–30). More telling is the fact that Bellamy did not see patriotism as incompatible with socialism. Yet as Strong's vitriolic prose suggests, others clearly did. Like Strong, newspaperman John Bell Boughton urged schools to lead the way in forming a "National Patriotic Cult" in his 1895 book *Uncle Sam's Church* (Bouton, 1895, p. iv). Bouton made clear, however, that certain political ideologies were not welcome in this new cult. "Socialists," he warned, "with deceptive olive branches . . . are menacing the institutions that are our heritage, bought by the Fathers with so great a price of blood and treasure" (Bouton, 1895, p. iii).

By the early 20th century, socialists had made considerable headway in American politics. While still a distinct minority, they became major political players in certain parts of the country, especially the American West. There, debates over how well socialism jibed with patriotism could be revealing. For example, in 1912, 13-year-old Lena Eyler, a student in Salt Lake City, Utah, refused to salute the American flag as part of her public school's daily reading of the "Pledge of Allegiance." In response, the city superintendent and school principal agreed to expel her. Eyler's protest was a planned political statement, not a spontaneous outburst. As she explained her action: "I will not salute that flag . . . if I must salute a flag it will be the red flag of Socialism because I think it stands more for liberty and justice than the Stars and Stripes" ("School Girl Is Expelled," 1912). After the city ruled that Eyler could return to school only if she agreed to salute the flag, she refused, reiterating that the American flag did not represent her values.

At the time of Eyler's suspension, the Church of Jesus Christ of Latter-day Saints, which still dominated society and politics even in comparatively secular Salt Lake City, had embraced antisocialist posturing as a way of distancing the church from its collectivist past (McCormick & Sillito, 2011). Still, the city school board questioned whether the suspension was fair. When the board convened in the wake of the suspension to see if they could agree on a policy, opinions were split. One member argued against compulsion, noting, "We love to salute the flag because of the freedom it insures [sic] us, but I would fight any flag that sought to compel me to salute it." Another countered that when the child "strays from the path of loyalty he should be brought back into the path by force if necessary" ("Flag Salute," 1912). The board walked away from the meeting without adopting a policy.

The headline in the *Salt Lake Tribune* the next day said it all: "Flag Salute Vexes Board of Education."

Socialists in Utah and across the country offered Eyler support but stopped short of encouraging similar protests. The *Daily People*, a newspaper produced by the New York–based Socialist Labor Party (SLP), cheered Eyler's "deliberately intense and intensely deliberate" protest. Yet the bulk of the SLP's energy went to chiding officials at the school and city authorities not for expelling Eyler, but for doing such a poor job of teaching history that she failed to appreciate "the freedoms" the flag afforded (De Leon, 1912). The SLP's view of the situation served as a reminder that many socialists at the time—including Socialist Party of America figurehead Eugene V. Debs— considered their politics compatible with American patriotism (Hansen, 2003).

Two years later and a few hundred miles north in the mining city of Butte, Montana, socialists had a firmer political foothold. The city had a socialist mayor, and socialists held three of the seven seats on the city school board. As the city worked to revamp its civics curricula, socialist board member H. L. Maury pushed the school board to introduce socialist literature into the schools. The *Anaconda Standard*—a nearby paper with close ties to the dominant copper industry—balked, arguing that such materials would spread a "doctrine of discontent" among the schoolchildren ("Socialist Mouths," 1914). Yet Maury was no radical. Indeed, most of his public pronouncements touted the school's utility as an Americanizing force. "The public schools," he argued that same year, "have taken the children of these immigrants and brought them to be civilized, respected American citizens approaching twentieth century standards" ("Public School System," 1914). While Maury's effort to create a class-conscious curriculum fell short, they suggest that left-of-center politics were not considered inimical to patriotic education in many pockets of the nation.

Once the United States entered World War I, the federal government and individual states took a sharp turn toward stifling any perceived dissent. Such efforts frequently targeted socialists, who were often vocal opponents of the war, and immigrants who displayed anything less than "100 percent Americanism" (Capozzola, 2008; O'Leary, 1999; Pfannestiel, 2004). These crackdowns on alleged seditionists had a far-reaching effect: Few leading educators or curriculum experts would publicly identify as socialists in the decades that followed. Yet controversies continued to swirl around the alleged influence of collectivist thinking in American classrooms. Often, these claims emanated from groups who wanted classroom materials to present American capitalism as an unvarnished success in contrast to the tyranny of Soviet communism and even, in some instances, the New Deal. Though the patriotic rituals and symbols championed by progressive reformers had become staples in classrooms and textbooks still presented the nation's history in an overwhelmingly positive light, some critics continued to chide schools for creating an insufficiently American atmosphere and accused individual teachers and textbook authors of disloyalty. Injecting patriotism into schools did not resolve debates over what economic policies the nation should pursue, but rather prompted demands from some critics that schools enforce a narrow idea of what true Americans should believe (Zimmerman, 2002).

While political and economic questions complicated efforts to teach patriotism in turn-of-the-century schools, so did military matters. As Jerome Landfield lamented, the Grand Army of the Republic stood at the forefront of efforts to wrap all public schools in the flag during these decades. They had assistance from the Woman's Relief Corps (WRC), an affiliated organization that grew out of woman-led Civil War voluntary associations. In their work with schools, the WRC worked to deliver flags to classrooms and teach children basic patriotic principles, while the GAR campaigned in favor of military drill. Despite their efforts, however, few states adopted measures that forced male students to participate in military activities. Instead, most opted to mandate "patriotic exercises," a purposefully vague designation usually consisting of flag salutes and patriotic songs (McConnell, 1992; O'Leary, 1999).

Utah, the same state where young Lena Eyler was expelled for refusing to salute the flag, was a notable exception to the general trend against mandatory military training. Ever since the state's first public high schools opened in the mid-1890s, it had required freshmen and sophomore boys to perform daily military drills. The cadet corps at Salt Lake High—which became West High School in 1915—was particularly popular, and even accompanied the governor on out-of-state trips on several occasions.

Many educational experts at the time, however, decried the physical demands required of military training and questioned its influence on students, casting militarism as antithetical to the aims of a public school education and American patriotism more generally. In 1915, for instance, the National Education Association (NEA) passed a resolution declaring compulsory military training "reactionary and inconsistent with American ideals and standards" ("Minutes," 1916). Others raised practical concerns about the cost of guns and uniforms and the physical toll that marching and lugging around military equipment had on developing boys. Yet not all educators agreed on this point. An editorial in *Educational Foundations* later in 1915 declared the NEA's decision was itself un-American. This missive argued that contrary to the NEA's claims, military training would prepare students to "perpetuate the sacrificial triumphs of our fathers, champion the cause of humanity against tyranny, and guard our territory, consecrated to Liberty, against the incursions of any redhanded foe" ("Danger," 1915).

Was military training patriotic or unpatriotic? This question split educators and average citizens in the years preceding the nation's involvement in World War I. Following Utah's lead, some American cities had instituted military drill programs after the war began under the aegis of preparedness. Most efforts to mandate these practices at the state level, however, fell short. As a result, educators who supported military training instead began pressing for mandatory physical education classes. Sure enough, 23 states had endorsed such programs by 1923. Debates over military training would continue to swirl for the next two decades, though in most cases, voluntary Reserve Officer Training Corps (ROTC) programs became the norm, not mandatory military drills (Zimmerman, 1999).

In the 21st century, patriotic education is often seen as a conservative practice, one associated with the glorification of national heroes and symbols and support for the military. Yet, over a century ago, a range of educators that held a diverse set of beliefs—including socialists and pacifists—also cheered the idea of making patriotism a more pronounced part of students' classroom experiences. Indeed, the question of what exactly patriotism is or what views make someone a patriot has never been settled. Those Americans who accept the notion that a simple dichotomy exists between education that seeks to unite and that which will inevitably divide might be surprised to learn that the first generation of educators to express a shared devotion to patriotic classroom practices found so much to disagree about.

In 1899, a prominent educator writing in the *School Review* critiqued what he saw as superficial efforts to teach patriotism. The author's chief concern was with what he deemed "spurious patriotism," or the tendency of educators to force children to spew nationalist platitudes without first allowing them to form their own opinions. "When I see schoolrooms full of children going through genuflections to the flag of the United States," he argued, "I am willing to bend the knee if I be permitted to understand what history has written on the folds of that flag." The author of that piece—who also emphasized that "this is a flag of liberty of opinion"—was then-Princeton University professor Woodrow Wilson, who would later fail to heed his own advice (Wilson, 1899, p. 603). As president during World War I, Wilson urged passage of legislation that imprisoned hundreds of Americans for acts as small as refusing to salute the flag and jailed anarchists and socialists—including many teachers—for the perceived threat they posed to the state. As Wilson's example makes clear, Americans should remain deeply suspicious of leaders who seek to impose narrow definitions of what it means to be a good citizen and to bar teachers and students from asking difficult questions. Patriotic education is today upheld as the antithesis of supposedly divisive modes of instruction that acknowledge past and present inequalities in American life. But as we have seen, in practice, patriotic education is never perfectly neutral. It is, instead, a contested—perhaps even divisive—concept.

REFERENCES

Bellamy, F. (1892). Americanism in the public schools. *Journal of Education, 36*(6), 107.

Bouton, J. B. (1895). *Uncle Sam's church: His creed, bible, and hymn-book.* Cambridge University Press.

Capozzola, C. (2008). *Uncle Sam wants you: World War I and the making of the modern American citizen.* Oxford University Press.

Danger: The illogical pronouncement of the National Education Association on the question of military training in the public schools. (October 1915). *Educational Foundations*, 71–75.

De Leon, D. (1912, November 13). "The flag" in Utah. *Daily People.*

Ellis, J. E. (2005). *To the flag: The unlikely history of the Pledge of Allegiance.* University Press of Kansas.

Flag salute vexes board of education. (1912, December 22). *Salt Lake Daily Tribune.*

Hansen, J. (2003). *The lost promise of patriotism: Debating American identity, 1890–1920.* University of Chicago Press.

LaGrone, L., & Phillips, M. (2022, August 25). Opinion: What the 1836 project leaves out in its version of Texas history. *Texas Monthly.*

Landfield, J. B. (1915, October 23). The patriotic teaching of history—a crime. *San Francisco Bulletin*, 9.

Mather, F. J. (1900, December 6). Patriotism by manual. *The Nation*, 440.

McConnell, S. (1992). *Glorious contentment: The Grand Army of the Republic, 1865–1900.* University of North Carolina Press.

McCormick, J. S., & Sillito, J. R. (2011). *A history of Utah radicalism: Startling, socialistic, and decidedly revolutionary.* Utah State University Press.

Minutes of the meeting of active members of the National Education Association for the year 1915–1916. (1916). *Yearbook and list of active members of the National Education Association* (p. 49). National Education Association.

O'Leary, C. E. (1999). *To die for: The paradox of American patriotism.* Princeton University Press.

Pfannestiel, T. J. (2004). *Rethinking the red scare: The Lusk Committee and New York's crusade against radicalism, 1919–1923.* Taylor & Francis.

The President's Advisory 1776 Commission. (2021). *The 1776 report.*

Public school system scored and praised. (1914, January 11). *Anaconda Standard.*

School girl is expelled in Salt Lake. (1912, November 2). *Ogden Standard.*

Smith, J. (2019, August 21). The 1619 Project's patriotic work. *Rolling Stone.*

Socialist mouths watering for jobs. (1914, June 5). *Anaconda Standard.*

Strong, J. (1885). *Our country: Its possible future and its present crisis.* Baker & Taylor.

Wilson, W. (1899). Spurious education versus real education. *School Review, 7*(10), 603.

Zimmerman, J. (1999). Storm over the schoolhouse: Exploring popular influences upon the American curriculum, 1890–1941. *Teachers College Record, 100*(3), 602–626.

Zimmerman, J. (2002). *Whose America? Culture wars in the public schools.* Harvard University Press.

About the Editors and the Contributors

Sherman Dorn is a professor at Arizona State University's Mary Lou Fulton Teachers College. His past works include *Creating the Dropout* (1996), *Schools as Imagined Communities* (2006, coedited with Barbara Shircliffe and Deidre Cobb-Roberts), and *Accountability Frankenstein* (2007). His current major project is the history of educational broadcasting in the United States since 1945.

David A. Gamson is professor of education in the Department of Education Policy Studies at Pennsylvania State University. He studies school reform past and present, and his research explores the history of school districts, academic standards, and efforts at providing equitable educational opportunities. He is author of *The Importance of Being Urban: Designing the Progressive School District, 1890–1940* (University of Chicago Press, 2019) and coeditor, with Emily Hodge, of *The Shifting Landscape of the American School District* (Peter Lang, 2018).

A. J. Angulo is a professor of education and a faculty affiliate in the Department of History at UMass Lowell. He is coeditor of the *History of Education Quarterly*, and his book projects include *Miseducation* (JHU Press, 2016), *Diploma Mills* (JHU Press, 2016), *Empire and Education* (Palgrave, 2012), and *William Barton Rogers and the Idea of MIT* (JHU Press, 2009).

Professor emerita at Wellesley College, **Barbara Beatty** is the author of *Preschool Education in America: The Culture of Young Children from the Colonial Era to the Present* and coauthor of *When Science Encounters the Child: Education, Parenting, and Child Welfare in Twentieth-Century America*. She has written many articles and chapters on the history of early childhood education. Her current focus is on the long debate over young children playing and learning to read.

Victoria Cain is an associate professor of history at Northeastern University whose research focuses on the history of education, media technology, and youth in the 20th-century United States. She is the author of *Schools and Screens: A Watchful History* (MIT Press, 2021), on the history of media technology in U.S. schools, and the coauthor, with Karen Rader, of *Life on Display: Revolutionizing U.S. Museums of Science and Natural History in the Twentieth Century* (University of Chicago Press, 2014), on life science display in American natural history and science museums. Her current research explores the history of adolescent privacy in the United States.

Kristen Chmielewski is an associate professor of health and human development at Western Washington University.

Larry Cuban taught high school history for 14 years in Cleveland and Washington, D.C., served as Arlington County (VA) superintendent for 7 years, and as a professor at Stanford University's Graduate School of Education for two decades.

Diana D'Amico Pawlewicz, PhD, is a historian of education policy and school reform at the University of North Dakota. She is the author of *Blaming Teachers: Professionalization Policies and the Failure of Reform in American History* and an editor at Made by History, *Time* magazine.

Neil Dhingra is a graduate academic advisor and a graduate student at the University of Maryland, College Park.

Dellyssa Edinboro is an assistant professor and chair of the Cultural and Ethnic Studies Department at Bellevue College, WA.

Linda Eisenmann is professor of education and history, and former provost of Wheaton College in Massachusetts, where her teaching focuses on gender and higher education. Her career has spanned professorial and administrative positions, from teaching doctoral students at UMass Boston to administering a research center at Harvard University to serving as dean of arts and sciences at John Carroll University in Cleveland. Trained at Harvard as an educational historian, her scholarship examines women in higher education, historiography, and the history of gender in higher education.

Ansley Erickson is an associate professor of history and education policy at Teachers College, Columbia University. She studies how racism and capitalism shape schooling in U.S. cities and how communities organize for educational justice. She is the author of *Making the Unequal Metropolis* (University of Chicago Press, 2016) and coeditor of *Educating Harlem: A Century of Schooling and Resistance in a Black Community* (Columbia University Press, 2019).

About the Editors and the Contributors

Cody Dodge Ewert is the author of *Making Schools American: Nationalism and the Origin of Modern Educational Politics* (Johns Hopkins University Press, 2022). He works as an associate editor at the Montana Historical Society.

Kenneth M. Gold is professor of educational studies and was the founding dean of the School of Education at the College of Staten Island (CUNY). He is the author of *The Forgotten Borough: Staten Island and the Subway* (2023), *School's In: The History of Summer Education in American Public Schools* (2002), and coeditor of *Discovering Staten Island: A 350th Anniversary Commemorative History* (2011).

Andrew R. Highsmith is an associate professor of history at the University of California, Irvine. A specialist in modern American history, metropolitan history, and the history of education, he is the author of *Demolition Means Progress: Flint, Michigan, and the Fate of the American Metropolis* (University of Chicago Press, 2015).

Judith Kafka is a professor of educational policy and history of education in the Marxe School of Public and International Affairs at Baruch College, City University of New York, where she also serves as faculty director for the Bachelor of Science in Public Affairs. Dr. Kafka's research focuses on urban education and the historical roots of current educational policies and practices. Her book *The History of "Zero Tolerance" in American Public Schooling* (Palgrave Macmillan, 2011) explores the history of school discipline.

Matthew Gardner Kelly is an assistant professor at Penn State University. His research examines K–12 school-funding policies, the history of those policies, and their intersections with inequities of race, ethnicity, income, and residence in the United States. He is the author of *Dividing the Public: School Finance and the Creation of Structural Inequity* (Cornell University Press, 2024).

Sharon S. Lee, PhD, is a teaching assistant professor in education policy, organization, and leadership (diversity and equity concentration) at the University of Illinois, Urbana-Champaign. Her research and teaching backgrounds are in the history of education, diversity and equity in higher education, and Asian American student experiences.

Joel Miller is an educator from Baltimore, Maryland. He is currently a graduate student at the University of Maryland, College Park.

Christine A. Ogren is professor in the Educational Policy and Leadership Studies Department at the University of Iowa. She is coeditor of *Rethinking*

Campus Life: New Perspectives on the History of College Students in the United States (2018); author of *The American State Normal School: "An Instrument of Great Good"* (2005); and has published articles in journals including *History of Education Quarterly* and *Paedagogica Historica*. Chris is a former president of the History of Education Society and is currently completing a book on the history of how U.S. teachers have spent their "summers off."

Yoon Pak is professor and head of education policy, organization and leadership at the University of Illinois Urbana-Champaign. Her research and teaching are in the history of American education.

Hope Rias, PhD, is an assistant professor of history at Siena College in Upstate NY. She researches St. Louis school desegregation. She is the author of the book *St. Louis School Desegregation: Patterns of Progress and Peril* (Palgrave Macmillan, 2019).

Kate Rousmaniere is professor of the history of education in the Department of Educational Leadership at Miami University, Oxford, OH. She writes about the history of American teachers and American schools.

John L. Rury is professor emeritus of education at the University of Kansas, where he also held appointments in history and African and African American studies. His work has focused on historical manifestations of educational inequality, and both of his adult sons graduated from Chicago public high schools.

Campbell F. Scribner is an associate professor of education at the University of Maryland, College Park, where he teaches educational history, philosophy, and law. He is the author of *The Fight for Local Control: Schools, Suburbs, and American Democracy* (2016), *A Is for Arson: A History of Vandalism in American Education* (2023), and, with Bryan R. Warnick, *Spare the Rod: Punishment and the Moral Community of Schools* (2021).

Joan Taylor is a retired teacher and district administrator. She has instructed classes at the University of Nevada, Reno, for the past 25 years and served as a consultant and state network director for the National Writing Project.

Jonathan Zimmerman is professor of the history of education and the Berkowitz Professor in Education at the University of Pennsylvania. A former Peace Corps volunteer and high school teacher, Zimmerman is the author of *Small Wonder: The Little Red Schoolhouse in History and Memory* and eight other books. He is also a columnist for the *Philadelphia Inquirer* and a frequent contributor to other popular newspapers and magazines.

Index

Aaron v. Cooper (1958), 94
Abbott, J., 130
Abbott Elementary, 110
Abott, C., 214
Adams, A., 146
Adams, D. W., 68
Agrarian myth: and the Depression, 35; expression of, 35; historical experience, 37; inchoate expressions, 35; origins of, 34–36; problem of, 36–38; and school calendars, 31–34; and summer vacation, 30–38; voicing of, 35
Agyepong, T. E., 68
Aids in English Composition (Parker), 130
Ailwood, J., 112
Alexander, G., 206
Allington, R. L., 129
Allison, C. B., 142
Allyn, R., 132
Alridge, D. P., 162, 163
American Annals of Education, 216
American educational system, 42
American Enterprise Institute, 30
American K–12 schools, 53
American school, 81–87: claims of decline, 82–83; curriculum improvement, 85–87; golden age in education, 83–84; school improvement, 84; school reformers, 81
Ames, M. G., 205
Amsterdam News (newspaper), 197
Anderson, J., 56, 66, 67, 83, 163, 192
Annamma, S. A., 119
Aoki v. Deane (1907), 183
Applebee, A., 131
Arenas, I., 183
Armstrong, S. C., 56

Artiles, A. J., 119
Asempapa, B., 115
Ashmore, H., 197
Asian American Legal Defense and Education Fund, 185
Asian American model minority myth: anti-Asian violence, 184; depiction of, 180; historical analysis of, 181; meritocracy, 184–185; origin of, 179–181; success and limitations, 182–183; trope of, 181
The Atlantic (magazine), 73
Aurner, C. R., 141

Back to School (film), 112
Badger, E., 73
Badillo-Goicoechea, E., 155
Bailey, L. H., 143
Bailyn, B., 24, 25
Baker, B., 214
Baker, D., 86, 87
Baker, K., 37
Baker, M., 227
Bal, A., 119
Baldwin, J., 191
Balogh, B., 43
Bangs, J. D., 25
Bardige, B., 227
Barkdoll, R., 154
Barnard, H., 34, 129, 217
Barnes, B., 155
Barnum, M., 214
Baron, J., 214
Barrett, M. J., 37
Barrett, S., 110
Baumgartner, K., 65, 225
Baynton, D., 119
Beatty, B., 55, 223–225, 228
Beech, G., 197
Beecher, C., 129
Belkin, D., 169, 176
Benjamin, K., 13
Bennett, W. J., 113
Berliner, D., 2, 81, 115
Berninger, V. W., 133

Berrey, S. A., 192
Bess Corey, 145
Best Kept Secret (film), 123
Biklen, D., 123
Blackboard Jungle (film), 73, 122
Black Lives Matter movement, 185
Black male educational thinkers: aims of education, 166–167; defense of teachers, 165–166; women's education, 163–165
Blair, C., 86, 87
Blakely, E. J., 76
Blaster, M., 209
Block, P., 119
Blount, J., 64, 112
Blum, E., 178
Boddie, E. C., 191
Bodino, A., 127
Boggs, G. L., 184
Bonomi, P., 22
Book of Virtues (Bennett), 113
Bosky, A., 198
Bowman, B. T., 227
Bowyer, V., 214, 215
Boyer, P., 21
Boyle, K., 193
Brand, D., 180
Breaux, R. M., 164
Breed, F. S., 134
Bremmer, F. J., 25
Brenzel, B., 76
Britzman, D., 114
Broening, A. M., 134
Brookfield, F., 130
Brown, E., 42
Brown, L., 225
Brown v. Board of Education (1954), 4, 46–47, 83, 90, 96, 102, 154, 191
Bruner, J., 208
Brunvand, J. H., 3
Bryan, W. J., 143
Bucalos, A., 115

243

Buchan, K., 127
Buchanan v. Warley (1917), 193
Buck, D., 61
Burbach, H., 111
Burger, W., 48
Burke, K. J., 118
Burke, L., 149
Burkholder, Z., 76
Burns, M. S., 227
Burrows, A. T., 131
Burrows, E. G., 33
Bush, G. H. W., 101
Bush, G. W., 101, 113
Bush, S., 115
Busteed, B., 82
Butchart, R., 67
Butler, J., 26

Cain, V., 205, 206, 208, 209
Campbell, F., 227
Candelaria, C. A., 214
Carey, A. C., 119
Carhart, D. E., 112
Carr, J. F., 131
Carr, S. L., 131
Carter, P., 112, 152
Carter, R., 197
Cascio, E. U., 214
Cassavetes, J., 121
Catt, C. C., 142
Caudill, K. R., 16
Cavanagh, S., 85
Cayton, H. R., 192
Cellini, S. R., 214
Chall, J. S., 133
Chambers, T. A., 33
Charlton, K., 35
Charters, W. W., 133
Child, B. J., 68
A Child Is Waiting (film), 121, 122
Children of a Lesser God (film), 121
Children ranking, in one-room schoolhouse, 17
Chinese Exclusion Act, 179, 183
Chmielewski, K., 113, 121
Chou, R. S., 183
City School Systems in the United States, 151
Civil Rights Act, 47
Civil Rights Movement, 180, 184, 206
Clark, C., 13
Clark, S., 93
Claxton, P., 143
Clifford, P. P., 140
Clinton, B., 101
Closson, T., 161

Cobbs, W., 15
Cohen, D. K., 52, 54
Cold War, 16
Coleman, J. S., 215
Collins, C., 113
Collins, J., 86, 87
Combs, S., 21
Commager, H. S., 84
Committee of Fifteen Report, 133
Common Core State Standards (CCSS), 85, 86
Common School Journal, 62
Common School Movement, 32, 83
Community events, in one-room schoolhouse, 13–14
Community school models, 48
Comprehensive Child Development Act, 227
Compton, F. E., 145
Computing Teacher (magazine), 209
Conant, J. B., 73, 75
Conard, S. S., 133
Concerned Parents Alliance, 95
Conlin, M., 214
Connecticut Common School Journal, 129
Connor, D. J., 119
Connors, R. J., 130
Conrads, M. C., 11
Cooper, A. J., 161–167: aims of education, 166–167; community's efforts, 167; defense of women's education, 163–165; Hampton-Tuskegee model, 166; teachers as professionals, 165–166; writings in 19th century, 164
Cooper, H., 35
Corcoran, R., 155
Co-teaching model, 52
COVID-19 pandemic, 38, 103, 155, 169, 178, 182, 184–185
Crabtree, C. A., 6
Creative Youth (Mearns), 134
Cremin, L., 23, 25, 128
Crip Camp (film), 120, 121
Cuban, L., 52–53, 55, 98, 134, 209, 224, 228
Culture wars, 44
Cummings, E., 86, 87
Cummins, L., 115
Cutright, P., 87

Dale, E., 205
Dalton, M., 114, 118
Daly, A. J., 119
D'Amico Pawlewicz, D., 141
Dangerfield, R., 112
Dangerous Minds (film), 110
Daniel, P., 192
Darling-Hammond, L., 114
Darrow, B. H., 205
Dash, E., 204
Davidson, J. D., 22
Dead Poets Society (film), 109, 110
Declaration of Principles, 152
De facto segregation: history of, 191; NAACP LDF lawyers, 197; NAACP report, 196; public discourse, 191, 198; shield, 199; in Southern courtrooms, 198; sword, 199; in United States, 192–195
Delmont, M. F., 47, 191, 194–196
DeVos, B., 42, 50, 55, 82, 83
Dewey, J., 54, 67, 142, 143, 152, 194
Dhingra, N., 121
Dinham, S., 114
Dix, J., 217
Dobson, M. J., 24
Dock, C., 128
Domenech, D. A., 37
Donovan, M. S., 227
Dorn, C., 171–173
Dorn, S., 54, 82, 119
Dougherty, J., 75, 195
Douglas, D. M., 194
Dow, P. B., 206, 208, 209
Downey, C., 149
Drake, S. C., 192
Draper, D. A. S., 133
Dresser, T., 33
Driver, J., 48
Drummond, S., 100
Duany, A., 75
Du Bois, W. E. B., 161–164
Dudley, T., 23
Duffy, J., 23
Duncan, A., 30, 50, 55
Dunn, R. E., 6

Earle, A. M., 129
Easy Exercises in Composition (Frost), 130
Eaton, N., 24
Eckert, S. A., 86
EdBuild, 213
Educating Peter (film), 123
Education funding, 213–220

Index

Education Policies Commission, 153
Edwards, G., 15
Eisenhower, D., 94, 153
Eisenmann, L., 172–174
Elementary and Secondary Education Act, 46, 223
The Elementary School Teacher, 141
Elementary writing instruction: colonial writing instruction, 128–129; creative writing movement, 134; cross-curricular writing assignments, 133; early 19th-century, 129–130; late 19th-century, 131–133; in 20th-century, 133–134; writing process, 127
Eliot, C. W., 142
Elliott, M., 112
Ellis, J., 51, 119
Ellison, H. A., 13
Entertainment, in schools, 15
Epstein, G. M., 20
Equality of Educational Opportunity (Coleman), 215
Erickson, A. T., 193–195, 199
Erskine, E., 185
Eurich, A. C., 208
Evans, S. Y., 162, 164, 165, 167
Evans, W., 15
Evers, F., 111
Every Student Succeeds Act, 101
Ewing, E., 48
Expression, agrarian myth, 35

Factory model of education, 55
Fairclough, A., 142
Falk, E. M., 134
Farran, D., 227
Farrar, E., 52, 54
Fass, P. S., 74
Faubus, O., 94
Faulty city schools, 73–78: ghetto and its schools, 76–78; suburban school advantages, 74–75; urban schools prevailed, 74
Fawcett, N. G., 36
Feagin, J. R., 183
Federal funding, 46, 47
Federal Housing Administration (FHA), 193
Fernquist, R. M., 87
Ferreira, F., 214
Ferri, B. A., 119

Ferrick, T., 20
Festivities, in one-room schoolhouse, 13–14
Feuerstein, A., 112
Fey, T., 146
Figgins, M., 111
Finkelstein, B., 56, 63, 64
First Lessons in Composition (Quackenbos), 131
First Lessons in Grammar (Greene), 130
Fitzgerald, J., 135
Flogging, 13
Folsom, M., 153
Forbes (magazine), 82
Foster, R. A., 15
Frankel, G., 61
Franklin, B., 128
Franklin, V. P., 91–94
Freedman, D., 114
Freedman's Bureau, 43
Freeman, R. A., 217, 218
Freund, D. M. P., 193
Frost, J., 130
Frostic, F. W., 134
Fuller, F., 145
Fuller, W. E., 12, 13
Fullilove, M. T., 194
Future Shock (Toffler), 50
Fyan, L., 144

Gamson, D., 86, 87
Garcia, D. G., 194, 195
Gardella, N., 33
Gately, S., 119
Gates, B., 2–3, 82, 83, 207
Gates, H. L., Jr., 161
Gates, M., 3
Geiger, R. L., 22–25, 65
Gelber, S. M., 111
Gender dominance: college enrollments, 171–172; in higher education, 169–176; impact of World War II, 170–171; impact on collegiate women, 173–175; long-term implications, 175; postscript, 175–176; veterans, 172–173
Gerber, P. L., 145
Gibson, W., 118
Gigliotti, P., 214
Glass, G. V, 2, 81
Glass, M., 191, 194, 196–199
Glass, R. E., 36
Glotzer, P., 193
Go, M. H., 81
Goe, L., 115
Goetz, P. M. B., 67
Goffman, E., 68

Gold, K. M., 30, 32–35, 140, 141, 145
Goldberg, E., 20
Goldfarb, B., 208
Goldsmith, W. W., 76
Goldstein, D., 208
Golub, A., 122
Gonda, J. D., 193
Gong Lum v. Rice (1927), 183
Goode, E., 109
Goodlad, J., 140
Good Without God (Epstein), 20
Goodykoontz, B., 133
Gordon, N., 214
Gordon, R. A., 227
Gordy, S., 94
Gorski, P., 184
Gorton, G. L., 142
Gou, A., 185
Gough, R., 144
Graduating Peter (film), 123
Graham, S., 135
Grand Army of the Republic (GAR), 232, 236
Graves, D., 133
Greathouse, S., 35
Green, A. A., 94
Green, K., 92
Green, S. K., 26
Greene, S. S., 130
Greenough, J. P., 64
Greenwald, R., 214
Gregory, J. N., 192
Grindal, T., 226
Grob, G., 119
Grobb, G. N., 23
Grove, M. J., 13
Grubb, W. N., 55, 224, 228
The Guardian, 20
Guiler, W. S., 134
Gulliford, A., 12, 14
Gutenberg, J., 204
Gwazdauskas, P., 123

Hall, D. D., 21
Hall, G. S., 143
Hall, S., 111
Hambrick, D., 114
Hammer, C., 119
Hampton-Tuskegee model, 163, 166
Hansen, J., 121
Hansot, E., 64
Hanushek, E. A., 214, 215, 226
Harlan, L. R., 163
Harper, W. R., 143
Harris, D., 37
Harris, K. R., 135

Harris, N., 169, 176
Harris, S. H., 133
Harris, W. T., 133
Hartman, A., 153
Harvard, J., 22
Harvard Educational Review, 226
Harvard University, 20–26: alternatives to popular origin story, 23–25; appointment of Nathaniel Eaton, 24; debates/assumptions about founding of, 26; economic motives of, 24–25; popular origin story of, 21–23; "promotional pamphlet" about, 24; selection of Greg Epstein, 20
Hatfield, W. W., 133, 134
Hawkins, L. K., 127
Hayes, D. P., 85
Haynes, G. E., 192
Haywood, F. J., 163
Haywood, H. S., 163
Heaney, G. W., 95, 96
Hechinger, F. M., 36
Heckman, J. J., 227
Hedges, L. V., 214
Heilman, R., 109
Heim, J., 82
Henke, W. A., 14
Herbst, J., 24
Hereford, N.-J., 207
Heroic teacher myth, 118–124
Herold, B., 204
Hess, F., 100
Hicks, H., 133
Higher Education Act, 175
Highlander Folk School, 93, 94
Highsmith, A. R., 193–194, 196, 199
Hill, E. M., 14
Hill, S. A., 76–78, 84
Hilliard, R., 206
Hillier, A. E., 193
Hillocks, G., 133
Hine, D. C., 165
Hirsch, A. R., 192, 194
Hirsch, E. D., Jr., 85
Historical myths *vs.* urban legends, 3
Hobbs, N., 51
Hoeveler, J. D., 22, 25
Holland, H. R., 33
Holmes, E. E., 133
Homer, W., 11
Hong, K., 214
Horn, M., 100

Horowitz, H. H., 171
Horowitz, H. L., 65
Horton, M., 93
Hosic, J. F., 133, 134
House and Garden, 16
Hudelson, E., 134
Hudson, W. S., 26
Hungate, W., 95
Hunter, E., 73
Hunter, T. W., 192
Hutchins, R., 152, 153, 155
Hutson, J. H., 21
Hutt, E., 65
Hylton, H., 37
Hyman, J., 214

Idol, L., 119
Illson, M., 153
Independent (magazine), 14
Individualized education programs (IEPs), 119
Industrial-era classrooms, 50–57: collaborative teaching, 52; history of, 54–55; open-classroom movement, 52; schooling and economy, 55–57; stable teaching practices, 53
Intensive Partnerships for Effective Teaching (IP) project, 2–3
Issel, W., 54
Itliong, L., 184

Jackson, C. K., 214
Jackson, K. T., 75, 193
James, E., 145
James, W., 143
Jansen, W., 198
Jefferson, T., 65
Jenkins, D., 193
Jensen, A., 226
Jeung, R., 178
Johanningmeier, E. V., 54
Johnson, C., 13, 14
Johnson, K., 162, 164–166
Johnson, L., 92, 110, 226
Johnson, Reynold, 208
Johnson, R. C., 214
Johnson, W., 51, 192
Johnston, A. M., 145
Johonnot, J., 12
Jones, K. M., 127
Jones, V., 185
Judd, C., 141
Juddson v. Board of Edu. of City of New York (1938), 141

Kaestle, C. F., 12, 31, 51
Kaestle, K., 62

Kafka, J., 61, 65
Kantor, H., 76, 77
Karch, A., 224
Katz, M., 56, 62
Kaufman, B., 110
Keating, A. D., 33
Keller, H., 118, 120, 122
Kelley, R. D. G., 192
Kelly, M. G., 213
Kelly-Gangi, C., 113
Kendrick, P., 225
Kendrick, S., 225
Kennedy, J. F., 120, 121
Kenyon, J., 18
Kephard, I. L., 64
Kett, J., 63, 64
Keyes v. School District No. 1 (1973), 94
Kilpatrick, W., 35
Kim, D., 77
Kinison, S., 112
Kirk, M., 98
Kirp, D. L., 224
Kiuhara, S., 135
Kleiman, G. M., 206
Kliewer, C., 123
Knipe, H., 86, 87
Kochiyama, Y., 184–185
Kogan, V., 214
Koretz, D. M., 3
Kramer, S., 121
Kreisman, D., 214
Krupnick, M., 169, 176
Kruse, K. M., 4
Kush, J. M., 155
Kwapis, J., 140

Laats, A., 45
Ladies Home Journal, 217
Lafortune, J., 214
Laine, R. D., 214
Lalvani, P., 119
Lancaster, J., 51
Lange, D., 15
Langer, J. A., 129
Lassiter, M. D., 191, 196
Lavertu, S., 214
Lazerson, M., 55, 224, 228
Lee, E., 179, 181, 182
Lee, J., 178
Lee, K.-G., 214
Lee, S., 182, 183
Legal Defense Fund (LDF), 197
Leiber, J., 118
Lemov, D., 114
Leon, J., 86, 87
Leonard, S. A., 134
Leslie, J., 206
Leukhina, O., 169

Index

Lewis, A. C., 17
Lewis, A. E., 183
Libit, H., 99
Liddell, M., 90, 95
Liddell v. Board of Education (1979), 90, 95
Lilienthal, M. E., 132
Lim, R., 178
Lincoln, A., 12
Lincoln Middle School, 52
Lindelow, J., 206
Lindsay, J., 35
Little House on the Prairie (Wilder), 15
Little red schoolhouse: myth of, 11–17; as symbol of united community, 14–17
Litwack, L. F., 192
Local control: constitutional law, 47; golden age of local democracy, 42; self-serving and reactionary myths, 48; state and federal funding, 46, 47
Locke, A., 196–197
Locke, B., 225
Loewen, J. W., 4, 184
Logan, E., 16
Lomawaima, K. T., 68
Lopez, M., 226
Lortie, D. C., 53, 140
Los Angeles Times (newspaper), 140
Lovern, M. F., 36
Lowe, R., 77
Lu, X., 86
Lynch, E. F., 217

MacArthur, C. A., 135
MacLean, N., 218
Mahmood, S., 112
Malikow, M., 114
Mamie Tape, 183
"Man: A Course of Study" (MACOS), 208 209
Mandernach, B. J., 112
Mann, H., 13, 31, 33, 63, 64, 129
Mardell, B., 227
Marshall, T., 90, 91, 96
Martinez, S. L. M., 76
Martorell, P., 214
Massachusetts Bay Colony, 21–24
Massachusetts Teacher (journal), 33
Mather, C., 129
Mathews, M. M., 85
May, F. B., 36
May, V. M., 162–164, 166
Mayo, A., 217

McAndrew, W., 218
McCaffrey, T., 121
McCarthy, K. E, 122
McCluskey, A. T., 165
McCulley, L., 52
McDowell, A., 112
McEntyre, D. E., 134
McFarlin, I., 214
McGeever, J. B., 61
McGuffey's Eclectic Readers (McGuffey), 85, 131
McGuire, W. H., 155
McIntyre, K., 210
McKeown, D., 135
McKnight, D., 115
McLain, J. D., 36
McMillan, J., 198
McWilliams, J. E., 23
Mearns, H., 134
Meckler, L., 155
Melby, E., 61
Memoir of the Life of James Jackson (Paul), 224
Ment, D., 197
Meredith, J., 95
Meskimen, A., 140
Metz, M. H., 53
Meyer v. Nebraska (1923), 45
Mika, H. K., 134
Milam, E. L., 209
Miller, C. L., 214
Miller, D. L., 33
Miller, J., 16, 121
Milliken v. Bradley (1974), 2, 48, 199
Mills, A., 145
Mino, J., 123, 124
The Miracle Worker (film), 118–120, 122, 124
Mirel, J. E., 76
Mitchell, R. W. S., 112
Moehlman, A. B., 215
Mongeau, L., 226
Monroe, P., 143
Montgomery, Z., 218
Morgan, D., 36
Morgan, L. D., 35
Morison, S. E., 26
Morison Myth, 26
Morley, C., 130
Morrell, E., 193
Morris, W. H., 68
Morrison, J. C., 35
Mort, P. R., 215
Moss, H. J., 225
Moursund, D., 209
Mr. Mayor (television comedy), 140
Muldoon, J., 23, 25
Murphy, M., 69
Musci, R. J., 155

Myers, D. G., 134
Myths: harmful impacts of, 2–3; historical, 3; origin. *See* Origin myths

Nagin, C., 127
Nalipay, M., 114
Nash, C. R., 54
Nash, G. B., 6
Natanson, H., 155
National Assessment of Educational Progress (NAEP), 77, 84
National Association for the Advancement of Colored People (NAACP), 90, 94, 154, 162, 196, 197, 199
National Association of Teachers in Colored Schools (NATCS), 142, 143
National Center for Educational Restructuring and Inclusion, 52
National Center for Education Statistics (NCES), 169, 171, 226
National Council on Year Round Education, 36
National Defense Education Act, 46, 206
National Education Association (NEA), 12, 142, 143, 145, 154, 155, 228, 236
National Kindergarten Association (NKA), 225, 228
National Science Foundation (NSF), 209
NEA Journal, 143
Neem, J., 43
Neilson, C. A., 214
Nelson, A., 127, 228
Nelson, M. J., 35
Nevin, A. I., 52
New Deal (Roosevelt), 15
New York Times (newspaper), 15, 20, 35, 36, 82, 180, 204
Ng, J., 183, 184
Nicolaides, B. M., 192
Nielsen, K. E., 118
Nine Country Kids, 15
Nixon, R., 47, 196, 198, 227–228
Northwest Ordinances (1787), 42
Novak, S. J., 65
Nye, B., 35

Oaks, S., 140
Obama, B., 101

"O Captain! My Captain!" (poem), 111
Ogren, C. A., 141, 142, 145, 146
One-room schoolhouse: children ranking in, 17; community events and festivities in, 13–14; decline of, 14; historical overview, 12–14; seating arrangements, 12; structure of, 12; for Whites, 14
Ong-Dean, C., 119
Ono, S. J., 183
Open-classroom movement, 52
Orcutt, H., 63
Organisation for Economic Co-operation and Development (OECD), 219
Orgeron, D., 206
Orgeron, M., 206
Origin myths: agrarian myth of summer vacation, 30–38; American individualism, 178–186; American school, 81–87; Asian American model minority, 178–186; Black male educational thinkers, 161–167; de facto segregation, 191–199; education funding, 213–220; elementary writing instruction, 127–134; faulty city schools, 73–78; gender dominance, 169–176; Harvard University, 20–26; industrial-era classrooms, 50–57; little red schoolhouse, 11–17; local control, 42–48; meritocracy, 178–186; patriotic education, 232–237; preschool education, panacea, 223–228; school reform failure, 98–104; special education teachers, 118–124; student behavior, 61–69; summers off, 140–146; teachers, 109–115; teacher tenure, 149–156; teaching technology, 204–211; U.S. schools desegregated in 1954, 90–96
Orr, R., 112
Ortlieb, E., 112
Osborne, S., 38
Osgood, R. L., 119
Oswego Movement, 131

Ouellett, M. L., 111
Ozawa v. United States (1922), 179

Pak, Y. K., 183
Palmer, A. T., 37
Pangle, L. S., 65
Pangle, T., 65
Papert, S., 207
PARC v. Commonwealth of Pennsylvania (1972), 120
Park, V., 119
Parker, F., 131, 143
Parker, R. G., 130, 132
Patridge, L., 132
Patriotic education: divisive concepts, 233; educator writing, 237; far-reaching effect, 235; military training, 236–237; NEA's claims, 236; SLP's view, 235; teaching patriotism, 232
Patterson, J., 113
Paul, S., 224
Paul, T., 224
Paumgarten, N., 20
Pawlewicz, D., 150, 152, 155, 156, 208
Payne, C., 144
Payson, T., 63
Peabody, E., 225
Pearson, P. D., 85
Pederson, J., 36
Peixotto, B., 151, 152
Pennington, K., 112
Perkins, L. M., 164
Perlstein, D., 122
Perry, C. A., 194
Persico, C., 214
Peskowitz, Z., 214
Pestana, C. G., 23
Petersen, A., 123
Petersen, W., 180
Phi Delta Kappan, 81
Philbrick, J. D., 151
Phippen, A. R., 130
Pierce v. Society of Sisters (1925), 45
Pieroth, D. H., 145
Pindell, H., 153, 154
Pinneo's Primary Grammar of the English Language for Beginners (Pinneo), 131
Plater-Zyberk, E., 75
Plessy v. Ferguson (1896), 183
Podgursky, M., 140
Pogue, G. C., 143
Polachek, S. W., 214
Popovic, T., 178

Porter, R., 119
Powell, A. G., 52, 54
Powell, L., 47
Powell, O. E., 215
Pratt, C., 225–226
Preschern, J., 112
Preschool education: children and families, 225–226; cost-beneficial societal outcomes, 226–228; overview, 223–224; reduce poverty, 226; reduce racism, 224–225
Pressey, S., 208
Preston, E., 144
Pritchett, H., 218
Progressive Era, 14, 15
Progressive Exercises in English Composition (Parker), 130
Provenzo, E. F., 16
Pruitt, B., 193
Pyle, R. E., 22

Quackenbos, G. P., 131
Quealy, K., 73
Quigley, I. B., 144

Racism, 14
Racism and White privilege, 47
Radke, A., 142
Rankin, N. R., 142
Raths, J., 114
Rauscher, E., 214
Ravitch, D., 69, 98, 100, 127
Razali, A. B., 127
Reagan, R., 61, 180
Reardon, S. F., 2, 78, 87
Reber, S., 214
Reese, W. J., 65–67
Reeves, R., 169, 176
Reformation-era education, 56
Rehabilitation Act, 119
Reich, J., 205, 208
Religiosity, in colonial America, 22
Reynolds, T., 129
Rias, H., 90, 92, 93, 95
Rice, D. F. R., 17
Rice, J., 67, 68
Rich, M., 82, 149
Rickford, R. J., 48
Rios, T., 112
Robbins, W. G., 23
Roberts, S., 224, 225
Roberts v. City of Boston (1849), 224
Robinson, J., 14
Roose, K., 204

Index

Roosevelt, F. D., 15
Rose, D., 175
Rose, E. R., 224, 226
Rosen, M., 127
Rothstein, J., 214
Rothstein, R., 191, 199, 200
Rousmaniere, K., 68, 112, 113, 119, 120
Roy, J., 214
Rudolph, J., 53, 208
Rugg, H., 131
Rury, J., 31, 47, 73–78, 84, 184
Rusk, H. A., 120

Saatcioglu, A., 74, 75
Saettler, P., 205, 206
San Antonio Independent School District v. Rodriguez (1973), 2
San Antonio v. Rodriguez (1973), 47
Sanders, S. H., 149
Scarborough, W., 183
Schanzenbach, D. W., 214
Schmalhausen, S., 152
Schneider, J., 155
Schoenfeld, A. H., 85
Schönholzer, D., 214
School Boys and School Girls, 15
School calendars in 19th-century, 31–34
School Days (song), 15
Schoolhouse in the Woods (Caudill), 16
School reform failure: bureaucratic time, 101–102; clocks, 100–101; home-based learning, 103; media time, 101; open space schools, 99–100; policymaker time, 101; practitioner time, 102–103; school-based learning, 103; student learning time, 103–104
School's In: The History of Summer Education in American Public Schools (Gold), 30, 34, 36
Schrag, P., 84
Schultz, L. M., 130, 131
Schumacher, B., 153
Schwartz, S., 85
Schweinhart, L. J., 227
Scotch, R., 119
Scott, C., 114
Scott, F. N., 134
Scribner, C. F., 2, 4, 44, 61, 63, 64, 69

Segall, A., 118
Seligman, A. I., 195
Selvig, C., 142
Serey, T. T., 111
Shackelford, O. M., 143
Shagaloff, J., 197
Shao, M., 210
Sheldon, E. A., 131
Shelley v. Kraemer (1948), 193
Shepard, M. A., 37
Shores, K. A., 214
Shriver, E., 121
Shriver, S., 121
Shumaker, A., 131
Sikes, R., 208
Simpson, M. E., 134
Singer, N., 204
Single-teacher classrooms, 51–53
Skinner, B. F., 208
Slums and Suburbs (Conant), 73
Smaldone, A., 169
Smith, E., 134, 169, 176
Snap the Whip (painting), 11
Snyder, E., 185
Social Education, 210
Sockett, H., 114
Solis, M., 52
Solomon, B. M., 175
Sorensen, L. C., 214
Sosina, V. E., 213
The Souls of Black Folk (Du Bois), 162
Southwick, M., 134
Spaeth, S., 15
Special education teachers, 118–124
Speck, J., 75
Spirko, R. C., 121
Spitz, E. H., 120
Squire, J. R., 133
Stand and Deliver (film), 110
Stange, K., 214
Stecher, B. M., 3
Steedman, C., 112
Steffes, T., 44, 65, 66
Steinberg, M. P., 214
Steineker, R. F., 65
Stephens, S., 169, 176
Sterngass, J., 33
Stewart, O. G., 112
Stilgoe, J. R., 14
St. Louis Public Schools, 93
Stout, H. S., 23
Stovey, P., 68
Strain, M., 30
The Strange Career of Jim Crow (Woodward), 197
Streible, D., 206

Strickland, D. S., 127
Strober, M. H., 112
Stuart, E. A., 155
Studebaker, J. W., 35
Student behavior: compulsory education laws, 66; discipline problem, 68; indiscipline, 63–66; need for control, 62–63; in 19th century schools, 66–67; turn of the 20th century, 67–69; undisciplined and uninstructed, 62–66
Students for Fair Admissions (SFFA) v. Harvard, 178
Students for Fair Admissions v. University of North Carolina (UNC), 178
Styfco, S., 226
Subcommittee on Summer Vacation Activities of the School Child, 35
Sugrue, T. J., 192, 194, 197
Sulé, V. T., 162, 164
Sullivan, A., 85, 118–122
Summers off: documented schoolteachers, 146; education policymakers, 140; NEA summer convention, 142; paternalistic administrators, 145; rural-school teaching methods, 141; scholars and public figures, 144; school leaders, 141; subject-matter knowledge, 141; teacher education, 143
Superfine, B. M., 2
Survey Graphic (magazine), 197
Swann, J., 94, 95
Swanson, E., 52
Swider, G., 140
Sykes, C. J., 82
Symonds, W. C., 37

Takagi, D., 181
Takahashi, P., 204
Takanishi, R., 228
Talks to Teachers (James), 143
Tanforan, V., 99
Tape, J., 183
Tape, M., 183
Tape v. Hurley (1885), 183
Tarbell, H. S., 133
Taylor, C., 153, 198
Taylor, J. O., 63
The Teacher (Abbott), 130

Teachers: attributes, 113; classroom instruction, 111; dispositions, 114; educational researchers, 114; elementary and secondary schools, 111; personality characteristics, 109; teaching skills, 111; work and commitment, 110
Teacher tenure: fears of, 149–150; myth of, 155–156; NEA report, 154; protection of, 151; public education, 155; recruitment and retention efforts, 153
Teaching technology, 204–211
Teaford, J. C., 75
Teranishi, R., 181
Theobald, P., 14, 48
Theoharis, J., 192
Things Taught: Systematic Instruction in Composition and Object Lessons (Lilienthal & Allyn), 132
The Third World Liberation Front, 184
Thomas, K., 115
Thomas Jefferson, 143
Thompson, C., 204, 206, 207
Thompson, P. N., 214
Thorndike, E., 143
Thousand, J. S., 52
Tillman, L. C., 154
Time (magazine), 30, 180
Times, 15–16
Todd-Breland, E., 48, 195
Toffler, A., 50
Trejos, N., 98
Treu, R., 149
Trier, J., 114
Troia, G. A., 135
Trotter, J. W., 192
Tyack, D., 17, 53, 54, 64, 66–68, 74, 112, 228
Tyson, T. B., 192

Uchitelle, S., 95, 96
Umemoto, K., 184
United States, de facto segregation, 192–195
United States v. Bhagat Singh Thind (1923), 179
Up From Slavery (Washington), 163
Up the Down Staircase (Kaufman), 110

Urban legends, historical myths *vs.*, 3
U.S. News and World Report, 180
U.S. schools desegregated in 1954, 90–96: enforce compliance with *Brown*, 93–94; NAACP support, 90; resistance to the *Brown* ruling, 91–93; St. Louis as microcosm, 95–96

Valente, J., 99
Van Engen, A. C., 21
Van Wagenen, M. J., 134
Vaughn, S., 52
Vergara v. California (1938), 149
Vermont Superintendent of Schools, 64
Villa, R. A., 52
Vinovskis, M., 23, 31
Virginia, 92
A Voice from the South by a Black Woman of the South (Copper), 163
Von Drehle, D., 30
Vorpe, W. G., 16

Walker, E., 66, 67
Walker, J., 128
Walker, V. S., 67, 93, 94
Wallace, M., 33
Walters, D. R., 143
Warnick, B. R., 61
Warren, K. C., 68
Warren, T., 210
Washington, B. T., 56, 161–163, 166
Washington Post (newspaper), 82
Watt, W. E., 144
Watters, A., 54, 205, 208
Wayland, F., 63
Wayne, A., 115
The Way We Go to School in Boston: Exclusion of Children in Boston, 223
Weathers, E. S., 213
Weathersby, C., 195
Weathersby, Y., 195
Weaver-Zercher, D. L., 16
Weeks, R. M., 133
Weiland, C., 227
Weiner, M. F., 69
Weisser, A., 52
Weld, A. H., 132
Wells, R. V., 24
Wentworth, G., 86

West, A., 122
West Virginia Board of Education v. Barnette (1943), 45
Whipple, G. M., 133
White House Conference on Child Health and Protection, 35
Whites, one-room schoolhouse for, 14
Whitman, W., 111
Whitney, M., 145
Wiggin, K. D., 225
Wilder, L. I., 15
Wilkerson, I., 192
Willcox, W. G., 149
Williams, H., 67
Williams, J. S., 64
Williams, R., 111
Willing, M. H., 134
Willis, B. C., 195
Wilson, W., 152
Winn, W. D., 133
Winslow, A. G., 129
Wired (magazine), 206
Wise, J., 154
Wolfe, M. F., 85
Wolfer, L. T., 85
Wollenberg, C., 184
Woman's Relief Corps (WRC), 236
Wonder (film), 122
Wong, A., 73, 78
Woodard, K., 192
Woodridge, W., 216
Woodward, C. V., 192, 197
Woollatt, L. H., 215
Works Progress Administration and Public Works Administration, 15
Worley, J., 153
Wynn, S., 109

Yang, M., 21
Yates, J. S., 225
Yellow Horse, A., 178
Yoshikawa, H., 227
Youngkin, G., 149
Youngs, P., 115

Zelizer, J. E., 4
Zhou, L., 184
Zigler, E. F., 226
Zimmer, R., 214
Zimmerman, J., 16, 43, 50, 64, 68, 82, 111
Zimmerman, S. D., 214
Zinsser, K. M., 225